OPEN SOURCE
WEB APPLICATIONS
for Libraries

Sorry about [illegible] ! Amanda

[illegible], [illegible]
[illegible]
[illegible]

OPEN SOURCE WEB APPLICATIONS *for Libraries*

Karen A. Coombs
Amanda J. Hollister

Information Today, Inc.
Medford, New Jersey

First printing, 2010

Open Source Web Applications for Libraries

Library of Congress Cataloging-in-Publication Data

Coombs, Karen A.
Open source Web applications for libraries / Karen A. Coombs and Amanda J. Hollister.
p. cm.
Includes bibliographical references and index.
ISBN 978-1-57387-400-7
1. Open source software--Library applications. I. Hollister, Amanda J., 1967- II. Title.
Z678.93.O65C66 2010
005.3--dc22

2010035599

President and CEO: Thomas H. Hogan, Sr.
Editor-in-Chief and Publisher: John B. Bryans
Managing Editor: Amy M. Reeve
Project Editor: Rachel Singer Gordon
VP Graphics and Production: M. Heide Dengler
Book Designer: Kara Mia Jalkowski
Cover Designer: Norma Neimeister

www.infotoday.com

Contents

Dedications and Acknowledgments vii

Introduction ix

PART I: INTRODUCTION TO OPEN SOURCE WEB APPLICATIONS

Chapter 1: What Is Open Source Software? 3

Chapter 2: The LAMP Stack 9

Chapter 3: Web Hosting Options 21

PART II: BLOGS AND WIKIS

Chapter 4: WordPress 39

Chapter 5: Movable Type 55

Chapter 6: PmWiki 71

Chapter 7: MediaWiki 81

PART III: CONTENT MANAGEMENT SYSTEMS

Chapter 8: WordPress as a CMS 97

Chapter 9: Joomla 115

Chapter 10: Drupal 137

PART IV: REFERENCE AND INSTRUCTION TOOLS

Chapter 11: Reference and Instruction Tools 163

Chapter 12: Subject Guide Tools 185

Chapter 13: LibData 201

PART V: RESOURCE DISCOVERY TOOLS

Chapter 14: Federated Search Tools 219

Chapter 15: NextGen Catalogs 229

Glossary 251

About the Authors 255

Index 257

Dedications and Acknowledgments

This book is dedicated to my parents. To my mom, who taught me to be independent and self-reliant. Your example instilled in me the value of having freedom and flexibility in as many things as possible. And to my dad, who showed me how to rip stuff apart and put it back together. Your fearless and curious nature has inspired me to want to know how stuff works and to be able to fix things.

—Karen A. Coombs

This book is dedicated to my husband and to my mother. To my husband for lighting a fire under my arse to get this book done. To my mother, from whom I received my sense of humor, combined with the faith that things will always work out. It's a powerful gift to be able to laugh at the crap life sometimes brings. Jag älskar dig och saknar dig mamma.

—Amanda J. Hollister

This book wouldn't have been possible without the help of the many colleagues who took the time to talk about their projects, answer questions, troubleshoot on the fly, and create patches so we could install, test, screen capture, etc. Many thanks to Casey Bisson, John Blyberg, Andrew Darby, Amanda Etches-Johnson, Sebastian Hammer, Mark Jordan, Demian Katz, Terry Reese, Nick Ruest, Bess Sadler, Kevin Stranack, and Ken Varnum. The authors would also like to thank Blake Carver and LISHost for providing us with much-needed testing space; Dan Chudnov for his assistance with Chapter 1, "What Is Open Source Software?"; and the Code4Lib community (code4lib.org), many of whom provided troubleshooting and answered questions.

Introduction

Open source software in libraries covers a wide range of applications that one could, in fact, write several books on. This book focuses on one piece of the puzzle: open source web applications and their use in libraries. A web application is a piece of software that is accessed via a web browser over a network (either the internet or an intranet). The majority of the web is made up of these web applications; sites such as Flickr and Gmail can be considered web applications. Libraries have increasingly worked toward deploying web applications to meet the needs of their users and to serve internal work processes. In our work as web librarians, we've witnessed this transition and have been asked to create or deploy an increasing number of web applications, many of which are open source.

As a result, over the course of our careers, we have encountered and used a variety of open source web applications in order to meet the changing needs of libraries. Sometimes we've worked with open source software out of financial necessity, but increasingly we've deliberately chosen to work with open source software. We prefer open source software because it provides us with more flexible and adaptable technologies to solve whatever problems we are working on.

We found it both serendipitous and ironic that, while we were completing this book, the transition of the whitehouse.gov site to Drupal (an open source content management system) was in the news. This announcement is just one of many indicators that open source software has become increasingly mainstream. Significant portions of the internet have open source components. Companies such as Google and Sony use open source infrastructure, and websites such as PBS Engage (www.pbs.org/engage), the Guggenheim Museum (www.guggenheim.org), IHOP (www.ihop.com), the University of Maine (www.umaine.edu), and Best Buy's local store blogs (stores.bestbuy.com/577) are powered by open source web applications.

Yet as web librarians we've also discovered a general lack of knowledge among our colleagues about the open source tools available to libraries and a general feeling of fear and uncertainty about open source software. We've found that libraries and librarians think of open source software as being difficult to install. Additionally, we often hear "there isn't any open source thing that does X," even when applications that provide such functionality do exist. It worries us that libraries lack good information when deciding which web tools (proprietary or open source) to implement.

Because of this information gap, we decided that one of our goals for this book would be to dispel some of the misconceptions about open source software in libraries. Most of the applications discussed in this book can be installed in 15 minutes or less. Some of the featured applications can easily be tried out with BitNami installations (www.bitnami.org), even without having access to a server.

Additionally, we'd like to shift the focus of open source software in libraries away from open source integrated library systems, such as Koha and Evergreen, to smaller web applications. There are many wonderful projects in this arena that can help libraries fulfill their goals and mission. We'll do our best to highlight the best of these web applications available for libraries.

The book's content builds in a progressive fashion, from discussing the basics—what is open source software—to providing an overview of the current open source "NextGen" catalog software. Although you are welcome to read the book from cover to cover, it is structured so that you can also choose to read just a particular chapter on a particular application. The first part gives an introduction to open source web applications. Chapter 1 provides an overview of the open source licensing model, the process by which open source software gets developed, and the culture of open source. Chapter 2 focuses on the LAMP stack (Linux, Apache MySQL, PHP), the backbone of most of the applications discussed later in the book. We examine the different pieces of the LAMP model and discuss what role each plays in the stack. Chapter 3 provides an overview of hosting options for open source software and will be helpful for libraries trying to decide where to host their software.

The remainder of the book is divided into four broad sections: Blogs and Wikis, Content Management Systems, Reference and Instruction Tools, and Resource Discovery Tools. In the Blogs and Wikis section, we discuss two blogging tools and two wiki applications. In Chapter 4, we discuss WordPress as a blogging platform. We demonstrate how to install the software and its basic features and talk about using WordPress as a platform for running multiple blogs. In

Chapter 5, we discuss another option for blogging software: Movable Type. We cover installation instructions, basic features, customizing the look and feel, and the current user community for the software. In Chapter 6, we shift gears to focus on wikis and discuss PmWiki. Chapter 7, the last chapter in this section, focuses on MediaWiki, the open source wiki tool that powers Wikipedia.

The next section of the book focuses on content management systems (CMS), building on the idea of librarians creating and updating their own content. While in Chapter 4 we discussed the use of WordPress as a blogging tool, in Chapter 8 we discuss how to implement WordPress as a CMS. We outline key plugins and themes for accomplishing this and provide examples of libraries that are using WordPress to power their library websites. Chapter 9 provides an overview of Joomla, a more traditional CMS, as we discuss the fundamentals of the application and provide examples of Joomla-powered library websites. Chapter 10 discusses the basic concepts and framework of the Drupal CMS. Here we outline key modules for libraries and provide examples of libraries that have implemented this powerful CMS.

The next section, Reference and Instruction Tools, covers tools for librarians in public services. Chapter 11 discusses a variety of useful tools, including the Assignment Calculator, Libstats, and refbase. Chapter 12 talks a bit about Pirate Source as well as SubjectsPlus, an open source subject guide tool. Chapter 13 highlights one last subject guide tool, LibData.

The final section of the book focuses on resource discovery tools. Resource discovery tools are search tools designed to solve three key problems with traditional library search interfaces: 1) siloization of library resources, 2) lack of Web 2.0 features and socially created content, and 3) lack of rich facets to facilitate browsable access for users. In this section, we discuss two different types of resource discovery tools: federated search tools and NextGen catalogs. Chapter 14 focuses on open source federated search tools. We describe three applications that libraries can implement to provide their users with federated searching. Chapter 15 covers NextGen catalogs such as Scriblio, SOPAC, VuFind, and Blacklight. This chapter compares and contrasts these four tools and provides examples of how each of them is currently being used in libraries.

We hope that this book is useful for a variety of librarians and library technologists in providing them with an overview of the tools available and examples of library implementations. If you are new to open source software, we encourage you to read the book cover to cover to get a bird's-eye view of the landscape of open source web applications for libraries. If you are already familiar with the landscape and are looking for information on a specific tool, just grab that chapter and get going.

Part I

Introduction to Open Source Web Applications

CHAPTER 1

What Is Open Source Software?

In recent years there has been a great deal of buzz in the library community about open source software (OSS). Open source integrated library systems such as Evergreen and Koha have gained popularity, as have open source next generation catalog tools such as VuFind and Blacklight. So what exactly is open source software, and what advantages does it present for libraries?

The term *open source software* can be confusing at times. Typically, people associate open source with software that you can download and install for free. This definition focuses solely on the cost aspect. However, while some OSS can be downloaded and installed for no cost, cost really isn't what OSS is about. At its core, OSS is about the freedom to adapt and customize software. For this reason, many people refer to open source software as FLOSS (free/libre open source software) to shift the focus to the freedoms that are inherent with this type of software. Dan Chudnov describes it best in a 2008 *Computers in Libraries* column when paraphrasing the GNU Public license (www.gnu.org/licenses/gpl.html): "FLOSS provides the freedom to run, study, adapt, improve, and redistribute software."[1]

So what does this mean in practical terms? With OSS, you have access to the raw source code files, so if you wish you can view these files and make changes. You have the ability to correct problems, add new functionality, or improve existing functionality. Any changes you make can be submitted back to the applications community and developers for others to try out and adopt. Our very ability to write a book like this and delve into the inner workings of the applications on the level we do is dependent on FLOSS.

Whether you know it or not, you have probably already made some use of OSS. A significant portion of websites run on OSS; in fact, major companies such as Amazon and Google use OSS. Moreover, if you browse the web with Firefox, check your email on Thunderbird, or blog using WordPress, you are already using OSS.

Principles of the Open Source Community

Open source software is very much about community; without a vibrant community, OSS often fails. This is because OSS is community developed, maintained, and supported. This means that code is often written by many different people throughout the world. While there may be some coordination of efforts on a project between open source developers and a core set of developers, there doesn't have to be. Each member of the software community can contribute in the way he or she sees fit.

This model has two advantages. First, many eyes and minds make for better software. The only way to find bugs in software is to look at the system intensively, which is a time-consuming process. Bugs are more likely to be caught when the process is distributed across a large group of people. (And, because a greater number of people have the ability to fix a bug once it is found, this model also increases the likelihood that the bug will be fixed.) Second, this cooperative development brings the "wisdom of the crowd" to open source projects. By bringing together a diverse group of people with different backgrounds and opinions, you get software that reflects a variety of perspectives and needs—in short, you simply get better software.

Another principle of the open source community is that participation is expected. Not only is it okay for developers to copy, correct, and enhance software, it is expected. In fact, if you want to redistribute or repackage open source code, most open source licenses require that you contribute any changes you make back to the community. Development of code is just one way to participate in an open source community, though. There are many other potential tasks, from reviewing code to answering questions in forums to writing documentation. Any kind of participation helps make the community stronger and more effective.

Costs

While in the open source model there is typically no cost for the software itself, *running* open source software is not without cost. The bulk of the cost shifts from the software itself to the expertise needed to run the software and, potentially, modify it. This is one of the most significant differences between OSS and commercial software. While using any software entails costs for implementation and support, with commercial products the software itself also costs money. By implementing OSS, libraries remove this cost and are able to invest that money elsewhere. Some have suggested if this money were reinvested in software development, the overall quality of library systems could be improved.

Many organizations argue against implementing OSS because they believe that the cost of supporting it is greater than the cost of a commercial software product. This argument makes the false assumption that commercial software doesn't come with a support cost and defers responsibility for support back to the vendor. Organizations that implement OSS choose to take responsibility for the software they run, but with this responsibility comes flexibility. OSS is not tied to a particular vendor; several vendors could choose to support the same open source product. Libraries thus have the flexibility to change vendors without changing their software. Additionally, they can change or modify the code to meet their individual needs as they see fit.

Strengths and Limitations

Open source software has myriad strengths. First, of course, is the cost of the software. Since open software itself typically has no cost, it allows libraries to invest these resources in other areas. Second, because the source code is freely available, libraries can inspect and evaluate the software on a deep level without having to purchase it first. Third, OSS provides libraries with the flexibility to adapt software to their specific needs. An in-house developer can customize OSS to meet the specific needs of the library or fix bugs. Libraries are no longer chained to the development priorities of vendors, which often don't agree with the library's priorities. Fourth, as mentioned previously, OSS is not tied to a single vendor. Therefore, libraries have the ability to change vendors without changing their software.

For all these strengths of OSS, it has its limitations as well. There is almost never a built-in support hotline to call, and the level of support from the community varies greatly from application to application. Some applications have extensive documentation, forums, IRC channels, and other forms of support, while with other applications, the only documentation might be the source code itself. Organizations need to do their homework before implementing an open source application to understand the level of support available.

Licenses

Open source software can be distributed under a variety of licenses. Currently, the most popular license for OSS is the GNU General Public License, also referred to as the GPL. Under the GPL users have the right to use, copy, modify, and distribute the software. However, if users choose to change or add to the software and redistribute it, it must be redistributed under the same license as the original software. This provision, which is known as *copyleft*, has helped to give OSS contributors confidence that their work would remain free for others and not be exploited by individuals or organizations that have no intention of contributing back to the community. Ironically, the GPL allows users to choose whether to charge a fee for redistributing the software, as long as the redistribution adheres to the terms and conditions of the GPL.

In addition to the GPL, there are a variety of other licenses for OSS, including GNU Lesser General Public License, BSD License, Mozilla Public License, MIT License, and Apache License. Some of these licenses are GPL-compatible, which means that applications with these types of licenses can have their code combined with GPL licensed software without creating a conflict. However, some of these licenses are not as strongly copyleft as the GPL license. For example, MIT and BSD-based licenses allow derivative works to be available under terms that are more restrictive than those of the original license. While each of these licenses is slightly different, they are all based on the same basic principles and ideals that users should have the freedom to use, copy, modify, and distribute software.

Open Source Business Models

Open source software has become so popular that several companies have developed business models based on it. The first business model, known as the *dual license* model, is the one used by Movable Type and MySQL. Dual licenses enable commercial entities to make two versions of their software available. One version is open source and typically provided at no cost. A second version with additional functionality and features, often designed as an enterprise solution, is available under a proprietary license. Using this model, organizations can both simultaneously support open source development and have a stable business.

This is the model under which the Movable Type blogging platform operates. Originally the Movable Type blogging platform was OSS, but in 2004, Six Apart, the company that developed Moveable Type, changed its licensing model to be strictly proprietary. This change created a huge backlash within the user community and prompted many Movable Type users to move to the WordPress platform. In response, Six Apart decided to dual license the software, offering both open source and proprietary versions for different user markets.

The second model, known as the software as a service (SaaS) model, is the one adopted by companies like LibLime and Equinox. This model differs from the dual license model in that revenue is generated not from selling the software itself but from providing support for the software. In this model, an organization chooses the OSS it wants to use, then finds a vendor to implement and support that software. Currently Equinox specializes in implementing and supporting the Evergreen open source ILS. LibLime provides support for a variety of products, including the Koha open source ILS; MasterKey, a federated search tool; and Kete, a digital library tool. However, LibLime's primary business is centered around supporting the Koha ILS. Outside of libraries, there are companies that specialize in supporting other OSS, such as the Drupal or Joomla CMSs. This support-based model seems quite successful, and libraries considering OSS should examine these types of options for external support.

Applications Discussed in This Book

We used several criteria when selecting the web applications to include here. The first two were ease of installation and server requirements. We wanted applications that were fairly simple to install and had fairly typical server requirements. For this reason, the majority of the applications in the books are LAMP-based (see more on the LAMP stack in Chapter 2). The next criterion was the level of use and the robustness of the user community. Because libraries installing OSS have to be self-supporting, we felt it was important to choose applications that were frequently used by libraries and that also had fairly active user and development communities.

Lastly, because of the breadth and variety of open source web applications available, we tried to focus on software that is universal to the tasks performed in nearly every library. For this reason, we have chosen not to cover tools related to digital libraries, special collections, or archives. We do understand that each library has individual needs, so where possible we will present more than one option for libraries to choose from in each category.

Endnote

1. Daniel Chudnov, "What Librarians Still Don't Know About Open Source Software," *Computers in Libraries* 28, no. 3 (2008): 40, 42–43. Library, Information Science & Technology Abstracts, EBSCOhost (accessed November 10, 2009).

References

Chudnov, D. 2007. The future of FLOSS in libraries. In *Information tomorrow: Reflections on technology and the future of public and academic libraries*, ed. R. S. Gordon. Medford, NJ: Information Today, Inc.

CHAPTER 2

The LAMP Stack

The LAMP stack is a set of open source software (OSS) that provides the principal components for a viable general purpose web server. The LAMP stack consists of four components, each of which serves a particular function. The first piece is Linux, which serves as the base operating system (OS). The second is Apache, which fulfills the role of web server. The third is MySQL, which functions as the database management system. The last piece in the LAMP stack is the server-side scripting language, which performs the task of providing dynamic webpages. The specific scripting language, though, varies across implementations. There are various popular, viable server-side scripting languages to choose from, including PHP, Perl, or Python, all of which run well as part of the LAMP module. The LAMP stack is extremely popular because it is free, adaptable, and bundled with most Linux OS distributions.

Linux

In the LAMP stack, a web server runs the Linux OS, which was originally developed in 1991 by Linus Torvalds. The operating system portion of LAMP handles the most basic functionality, including network access, file and data storage, and other baseline functions. Like most OSS, Linux is collaboratively built and managed by programmers and testers from around the world, and can be customized, modified, and tweaked. As a result, there are many different flavors of Linux available. A few of the most popular are Red Hat, Fedora, Debian, SUSE, and Ubuntu; while each is slightly different, they all perform the same basic operations. Some versions, such as Red Hat Enterprise, are licensed in software with support fashion, meaning that although they are based on open source code, the license itself is not free and those who purchase Red Hat Enterprise receive a guaranteed level of support. Many other flavors of Linux, however, are both open source and free.

Many who use the LAMP model feel that it offers significant advantages over other ways of running web servers. One argument is that open source and freely available software is inherently more secure, because bugs and security flaws are found more quickly and fixed by the community. Another potential advantage is that the baseline configuration of the Linux server OS is very simple and stripped down, so only the basic functionality is installed by default. Two things are gained by keeping the server lean. First, server resources are not devoted to unnecessary applications, so the full power of the server can be used to run those applications that actually need to be run. Second, a server running fewer applications is open to fewer security issues. Eliminating unnecessary applications reduces the potential for security flaws and bugs. If additional software is necessary for a given application, then it can be added to the server as needed.

The Windows OS follows a different model. The default installation of a Windows server adds much more rich functionality, which may or may not be needed on a given server. While this setup may be advantageous if you're not sure what you need, it requires additional resources and theoretically increases the chance of security issues. This is not to say, though, that you can't run OSS on a Windows server. While a LAMP stack uses Linux as the operating system, the Apache, MySQL, and PHP/Perl combination can also be run on other operating systems. Using the Windows OS (the WAMP model) or the Mac OS (the MAMP model) are both viable options if an organization is unable or unwilling to use a Linux OS.

Apache

Apache is an open source web server developed in 1995 by a core group of developers who used as their base the National Center for Supercomputing Applications (NCSA) httpd 1.3 web server developed by Robert McCool. The software is currently maintained by the Apache Software Foundation, which also supports a number of other open source projects. Apache is the only web server to run on all the major platforms. Since 1996, it has been the most popular web server, and its market share continues to grow each year. Within the LAMP model, Apache is responsible for the delivery of webpages. It takes

HTTP requests from web browsers and other software and sends back the file requested. For older, static, HTML-only pages, Apache is the only component necessary on the server. For more dynamic, database-driven sites and applications, it is necessary to install add-ons, better known as modules, to Apache.

Many modules can be added to extend Apache's baseline code. Some are in fact packaged as part of the standard Apache distribution but need to be enabled in order to function properly. One important set of modules are those that handle server-side scripting languages. Server-side scripting allows web developers to create dynamic and interactive webpages, which often draw information from and add information to a database management system. All of the applications in this book employ a server-side scripting language. For the purposes of our discussion, the two main modules supporting server-side scripting that are necessary in a LAMP module are mod_php and mod_perl. These two modules allow Apache to handle requests for files that incorporate the PHP and Perl programming languages, respectively. Apache modules are also available to support other server-side scripting languages, such as Python and Ruby on Rails.

In addition to modules that extend Apache to handle scripting languages, there are several modules that deal with authentication and access control, so that access to a particular page (or pages) can be limited based on a username and password. Some frequently used modules in this area include mod_access, mod_auth, mod_digest, and mod_auth_digest.

Another extremely important module is mod_rewrite, which allows URL requests sent to Apache to be "rewritten." Often it is necessary for a web server to rewrite URLs in order to redirect people to a different page or to make URLs more easily read and remembered by humans. Sometimes this means simply forwarding a request for page A to page B. However, URL rewriting also allows this to be done in a more complex fashion, by taking pieces of the first URL and using them to create the URL to which the person is being forwarded. So, for example,

http://www.librarywebchic.net/someform.php?name=Karen

could be redirected to

http://www.librarywebchic.net/newform.php?name=Karen

This technique of URL rewriting is used by several of the applications discussed in this book.

MySQL

MySQL is an open source multithreaded, multiuser, relational database system maintained by the MySQL AB group, now a subsidiary of Sun Microsystems. Initially released in 1995, the software has gone through many changes. The most recent was the transition from version 4.x to 5.x, which added many new enterprise level features, including cursors, stored procedures, triggers, and views. As of September 2010, MySQL had more than 11 million installations. It is used to power a number of popular websites, including Flickr, Wikipedia, and Facebook, as well as popular open source web applications such as WordPress, MediaWiki, and Drupal.

MySQL can be administered via basic command line tools, which allow users to perform all the basic administrative tasks such as creating users, setting permissions, and managing databases. In addition, a GUI version of the MySQL administrative tools (dev.mysql.com/downloads/gui-tools/5.0.html) is available for a variety of platforms, including Windows, Mac, and several Linux distributions. phpMy Admin (www.phpmyadmin.net) is a web-based tool that also allows users to administrate MySQL databases (Figure 2.1).

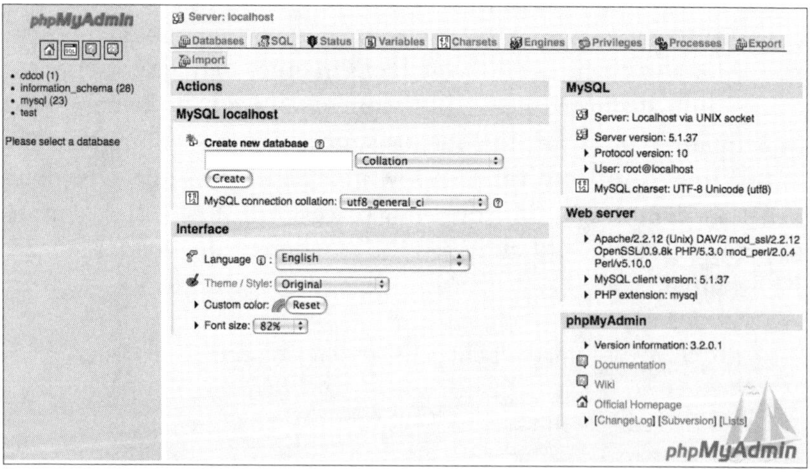

Figure 2.1 phpMyAdmin

In the LAMP model, MySQL is responsible for storing and serving data that is being accessed via SQL (Structured Query Language). SQL allows a web scripting language (PHP, Perl, or Python) to perform operations on specific portions of the data within the MySQL database. Typical operations include select, update, insert, and delete. Select brings back a specific set of data from the database and makes it available for display. Update changes existing data within the database. Insert adds new data to the database, and delete removes existing information from the database. These four basic operations are the backbone of most web applications. As a result, many of the applications discussed within this book use MySQL to store their data.

PHP

PHP is an open source server scripting language that is used to produce dynamic webpages. It was developed in the mid-1990s specifically for creating webpages, and currently more than 10 million sites use PHP. The language is capable of creating a variety of outputs on the fly, from HTML and XML to images and PDFs. It can natively connect to a variety of database management systems, including MySQL, PostgreSQL, and SQLite, and has evolved to include command line interface capabilities. As a result, it is extremely flexible. In the LAMP model, on the most basic level, PHP is responsible for rendering pages based on information within the database. However, it is also used to create interactivity within web applications. For example, PHP allows information to be taken from a web-based form and added to a database.

Like the other parts of the LAMP model, PHP is also modularized. The language comes with a core set of functions and operations, but these can be added to via extensions. There are two ways to extend PHP: PEAR and PECL. The PHP Extension and Application Repository (PEAR; pear.php.net) is a code repository that contains packages that extend PHP's functionality. PEAR packages are essentially script libraries written in PHP, which can easily be downloaded as compressed tar.gz files. (Mac users can extract tar.gz files natively, but PC users will need to download a program like 7-Zip at 7-zip.org.) In contrast, the PHP Extension Community Library (PECL; pecl.php.net) contains PHP extensions written in the C language. These are compiled to make them run more efficiently than PEAR extensions. Both types of extensions can be downloaded, installed, managed, and updated using the PEAR package manager. Depending on your operating system, there are a variety of ways to download and install PEAR. You can always, however, download it from the PEAR website and install it manually by following the instructions there.

PHP code must be enclosed in opening and closing PHP tags in order to be parsed. These tags separate the PHP code from the regular HTML code (Figure 2.2)

```
<?php

$bm = get_bookmarks( array(
          'orderby'         => 'name',
          'order'           => 'ASC',
          'limit'           => -1,
          'category'        => null,
          'category_name'   => 'Sites Hosted',
          'hide_invisible'  => 1,
          'show_updated'    => 0,
          'include'         => null,
          'exclude'         => null,
          'search'          => '.'));
     foreach ($bm as $bookmark){
          echo '<div style="float:left; padding-right:1em;">';
          echo '<img src="' . $bookmark->link_image . '" alt="' . $bookmark->link_name . '">';
          echo '</div>';
          echo '<h4><a href="' . $bookmark->link_url . '">' .  $bookmark->link_name . '</a></h4>';
          echo '<p>' . $bookmark->link_description . '</p>';
          echo '<br clear="all"/>';
        }

?>
```

Figure 2.2 PHP code example

There are two different types of tags you will typically see in PHP: <?php ?> and <? ?>. The latter is the short form, and although valid, it makes PHP code less portable. In addition, the short form can be disabled in an individual PHP configuration, so the use of this form of tag is discouraged. Variables are prefixed with a dollar sign and are case sensitive, so for instance $variable and $Variable are not equivalent. In general, PHP code is similar to the C programming language, which makes it relatively easy to learn. It uses comparable syntax, such as if and elseif conditions, and for and while loops. Here is an example of PHP code:

```
<html>
<body>
<?php

if ( strlen($_REQUEST[ 'Name' ] ) > 0) {
  echo '<p>Hello ' . $_REQUEST[ 'Name' ] .
  '</p>';
```

```
    }
?>

<?php
} else {
?>
<form action="name_collect.php"
method="get">
<p>
  <label for="AddWorldCatSearch-
  SearchString">Name </label>
  <input type="text" id="Name" name="Name"
  value="" />
</p>

<input type="submit" value="Search"/>
</form>
<?php
}
?>
</body>
</html>
```

Several open source frameworks can be downloaded and installed to facilitate rapid application development with PHP. Some of the more popular frameworks are CakePHP (cakephp.org), Symfony (www.symfony-project.org), CodeIgniter (codeigniter.com), and Zend Framework (framework.zend.com). The purpose of these is to enable developers to produce projects much faster by providing a standard set of code for commonly needed tasks. In addition, several of these frameworks utilize the Model-View-Controller (MVC) paradigm, which separates the business logic from input and presentation. Using a framework cannot only speed development but also improve application performance.

Perl

Perl is another open source programming language, which was originally developed around 1987 to handle text manipulations. Over time, it has developed other functionalities and features, but its strength still lies in data manipulation and handling text files. Early on, Perl was often used to process data submitted from a web-based form. From this starting point, it was increasingly used to add interactivity to websites, and today Perl is used for a variety of tasks, from text handling to graphics programming to dynamic webpage creation. It can also be run from the command line using a Perl interpreter, which makes the language extremely versatile and flexible.

Like PHP and Apache, Perl is also extensible. Its functionality can be expanded using Comprehensive Perl Archive Network (CPAN; www.cpan.org) modules. CPAN is an archive of Perl modules, which can be downloaded and installed. There is also a program called CPAN, which acts as a package manager to facilitate the download and installation of packages from the CPAN repository. Many of the modules in CPAN are essential to creating web applications with Perl. In particular, the functionality to interact with databases is not a core part of Perl; in order to interact with databases, it is necessary to install the Perl:DBI module from CPAN.

As with PHP, in the LAMP model, Perl is responsible for rendering dynamic pages and providing interactivity. Very few of the applications discussed in this book are Perl-based, the primary exception being Movable Type, an open source (but not completely free) blogging platform.

Ruby on Rails

While nearly all of the applications discussed in this book are PHP-based, a select few are written using Ruby on Rails. While Ruby on Rails is not part of the LAMP model itself, it uses nearly all the same technologies: Linux, Apache, and MySQL. The main difference here is that, instead of the coding layer being PHP or Perl, Ruby is used. Rails is a relatively new web application framework, developed in 2004 by David Heinemeier Hansson. Like many other frameworks, Rails uses the MVC architecture pattern, which separates code logic from presentation.

Ruby is also extensible; packages called "gems" are used to add functionality and libraries of code to Ruby. Like PHP and Perl, Ruby uses a package manager to add and manage additional functionality. Using the RubyGems package manager, code can be added to Ruby that adds a variety of features. Some Rails developers within the library community have been working to develop gems that provide specific library-related code, one example being the WorldCat Search API gem developed by Terry Reese at Oregon State University Library. Ruby libraries for working with MARC records are also available.

The main challenge with Rails is creating a scalable server environment. Rails has been critiqued in the past for not scaling up well; however, recent changes have made it more scalable and reliable. Rails comes with an integrated web server, WEBrick, and a build tool, Rake, which provide a basic development environment. When running Rails applications in a production mode, there are several options for web servers. Mongrel is extremely popular for serving Rails applications. However, if you are already running an Apache web server, a better choice is to install mod_rails, which allows Apache to handle the Rails scripts.

XAMPP

Not everyone will have a server at their disposal for configuration or will be comfortable installing these foundational programs. However, if you fall into either of these categories, you can still try out the applications featured in this book. Another possible way to run a LAMP model setup is by using XAMPP, which stands for cross-platform, Apache, MySQL, PHP, Perl. XAMPP can be downloaded at sourceforge.net/projects/xampp. This cross platform installer for Apache, MySQL, PHP, and Perl allows you to install a basic setup on a Linux, Windows, or Mac OS machine for testing purposes. XAMPP can even be run from a USB drive.

XAMPP is extremely easy to install and set up, and can be a huge time saver because it makes sure all the parts of the LAMP stack play nicely together. Installing all of the pieces of the LAMP stack and configuring them to work with each other properly can be a challenge, particularly if it is done from source files. XAMPP removes this complexity and transforms the process into literally two steps. Once XAMPP is installed, you will be presented with a welcome screen when you visit http://localhost in your web browser. Then, just choose a language to see a dashboard for XAMPP (Figure 2.3).

XAMPP is extremely popular and widely used. It is often used by instructors who teach classes on PHP because it provides students with the same baseline environment to work in. Additionally, XAMPP is used by many developers to easily test new code and applications because it saves them from having to spend time configuring a development server. XAMPP comes with several built-in development

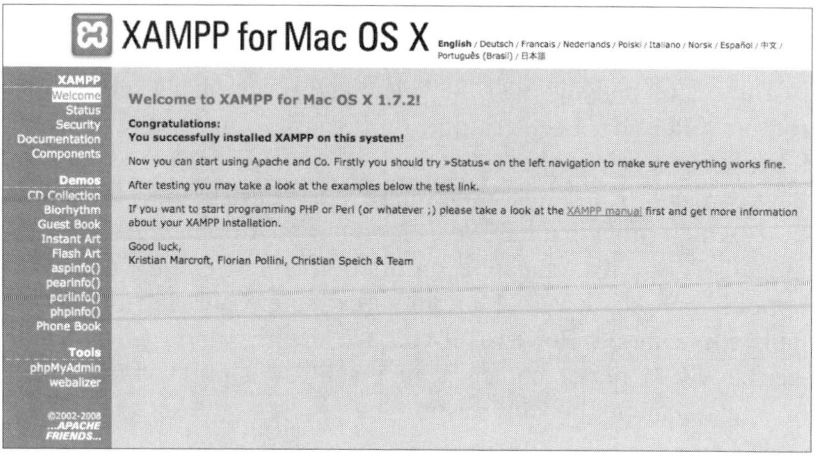
XAMPP for Mac OS X
English / Deutsch / Francais / Nederlands / Polski / Italiano / Norsk / Español / 中文 / Português (Brasil) / 日本語
XAMPP
Welcome
Status
Security
Documentation
Components
Demos
CD Collection
Biorhythm
Guest Book
Instant Art
Flash Art
aspInfo()
pearInfo()
perlInfo()
phpInfo()
Phone Book
Tools
phpMyAdmin
webalizer
©2002-2008
...APACHE FRIENDS...
Welcome to XAMPP for Mac OS X 1.7.2!
Congratulations:
You successfully installed XAMPP on this system!
Now you can start using Apache and Co. Firstly you should try »Status« on the left navigation to make sure everything works fine.
After testing you may take a look at the examples below the test link.
If you want to start programming PHP or Perl (or whatever ;) please take a look at the XAMPP manual first and get more information about your XAMPP installation.
Good luck,
Kristian Marcroft, Florian Pollini, Christian Speich & Team

Figure 2.3 Default XAMPP web server

tools, including phpMyAdmin for managing MySQL databases, a script to easily switch between versions 4 and 5 of PHP, and Webalizer for analyzing web server log files. These tools make developing applications within a LAMP environment much easier.

However, XAMPP is not without its disadvantages. It is not designed to operate in a production environment, as many important security features are disabled by default in order to make testing easier. Also, it provides just a basic install of Apache, MySQL, PHP, and Perl, so particular add-ons or configurations needed for various applications may be missing. Lastly, it does not provide an environment for testing Rails applications.

XAMPP, though, is not the only packaged installer for Apache, MySQL, PHP, and Perl. A variety of installers are available for both the Windows and Mac operating systems. A good alternative to XAMPP for Windows is WampServer (www.wampserver.com/en). In Mac OS versions 10.5 and higher, an installer isn't really necessary, as the basic Mac OS ships with Apache, MySQL, and PHP. However, for those who prefer to avoid potential configuration issues, MAMP (www.mamp.info/en/index.html) is a packaged installer for the Mac OS.

These package installers are the best solutions for those who want a quick and easy way to try out open source web applications.

References

About the Apache HTTP Server Project. Apache HTTP Server Project. Retrieved July 13, 2010, from httpd.apache.org/ABOUT_APACHE.html

Sobel, J. (December 21, 2007). Keeping Up. The Facebook Blog. Retrieved July 13, 2010, blog.facebook.com/blog.php?post=7899307130

Top Reasons for Product Managers to Embed MySQL. MySQL. Retrieved July 13, 2010, from www.mysql.com/why-mysql/topreasons_pm.html

YouTube, Flickr, and Wikipedia to Share Their Secrets of Success at the 2007 MySQL Conference & Expo. MySQL. April 10, 2007. Retrieved July 13, 2010, from dev.mysql.com/tech-resources/articles/mysqluc-2007.html

CHAPTER 3

Web Hosting Options

The basic prerequisite for using open source web applications is access to a web server or web space. At minimum, a web server provides space to store the files associated with a website and provides access to those webpages via the internet. Preferably, a library will have at least two web servers: a production server that hosts the live website, and a development server for testing web applications before they go live. Web server access will vary greatly from library to library. Smaller libraries may only have access to a single folder on a web server that contains their website's files, while larger libraries may have full, or root, access to multiple web servers.

There are two basic reasons why a library might choose to use an outside web hosting company: no access to a web server, or no access to a server that will support open source web applications. A library or its parent organization may not have the funds to purchase and support an in-house server, the technology personnel to set up and support a web server, or the personnel to set up and maintain a website. Under these circumstances, they need a permanent web hosting solution.

Lack of server support for open source web applications is another reason to use a web hosting company. A library may be in an environment where access to servers is strictly controlled. For example, a library in a corporate or government setting may have a very locked-down web environment and therefore not have the ability to set up development servers to explore open source web applications. Running open source web applications usually requires access to a server running Apache/MySQL/PHP. If your organization is heavily invested in a Microsoft server environment or cannot provide access to development servers with a LAMP environment, you may wish to use a web hosting company. The majority of web hosting companies provide access to either a LAMP or WAMP environment. It is not uncommon to use web hosting for a development server or to provide a "proof of concept" site. A proof of concept site can demonstrate the need for a LAMP server environment to your library director and IT.

Free Web Hosting

Free web hosting services offer the ability to create a website using tools provided by the site host. WordPress (wordpress.com) and Google Sites (sites.google.com) are examples of free web hosting sites. Both offer the ability to create simple sites. WordPress gives you option of various themes and layouts, and the ability to add your own domain name. Google Sites gives you all of this and adds the ability to add modules that interact with other Google tools, such as Google Docs, Calendar, Maps, and Picasa. Both sites are limited as to theme customization, although both provide a number of templates or themes to pick from. One thing to keep in mind about free hosting services is that most generate revenue either by placing ad banners on your site or by charging a fee to add extra features to your site. For example, for a fee, WordPress will allow you to customize the CSS of a theme, block ads from appearing on your site, or add more server space to your account. Due to the limitations of free web hosting sites, we recommend that free web hosting sites be used only for personal websites or blogs, not for a library site.

Domain Names

Once you have made the decision to sign up with a hosting service, you will need to acquire a domain name. Computers and web servers are identified by their internet protocol (IP) addresses on the internet. But as IP addresses are difficult to remember, a domain name is used to provide a user-friendly alias for the IP address of a website. Web hosting companies usually require that you either provide or register for a domain name when you sign up for a hosting service. While many hosting companies offer free domain registration when you sign up for a hosting package, we recommend that you register your domain name with a separate company. A "free" domain name provided by a web hosting company may not actually be registered to you but to the hosting company itself. This makes it very difficult to move the domain name to a different web hosting company should you want to change to a new host in the future.

Signing up for a domain name is a very simple process; the challenge is creating a name that is memorable and around five to 20 characters in length. You also have to decide on the domain extension. If you are signing up for a domain for an official library website, then you should probably try to get a domain such as "yourlibrary name.org." If you are registering a domain for a development site, then consider the popular domain extensions of .com or .net. While the .com domains are harder to register due to their popularity, .com is the default extension that your users and web search tools will add to the end of your domain. Domain name generator sites like BustAName (www.bustaname.com) can help you brainstorm available combinations of domain names and extensions (Figure 3.1).

Once you have a domain name in mind, you will need to register that domain with a domain registrar. Numerous domain registrars are available on the internet, such as Namecheap (www.namecheap.com), Network Solutions (www.networksolutions.com), and Moniker (www.moniker.com). Most registrars will also show you what other

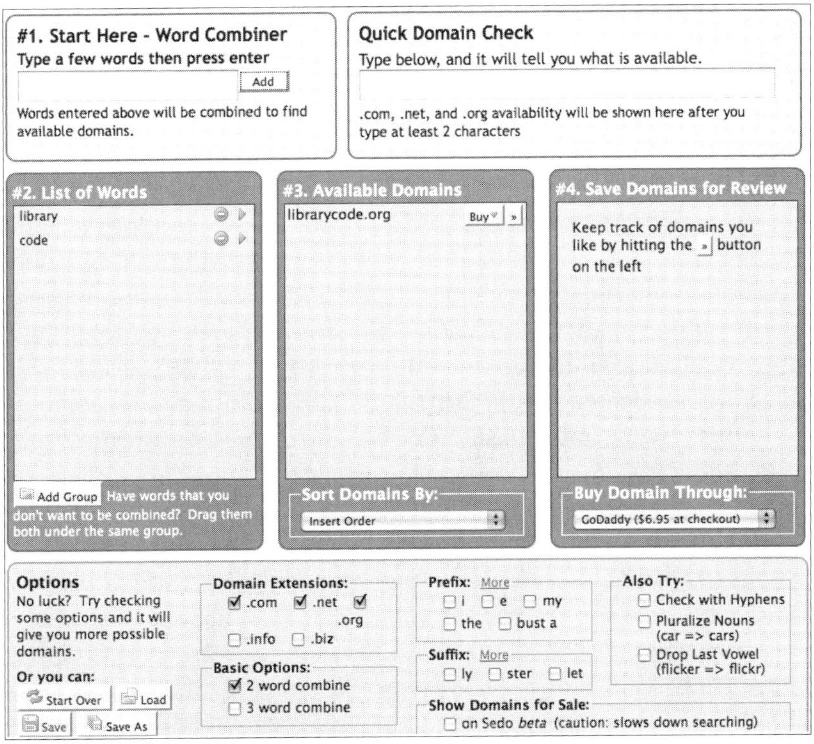

Figure 3.1 BustAName

extensions are available for your selected domain name. While this is an additional expense, it is often good idea to buy your name with multiple domain extensions. This gives you the ability to use "your libraryname.org" as your live site and "yourlibraryname.net" as your development site. It will also prevent anyone from setting up "your libraryname.net" as the type of site your users may not want to stumble upon.

There are some precautions to keep in mind while signing up for a domain. You can register the domain name for up to 10 years at a time. Doing this can save you expense and the trouble of renewing your domain yearly. Make sure that you register with an email account that you use frequently; the domain registrar will send notifications to your email account as the time to renew your domain approaches. You don't want to miss the renewal deadline, as many domain registrars allow people to backorder domain names; your domain could potentially be snatched away as soon as you let it expire.

The Need for Speed: Bandwidth

Before choosing a web host you should determine how much bandwidth your site will need. If you are using the server as a proof of concept or for development, then your bandwidth requirements will most likely be low. If this is to be a live site for your library, you will need to estimate how much bandwidth your site will use. While many hosting companies claim to offer unlimited bandwidth, this is rarely the case. All web host providers will have a proviso in your user agreement that they may throttle your site's bandwidth or shut down your site entirely due to high bandwidth or web server CPU usage. This issue is complicated by the fact that hosting companies often automate this process and will shut down your site without warning you.

Before you sign on with a web host, you can calculate the estimated bandwidth you will need based on the usage statistics of your current site. As web hosts bill based on bandwidth used per month, a common formula used to determine how much bandwidth you will need is: visits a day x page views per visit x average page size x 30 (number of days in a month). For example, the SUNY Cortland library site gets an average of 1,500 visits per weekday, each visitor looks at an average of 5 pages per visit, and each webpage has an average page size of 30KB. Therefore the bandwidth needed by the SUNY

Cortland library site for one month equals: 1,500 x 5 x 30KB x 30 = 6,700,000KB = 6,700 MB = 6.7 GB. So the SUNY Cortland library site would require a hosting plan with at least 6.7 GB of bandwidth a month. However, you should anticipate that redesigning your website will result in an increase in the number of users visiting your site and also factor in that an image-rich site with multimedia, especially video, will use additional bandwidth.

There are a few things that you can do to reduce bandwidth usage. The first is to keep an eye on your site's usage. Many hosting companies will provide a means to monitor your site's traffic. For example, once you have logged into your web host, you may see a panel with monthly usage data (Figure 3.2).

Web hosts will often provide access to a stats package like AWStats or Webalizer. These tools can provide a month-by-month analysis of bandwidth usage (Figure 3.3).

A good way to reduce bandwidth is to host your site's multimedia files elsewhere; for example, you can use Flickr, YouTube, and/or Amazon S3 to host your images and video files. Lastly, a robots.txt file can help to reduce your site's bandwidth. A robots.txt file is a text file you save on the root of your web server that either permits or forbids search engine spiders to crawl your site or part of your site. Writing the robots.txt file so that it permits only a few search engines to crawl your site will help reduce your bandwidth usage. Here is a sample robots.txt file that allows only Google, Yahoo!, and Microsoft to crawl your site:

```
User-agent: MSNbot
Disallow:
User-agent: Slurp
Disallow:
User-agent: Googlebot
Disallow:

user-agent: *
disallow: /
```

To use this example, simply create a text file named "robots.txt" using this sample text. Save or copy that file to the root, or main directory of your website. If you wish to further customize your robots.txt file, the Web Robots Pages (www.robotstxt.org) provides instructions on how to create a robots.txt file as well as a list of current bots.

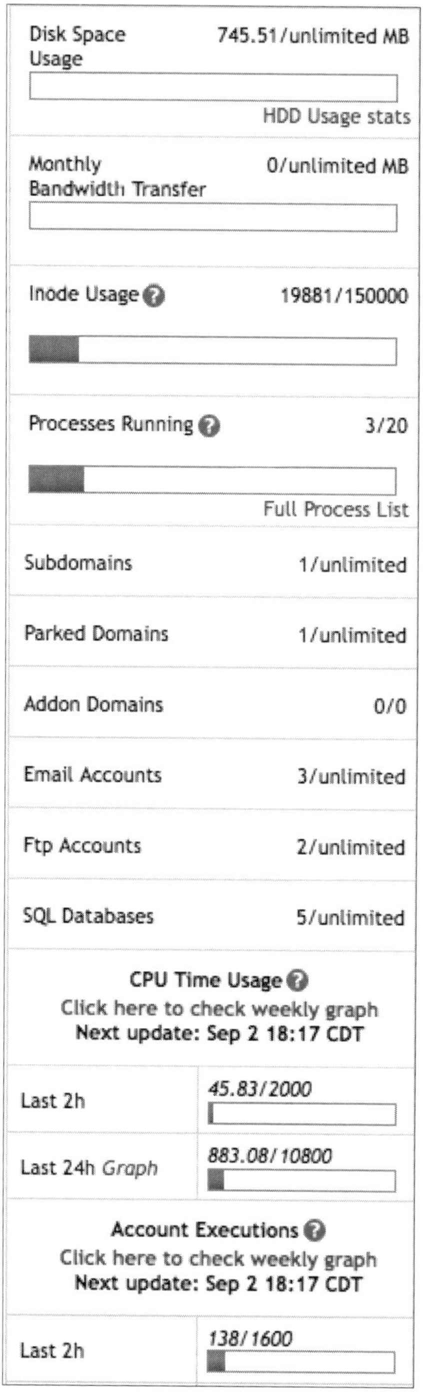

Figure 3.2 SiteGround usage data

Reported period	Month Apr 2009				
First visit	01 Apr 2009 - 00:00				
Last visit	30 Apr 2009 - 23:59				
	Unique visitors	Number of visits	Pages	Hits	Bandwidth
Viewed traffic *	**9300**	**31497** (3.38 visits/visitor)	**151407** (4.8 pages/visit)	**1011327** (32.1 hits/visit)	**3.56 GB** (118.42 KB/visit)
Not viewed traffic *			**19812**	**21330**	**465.16 MB**

* Not viewed traffic includes traffic generated by robots, worms, or replies with special HTTP status codes.

Figure 3.3 Example of AWStats usage data

Determining Server Needs

Now that you have an idea of how much bandwidth your site will need, you can start making a checklist of features you need your web host to have. You will need to think about the server requirements of the software that you will be using, what access you will have to the server, and how often the web host updates the server software. Here are some points to consider:

- What operating system will your server be running? While most servers run some flavor of Linux, if you need the ability to work with ASP or ASP.NET code, you will need a Windows server.
- What programming languages will the server support? Most of the software mentioned in this book requires PHP; some also requires Perl and/or Ruby.
- What database software is available, and how many databases can you have? Most web hosting companies will have MySQL and possibly PostgreSQL. Some hosting companies limit the number of databases you can create; if so, make sure that this limit meets your needs.
- Will you have secure FTP (sFTP) and secure shell (SSH) access to your server? You will need sFTP and SSH to upload, unpack, and set up software on your server.
- What permissions will you have on your server? You may need super user or root access to run software install scripts, edit your .htaccess files, and so on.
- Is there an administration GUI such as cPanel or Plesk? An administration GUI will make managing user and email accounts easy, and allow quick access to website usage statistics.

- How much bandwidth and storage will you have?
- Does the hosting company offer an upgrade path? If your site starts to attract more visitors, you may need to upgrade your plan to increase your monthly bandwidth.
- Does the web host have a tool for software installs? For example, Fantastico is a common tool that allows users to install software easily; it will install the software and set up any MySQL databases associated with it. This is an excellent way to explore open source software and to set up and run quick software demonstrations. Fantastico software installs are not recommended for live (production) servers, though, as you are dependent on your web hosting company for security patches and upgrades.

Types of Web Hosting

As you go hunting for a web host, you may find the number of choices confusing. For a development site, you will most likely be looking for a shared or cloud hosting service. For a live (production) site, you will be looking for a virtual private server (VPS) or a dedicated server.

Solutions for Development Sites: Shared and Cloud Web Hosting

Shared web hosting packages are usually the starting place for most new websites. Shared hosting is exactly what it sounds like: Your website is sharing a server with up to hundreds of other websites. Shared hosting plans are the cheapest, starting at about $5 to $10 per month. Most shared hosting plans feature an administrator's panel to configure software and site settings, limited or no root access, and limited sFTP and SSH access. One of the potential downsides of shared hosting is that high traffic on one or more of the websites on a shared server will slow down page load times for all the websites on that server.

Shared servers are a good place to learn the basics of working on a web server. Example web hosting companies that offer shared hosting plans are SiteGround (www.siteground.com), HostGator (www.hostgator.com), and WestHost (www.westhost.com). SiteGround and HostGator provide a wide range of configurable options in the administrator's panel, cPanel. Installing a content management system such as Drupal or Joomla takes less than five minutes on HostGator (see Figures 3.4 through 3.6).

SiteGround provides a good example of the kinds of tutorials and help possible on a web hosting site. SiteGround has walk-through tutorials and videos to get you started, including information on how to install and configure software, web server basics, and managing your account (Figures 3.7 and 3.8).

WestHost does not use the common administrator software cPanel, but instead uses a customized administrator's panel. It's quite a bit slower than cPanel but offers one big advantage: the ability to install and upgrade MySQL, PHP, Perl, and Java at your choosing. The ability to choose which PHP and MySQL version you are running on your web server can be important if you are using a library software package that uses older versions of PHP or MySQL (Figure 3.9).

Web Hosting in the Cloud

Cloud computing is a buzz term that has sprung up within the past few years. In terms of web hosting, a simplified definition of cloud

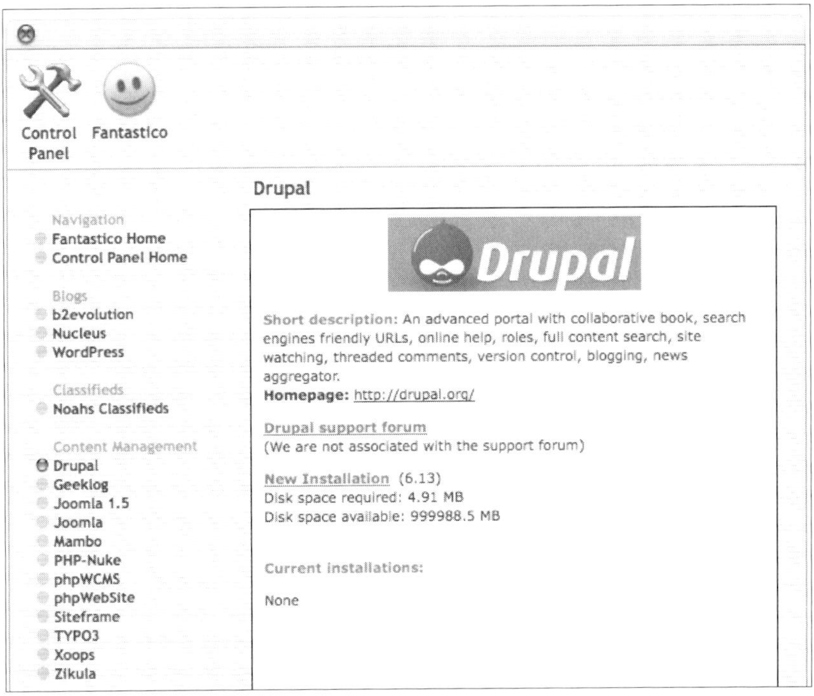

Figure 3.4 HostGator installation step 1

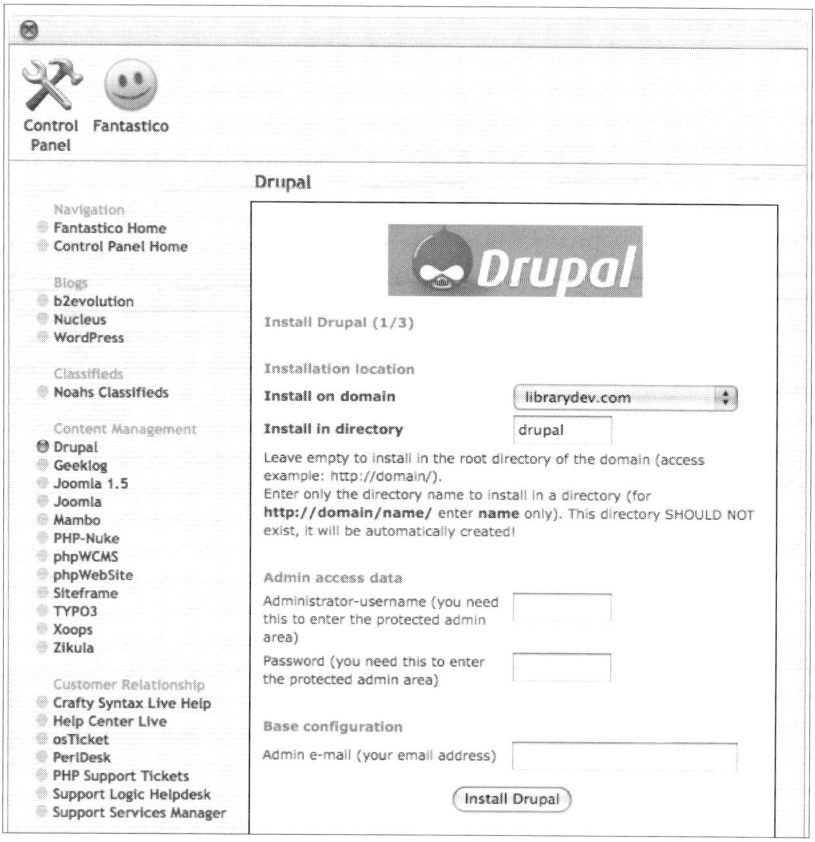

Figure 3.5 HostGator installation step 2

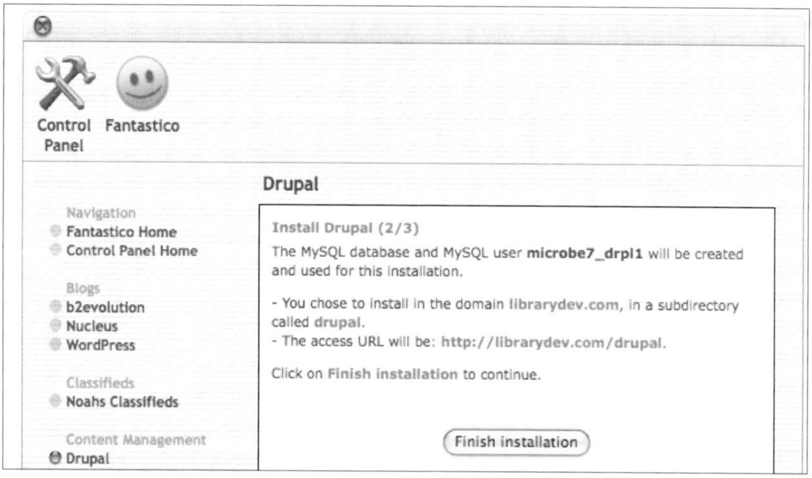

Figure 3.6 HostGator installation step 3

Figure 3.7 SiteGround tutorials

computing is that it is a network of virtual servers on the internet. Cloud computing involves several common assumptions: Cloud computing service charges are based on usage (often calculated by the minute), cloud computing is scalable to the user's needs, and the technology behind the cloud is hidden from the user (i.e., all the user needs to access the cloud is an internet connection and a web browser).

Amazon Web Services (AWS) has been offering the cloud computing web host service Amazon Elastic Compute Cloud (EC2) since 2006. Amazon EC2 offers virtual machine instances intended to provide users with computing resources that are scalable for on-demand computing power. However, these virtual machine instances can also

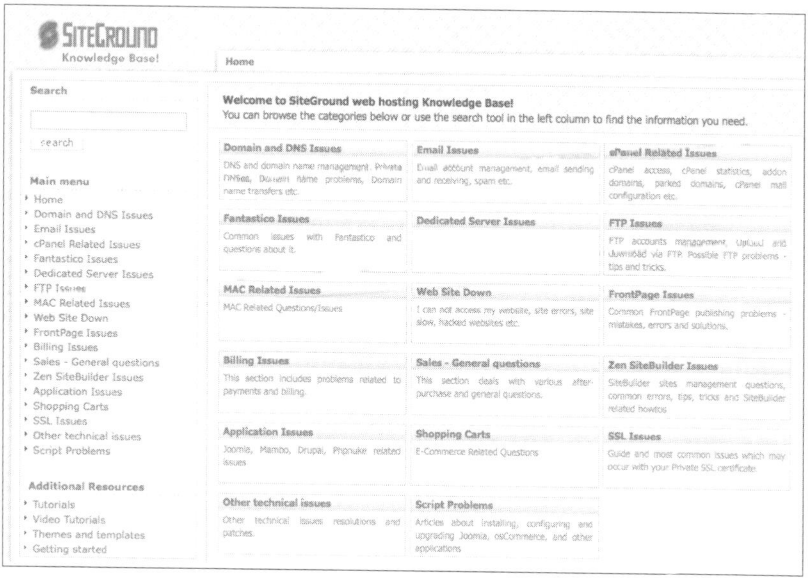

Figure 3.8 SiteGround knowledge base

serve as development servers. Amazon allows the users to select the virtual server specifications they need and to install an Amazon machine image (AMI; Figure 3.10). The ability to quickly create server instances provides an excellent development platform for testing software. After completing the sign-up process with AWS, you can search for and install machine images. For example, if I wanted to test Drupal, I would simply find and launch a Drupal image.

After the instance launches, Amazon provides you with a URL for your web server and SSH access to the virtual server. Amazon EC2 has thousands of machine images configured with many types of Linux and the various open source content management systems mentioned in this book.

Solutions for Production Sites: VPS Grid and Dedicated Servers

For a production server, you will probably need a virtual or dedicated server. A shared web hosting package may not be able to handle a website that gets thousands of hits per day. Either the site will load slowly, or it will fail to load at all. The next step up from a shared web hosting service is a VPS or a dedicated server.

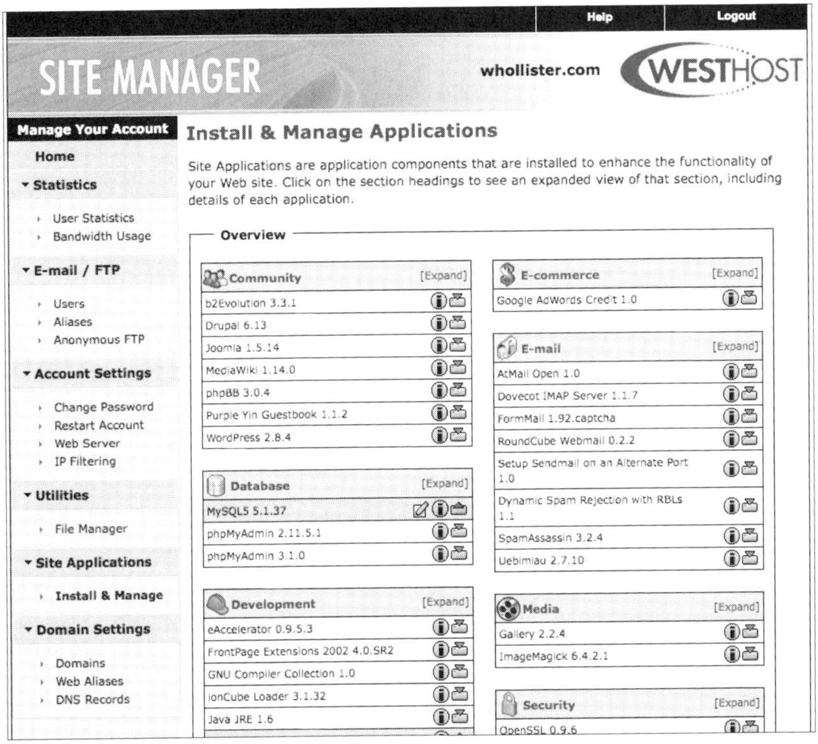

Figure 3.9 WestHost site manager

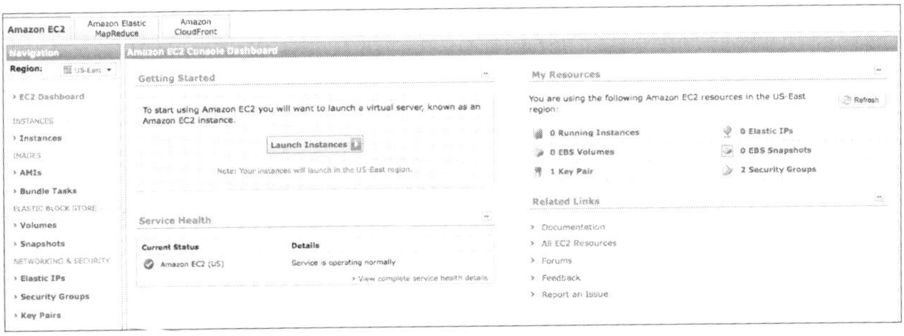

Figure 3.10 Amazon EC2 AMI

Virtual Private Server

A VPS is the next step up from a shared hosting plan. A VPS server uses virtualization software to divide a single server into several virtual servers and is a middle ground between a shared hosting plan and a dedicated server. Each VPS simulates a dedicated server; you have root access, which gives you full control over the VPS, including the ability to run scripts and restart Apache. While a VPS will have lower server specifications than a dedicated server, a VPS will give far more flexibility than a shared hosting plan. VPS plans start at about $30 per month for an unmanaged VPS to $50 for a managed VPS. If you are comfortable handling server management tasks such as running updates and security patches and performing backups, then an unmanaged plan will work for you.

Dedicated Server

Many web hosting companies offer both shared hosting and dedicated server packages. The companies mentioned previously, SiteGround, HostGator, and WestHost, all offer dedicated hosting packages that start at about $175 per month. As with VPS hosting, dedicated servers are available as either unmanaged or managed servers. The advantages of a dedicated server are that you are not sharing resources and that the server itself may be more robust than a VPS. Ironically enough, dedicated servers are most likely only needed by high-traffic academic or public library sites, which most likely have their own in-house servers.

LISHost

LISHost (lishost.net) falls outside of the types of hosting mentioned so far. LISHost is a web hosting company for librarians, run by librarians, which has grown to host several hundred sites, including several public library websites and librarians' personal blogs. Signing up for an account on LISHost is not quite an automated process; there will be some discussion back and forth as to what web applications you will be running.

LISHost has only one hosting "plan" to choose, which as of this writing is $10 a month. Many web hosting companies claim to offer unlimited bandwidth and storage and hide the actual amounts in the small print of the user agreement. LISHost offers "almost unlimited space" and bandwidth. Most sites on LISHost have no limits on storage or bandwidth; a small number of very large sites are charged an additional fee for their heavy bandwidth usage. LISHost offers server space on a Linux server that supports PHP, Perl, Python, MySQL, and PostgreSQL. As of this writing, LISHost does not support an administration panel such as cPanel; all server configurations and software installs are done via sFTP and SSH.

One of the big advantages of using LISHost as a web host is the support since the support team is comprised of librarians who are experienced at server management. If you have little experience setting up blogging software or a content management system, the support team can do this for you. Need a little help tweaking or fixing something on your site? LISHost support can also assist you with this. There is a definite advantage to getting support for your site from a fellow librarian as opposed to refreshing your email as you await the next trouble ticket update.

Summary

Libraries that do not have access to a server that supports open source web applications can choose from many hosting solutions. Amazon's EC2 service seems like an excellent route for librarians needing a development server or a server to show proof of concept of what can be done with open source web applications. LISHost or a VPS server is the suggested route for libraries needing server space for their production (live) websites.

Part II

Blogs and Wikis

CHAPTER 4

WordPress

Library blogs and wikis allow librarians and staff to easily create and edit web content. A blog (short for "weblog)" is written in a journal format that presents content in a reverse chronological order (the most recent items first). In recent years, blogging has become extremely popular with libraries and librarians. Typically libraries use blogs as a tool to communicate effectively with their patrons. Libraries' blogs often contain news items or other information that is updated on a regular basis, such as book reviews, events, and announcements.

In contrast, wikis are used for content that is more static in nature. Wikis originally developed as a way to allow everyday users to create, format, and present content easily on the web without having to know HTML. Content in wikis is formatted via wiki-markup, which is much simpler and easier to use than HTML. Wikis can be set up so that anyone can edit a given page, or they can be limited to a specific group of people. In addition, wikis keep track of page revisions, which allows content to be reverted to a previous version in the case of improper or accidental changes. Wikis can be used in a variety of ways in libraries. Some libraries use wikis to create and edit the content on their staff intranet or even to manage all the content on their library website. Other libraries use wikis for more specific functions, most commonly as subject or course guides.

The most popular open source solution for blogging is WordPress (wordpress.org), which was first developed in 2003 as a fork of the blogging software b2\cafelog. It is written in PHP and uses a MySQL database to store information. WordPress grew significantly in popularity as a blogging platform in 2004, when the licensing terms of Movable Type changed, placing greater restrictions on users who weren't paying a licensing fee. WordPress.com provides a hosted version of the WordPress software, which has also spurred its popularity.

WordPress has many features that make it attractive to bloggers. First, it contains a WYSIWYG (What You See Is What You Get) editor that creates XHTML and CSS standards compliant code, and allows bloggers to easily format posts and pages. Second, WordPress has a pages feature that allows bloggers to include regular webpages as part of their blog with little coding effort. This means that WordPress can easily be used to host small websites or blogs that have more static content. WordPress supports comments and trackbacks, and allows authors to control which posts and pages users can add comments or trackbacks to. WordPress also offers a number of options for dealing with comment spam. You can moderate comments, with the option to bypass moderation if the user supplies an email address or has posted a comment before. You can configure a set of blacklist words, so that a comment containing any of these words is sent to moderation. As a final measure, the spam-catching plugin Askimet can be installed. Using these features in concert will help keep the amount of spam posted to a blog low. It is important to note that if you choose to moderate comments, you will need to check the moderated comments queue to approve valid comments and delete spam comments. Doing this on a regular basis is essential so that readers know their comments are being read.

Another important feature of the WordPress software is the ability to assign different roles to different users of a WordPress blog. There are five different roles: administrator, editor, author, contributor, and subscriber. Each has a different set of permissions, with administrators having the most permissions and subscribers the least. More information on WordPress roles can be found in the WordPress codex (codex.wordpress.org/Roles_and_Capabilities). This system of roles allows an administrator granular control over what different users can do on a given blog. Many community-created blogs use this feature extensively because of the number of users who participate. The idea is that different users have different roles and responsibilities. Some can publish content, while others can only submit content to be reviewed by users with editorial rights who will review the content and publish it. WordPress's user roles system provides the functionality to easily manage all of these users by assigning them different permissions.

Installing WordPress

WordPress is extremely easy to install, and the WordPress website offers a five-minute installation guide for the tech savvy. Even for the less technically adept, a typical installation should take just 15 to 20 minutes.

There are two basic requirements for a web server to run the current version of WordPress (at the time of writing, version 3.0.1): PHP 4.2 and MySQL 4.0 or higher. To begin installing WordPress, you first need to create a database in your MySQL installation for WordPress to use. This is done by going into the MySQL console and entering the following commands:

```
CREATE database database_name;
GRANT ALL on database_name.* to
username@' localhost' identified by
'password' ;
```

Make sure to write down the database name and the username and password needed to access it. You will need these later in the installation process.

You should then download the latest version of WordPress from wordpress.org/latest.tar.gz to the web root of your web server:

```
wget http://wordpress.org/latest.tar.gz
```

Extract the package using the following command:

```
tar -zxf latest.tar.gz
```

This will create a folder named wordpress. Navigate to the WordPress directory by typing the command `cd wordpress`, then display the files and folders in that directory with the command `ls -l`. You will see many files and folders. However, the one we are interested in is named wp-config-sample.php. In order to get your WordPress installation working, you need to make a copy of this file and edit several lines in it. So make a copy of the file name wp-config.php:

```
cp wp-config-sample.php wp-config.php
```

Then open the file using a text editor; in this case I'm using Pico:

```
pico wp-config.php
```

When the file is opened, you'll see several lines of code that look like this:

```
<?php

// ** MySQL settings ** //
define('DB_NAME', 'database_name'); // The
name of the database
define('DB_USER', 'username'); // Your
MySQL username
define('DB_PASSWORD', 'password'); //
...and password
define('DB_HOST', 'localhost'); // 99%
chance you won't need to change this value
define('DB_CHARSET', 'utf8');
define('DB_COLLATE', '');

// You can have multiple installations in
one database if you give each a unique
prefix
$table_prefix = 'wp_'; // Only numbers,
letters, and underscores please!
```

There are three lines that you need to edit in this file. The first three lines under the MySQL settings entry should be changed to reflect the name of your database and the username and password associated with it. For example, if your database was named `recipes` and your username and password were `karen` and `cooking`, the resulting wp-config-sample.php file would look like this:

```
<?php

// ** MySQL settings ** //
define('DB_NAME', 'recipes');    // The
name of the database
define('DB_USER', 'karen');     // Your
MySQL username
define('DB_PASSWORD', 'cooking'); // ...and
password
```

Once you have made those changes to the file and saved it, the file will tell WordPress how to connect to the database, where it will store all of the information for your blog. Without it, WordPress won't function correctly. Now that you've made these changes, you're ready to install.

Open a web browser to the WordPress installation script (Figure 4.1):

```
http://www.yourwebsite.com/wordpress/wp-
admin/install.php
```

You will first be asked to enter your blog's title and your email address. Then, you will be able to click the Install button. If you have entered the MySQL settings correctly, you should see the page shown in Figure 4.2

WordPress is just that easy to install. You will see your login and password on the resulting screen, and you should copy that password to a text file or write it down so that you don't forget it. Click the login link, and enter your login and password to get to the administration screen for your blog. At that point, you can change the password to something that is easier to remember.

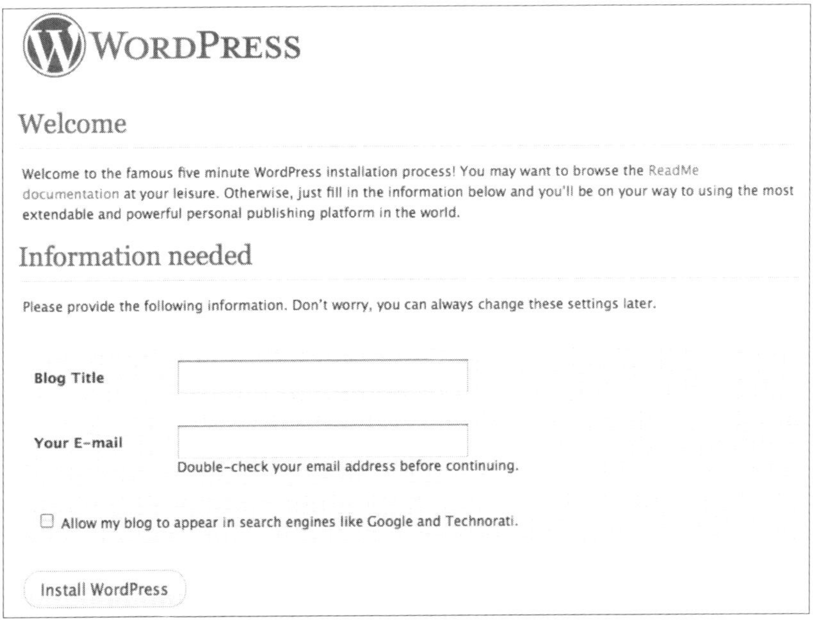
WordPress
Welcome
Welcome to the famous five minute WordPress installation process! You may want to browse the ReadMe documentation at your leisure. Otherwise, just fill in the information below and you'll be on your way to using the most extendable and powerful personal publishing platform in the world.
Information needed
Please provide the following information. Don't worry, you can always change these settings later.
Blog Title
Your E-mail
Double-check your email address before continuing.
Allow my blog to appear in search engines like Google and Technorati.
Install WordPress

Figure 4.1 WordPress installation screen

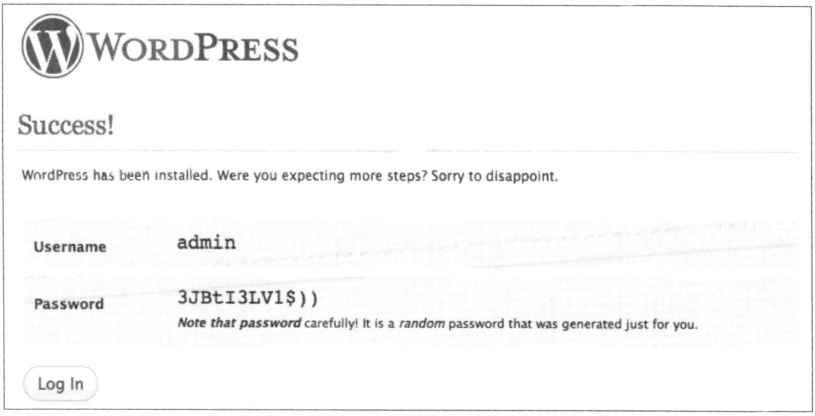

Figure 4.2 WordPress installation complete

Administering WordPress

Once you have successfully installed WordPress, you will see a number of sections on the administration screen that will allow you to add to and edit the content of your blog; control its look and feel; and install additional features. The Posts section allows you to add and edit posts to your blog. The Pages section allows you to do the same for pages. The Comments section allows you to manage comments and the Links section links. The Media section allows you to upload and manage different types of media: photos, videos, sound files, and PDFs (Figure 4.3).

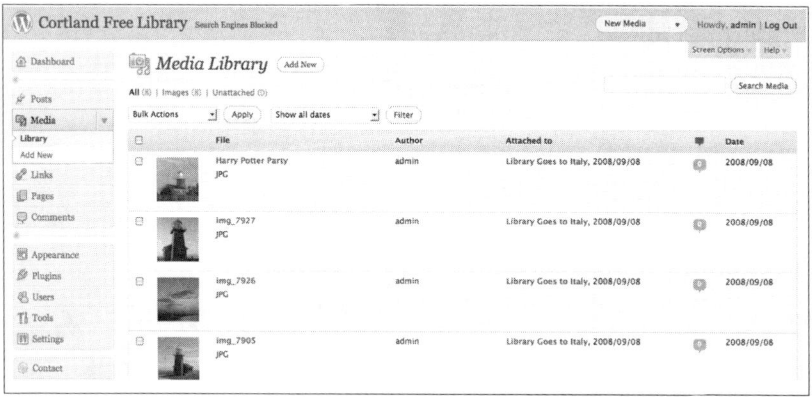

Figure 4.3 WordPress media screen

Creating a Post

Once you've set up your blog, you can log in and start posting to it. To create a new post, simply select the Post link and click Add New. WordPress makes the process of creating a post extremely easy by incorporating a WYSIWYG editor, which allows you to create and format text in a Word-like interface. The interface has buttons for making lists, adding links, centering text, and adding images. Once you've added the basic content of your post, you can select a category for the post and/or add tags (which are similar to keywords). After adding categories and tags, you can either publish your post immediately using the Publish button or save it for later using the Save as Draft button. You can also schedule the post to be published in the future by changing the post's Published Date to a future time and date, and then selecting the Publish button.

In addition to blog posts, WordPress also allows users to create pages with more static content as part of their blog. This process is very similar to creating a post and is also done via Pages > Add New. Users can also upload files from within an individual post or page (Figure 4.4). This integration makes file management a seamless part of content creation.

Media

WordPress also allows you to create a gallery of images within a post or page. To do this, upload the images you want to appear in the gallery to the editor interface for the post or page. You can then customize the order in which the images will appear. Next, insert

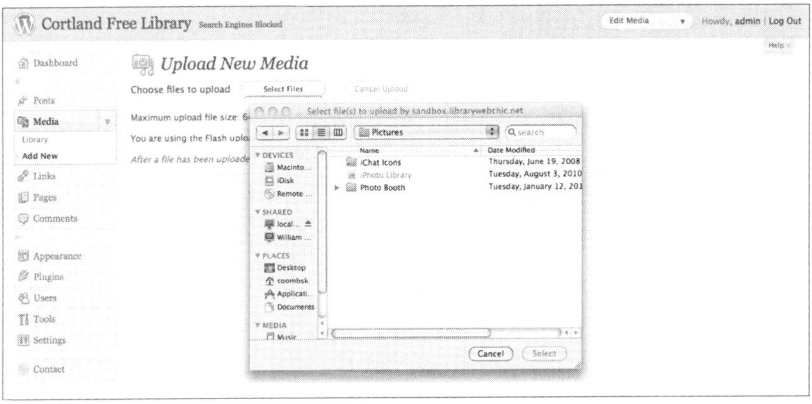

Figure 4.4 Uploading media in WordPress

[gallery] into the post or page. This will display a gallery of those images within the post or page. You can configure the number of columns of images in the gallery and the size of the images using columns= and size=. When you click on an individual image, it will take you to a page that displays a full-sized version of that image. In addition to this built-in gallery functionality, there are a number of WordPress plugins that provide gallery features. The most full featured of these is NextGEN Gallery (wordpress.org/extend/plugins/nextgen-gallery), which allows you to create galleries of images within your WordPress blog and display them in a number of ways, from an individual image to slideshows to a sidebar widget. For Flickr users, there are a number of plugins that allow for adding images or sets of images from Flickr. Two particularly good options are WordPress Flickr Manager (wordpress.org/extend/plugins/wordpress-flickr-manager) and Flickr Gallery (wordpress.org/extend/plugins/flickr-gallery). WordPress Flickr Manager is easier for novices to use because of its GUI. You can add a single photo, several photos, or a photoset to your WordPress post or page. You can also use WordPress Flickr Manager to post photos to Flickr from within WordPress, which is a significant time saver. Flickr Gallery, on the other hand, is great for power users who are comfortable with shortcodes and want to add photos by tag, group, set, or even search term.

With WordPress's support for media comes support for enclosures in RSS and Atom feeds, which means that WordPress can be used as a tool for podcasting. Using the media library features, you can easily attach audio files to posts. However, most podcasters prefer more robust podcast support and choose to download the podPress plugin (wordpress.org/extend/plugins/podpress). This plugin adds built-in iTunes support and a built-in Flash MP3 Player to WordPress.

Videos can also be uploaded and posted to WordPress. For those who want to embed content from video-sharing sites such YouTube, Blip.tv, or Vimeo, there are several plugins that simplify this process. Viper's Video Quicktags (wordpress.org/extend/plugins/vipers-video-quicktags) allows users to embed video from video sharing sites and can also be used to embed Flash video from any website or a variety of other video formats (QuickTime, AVI, MPEG, WMV) located locally. wordTube (wordpress.org/extend/plugins/wordtube) is another alternative for uploading and managing local video and audio files. An especially useful feature is that it allows you to create playlists of your content and then embed a specific playlist within a post or page.

All in One Video Pack (wordpress.org/extend/plugins/all-in-one-video-pack) is another extremely useful plugin for video bloggers (Figure 4.5). Created by Kaltura, this plugin allows you to create, upload, and manage video via Kaltura. The video creation and editing tools are simple but pretty powerful. You can use your computer's webcam or other input device to capture video, or you can upload video clips. The plugin can also be used to add audio content or images. Overall, this tool is one of the best all-around media management plugins.

The User section of the WordPress Administration panel allows you to manage users, assign roles, and create new user accounts. From this section you can also update your profile within the blog. Your profile contains information such as your name, contact information, and bio. In the Profile section, you can also change your password. The Settings section contains the basic blog settings, including its title and tagline, along with more advanced configuration options for feeds, comments, media, remote posting, permalinks, and any additional plugins you may have installed.

Appearance and Plugins

Two other key sections in the WordPress Administration screen are Appearance and Plugins. The Appearance section allows you to control the look and feel of your blog via themes and widgets. By default, WordPress comes with a standard set of themes and widgets, but you

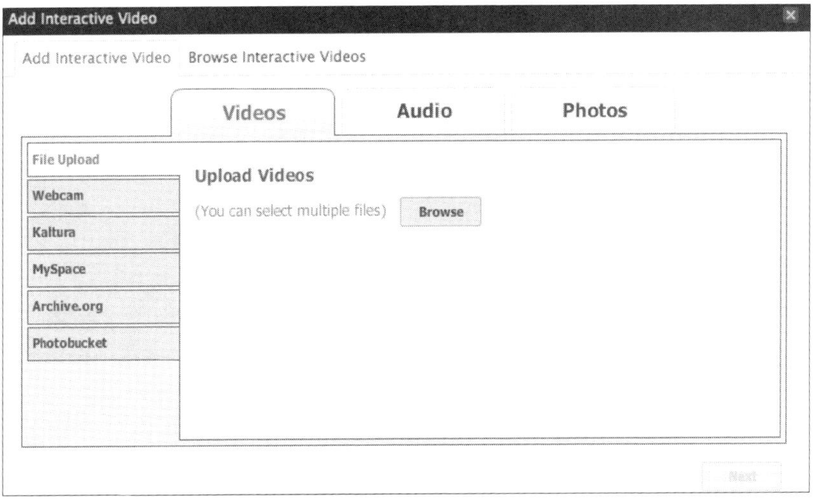

Figure 4.5 All in One Video Pack

are not limited to using only these themes; additional themes can be downloaded at wordpress.org/extend/themes. In order to install a new theme, you need to download it from the WordPress site, unzip it, and then upload the theme to wp-content/themes. Once you have done this, you will see the theme listed as a choice in the Appearance section; you can change the look of your blog to this theme simply by clicking on it. Two extremely flexible themes that allow you to customize your blog's look and feel without editing code are Atahualpa (wordpress.org/extend/themes/atahualpa) and Vigilance (wordpress.org/extend/themes/vigilance). Atahualpa allows you to customize the look and feel of your blog extensively, including changes to colors, fonts, header and footer content, and layout. The theme allows a site to have a fixed or fluid layout and highly customized sidebars (Figure 4.6).

Vigilance allows you to customize fonts, colors, the logo image, and footer. It also has the advantage of allowing you to customize which pages appear in the navigation. This is a significant advantage if you don't want all your top-level pages to appear in the navigation menu. In other themes, this would have to be overridden in the theme code. Vigilance makes this customization simple through use of its options (Figure 4.7)

If you are familiar with CSS, you can further customize the theme using the Theme Editor. This tool also allows you to build and test your own theme. There are several good starter themes for WordPress including Cutline (cutline.tubetorial.com) and Whiteboard (plainbeta.com/2008/05/20/whiteboard-a-free-wordpress-theme-framework). We will discuss custom themes at more length in Chapter 8, "WordPress as a CMS."

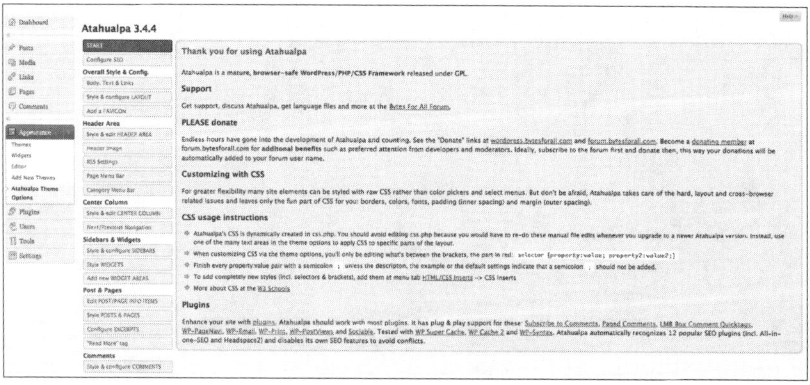
Dashboard
Posts
Media
Links
Pages
Comments
Themes
Widgets
Add New Themes
Atahualpa Theme Options
Plugins
Users
Tools
Settings
Atahualpa 3.4.4
START
Configure SEO
Overall Style & Config.
Body, Text & Links
Add a FAVICON
Header Area
Style & edit HEADER AREA
RSS Settings
Page Menu Bar
Center Column
Style & edit CENTER COLUMN
Sidebars & Widgets
Style & configure SIDEBARS
Style WIDGETS
Add new WIDGET AREAS
Post & Pages
Edit POST/PAGE INFO ITEMS
Style POSTS & PAGES
Configure EXCERPTS
"Read More" tag
Comments
Style & configure COMMENTS
Thank you for using Atahualpa
Atahualpa is a mature, browser-safe WordPress/PHP/CSS Framework released under GPL.
Support
Get support, discuss Atahualpa, get language files and more at the Bytes For All Forum.
PLEASE donate
Customizing with CSS
For greater flexibility many site elements can be styled with raw CSS rather than color pickers and select menus. But don't be afraid, Atahualpa takes care of the hard, layout and cross-browser related issues and leaves only the fun part of CSS for you: borders, colors, fonts, padding (inner spacing) and margin (outer spacing).
CSS usage instructions
To add completely new styles (incl. selectors & brackets), add them at menu tab HTML/CSS Inserts --> CSS Inserts
More about CSS at the W3 Schools
Plugins

Figure 4.6 Atahualpa theme options

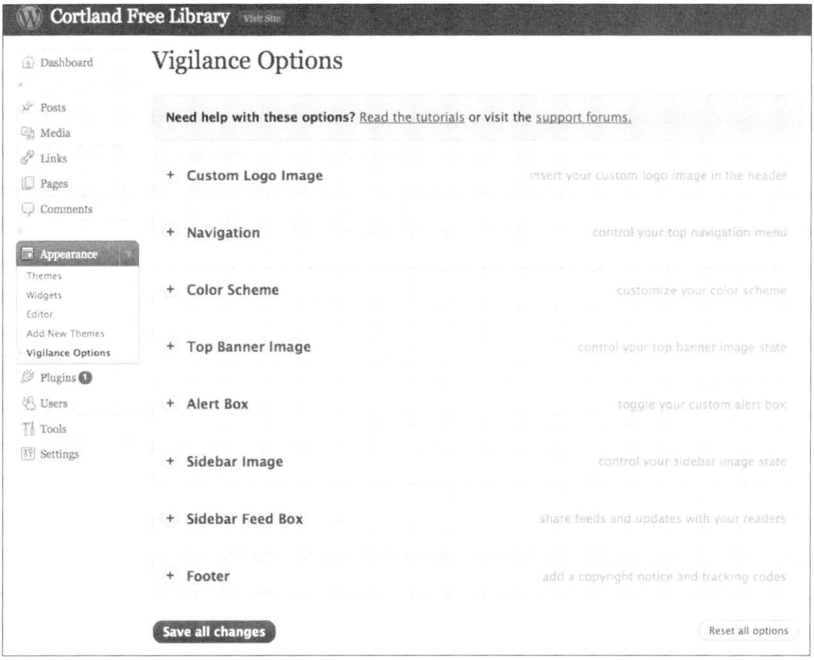

Figure 4.7 Vigilance theme options

The Plugins section allows you to extend the capabilities of WordPress by adding plugins (plugins are available for download at wordpress.org/extend/plugins). One way in which plugins extend functionality is by adding snippets of content known as widgets. By default, WordPress comes with the following widgets: Archives, Calendar, Categories, Links, Meta, Pages, Recent Comments, Recent Posts, RSS, Search, Tag Cloud, and Text. Additional widgets, such as Category Posts Widget (wordpress.org/extend/plugins/category-posts), can be added via plugins.

You can control where widgets appear within your blog through a variety of methods. One method for positioning widgets is via the Administration screen portion of your WordPress site. Simply click on the Design tab, then Widgets. From here, widgets can be dragged and dropped into place. Another method for controlling widgets is by incorporating them into WordPress templates. More detailed information on themes and templates can be found in Chapter 8.

When choosing to install a plugin, it is extremely important to read any installation instructions carefully for system requirements. Additionally, make sure the plugin you want to install is compatible

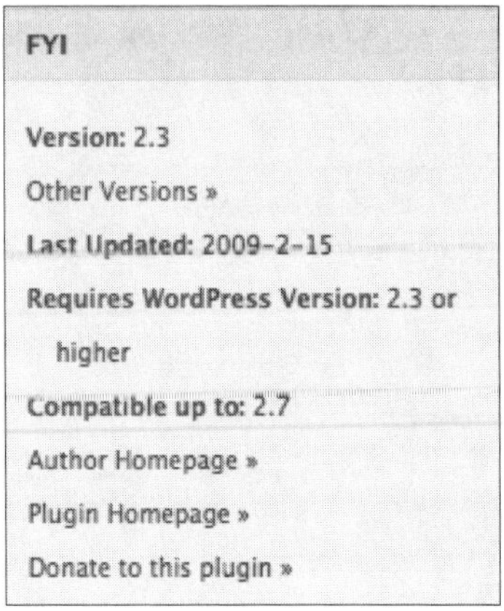

Figure 4.8 Plugin compatibility chart

with the version of WordPress you are running. If you are downloading plugins from the WordPress site, their descriptions tell you which version of WordPress they are compatible with (Figure 4.8).

Once you have decided to install a plugin, download it from the WordPress site, unzip it, and then upload the entire folder created to /wp-content/plugins. Once you have done this, activate the plugin in the Plugin Administration page. As with any software, there is a chance that the plugin won't work as desired. In extremely rare cases, a plugin may even cause your blog to not render properly. There are two simple ways to fix this. First, try to disable the plugin via the Plugin Administration page. If this doesn't work, then delete the plugin from the plugin directory. This will also disable it and remove the problems it caused.

Strengths and Limitations

As a blogging platform, WordPress has several distinct advantages. Creating a customized look and feel for your blog is relatively simple using the templates. Moreover, WordPress is an extremely flexible tool that can be extended and modified to meet a variety of user needs. There is an extensive developer community that is both maintaining and updating the WordPress code, so bug fixes and updates are released on a regular basis.

WordPress and Multiple Blogs

Many organizations use WordPress to support multiple blogs including Edublogs, Harvard University, and a number of libraries such as at McMaster University and University of Houston. As of version 3.0, WordPress has added the ability for users to run multiple blogs on a single instance of the software. Prior to this version, multiblog functionality required a separate application called WordPress MU. The code bases of WordPress and WordPress MU merged in version 3.0, greatly simplifying maintenance and development for end users.

In order to enable multiblog support in WordPress, several steps are necessary. First, WordPress must be installed in the root of your website. This means that when you access the software, its address will be something like: http://www.mycoolsite.net. Second, you need to open your wp-config.php file and add the following line:

```
define('WP_ALLOW_MULTISITE', true);
```

Next, go to the Tools section of your Administration screen and select the newly appearing Network link. Check to make sure that the information displayed is correct, then click the Install button, as shown in Figure 4.9.

Follow the instructions on the Enabling the Network screen, which guides you through updating your wp-config.php and .htaccess files (Figure 4.10). This will turn on networked sites. Now go to the Super Admin panel where you will be able to create additional blogs.

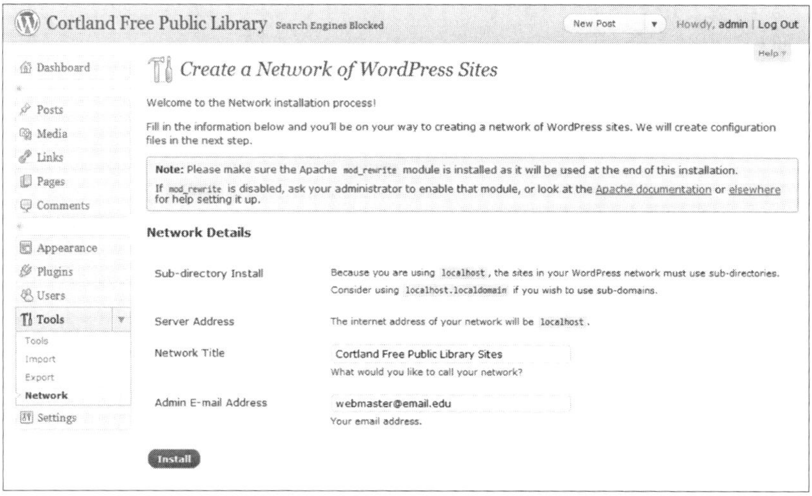
Cortland Free Public Library
Search Engines Blocked
New Post
Howdy, admin | Log Out
Help
Dashboard
Posts
Media
Links
Pages
Comments
Appearance
Plugins
Users
Tools
Tools
Import
Export
Network
Settings
Create a Network of WordPress Sites
Welcome to the Network installation process!
Fill in the information below and you'll be on your way to creating a network of WordPress sites. We will create configuration files in the next step.
Note: Please make sure the Apache mod_rewrite module is installed as it will be used at the end of this installation.
If mod_rewrite is disabled, ask your administrator to enable that module, or look at the Apache documentation or elsewhere for help setting it up.
Network Details
Sub-directory Install
Because you are using localhost, the sites in your WordPress network must use sub-directories.
Consider using localhost.localdomain if you wish to use sub-domains.
Server Address
The internet address of your network will be localhost.
Network Title
Cortland Free Public Library Sites
What would you like to call your network?
Admin E-mail Address
webmaster@email.edu
Your email address.
Install

Figure 4.9 Creating a new network of WordPress sites

Figure 4.10 Adding a new WordPress site

For libraries providing multiple blogs to a large group of users, authentication is a crucial issue. It is often not scaleable to create WordPress accounts for each individual user, approve registrations, or manage accounts that are solely for the WordPress system. As a result, many institutions choose to use plugins that enable the use of an external system for authentication. There are several authentication plugins that may be of interest to institutions providing multiple blogs:

- wpDirAuth (wordpress.org/extend/plugins/wpdirauth)
- Simple LDAP Login (wordpress.org/extend/plugins/simple-ldap-login)
- Shibboleth (wordpress.org/extend/plugins/shibboleth)
- wpCAS (wordpress.org/extend/plugins/wpcas)
- OpenID (wordpress.org/extend/plugins/openid)

Libraries Using WordPress

WordPress is extremely popular in libraries. Many libraries use it simply for blogging, while others use it as a full-fledged content management system. (For more information on using WordPress as a CMS, see Chapter 8.) Dartmouth Public Library (www.dartmouthpublic

libraries.org) uses WordPress, as does the Park County (WY) Library System (parkcountylibrary.org) and the University of Houston Libraries (weblogs.lib.uh.edu). The software is also used for the blogs of many library professional organizations, including LITA (Library and Information Technology Association) Blog (www.litablog.org), PLA (Public Library Association) Blog (plablog.org), and ACRLog, a blog from the Association of College and Research Libraries (acrlog.org). McMaster University uses WordPress MU to support campus blogging as part of its 2.0 Toolbox initiative (blog.lib.mcmaster.ca).

Movable Type

Movable Type is a server-based blogging program that was developed by the software company Six Apart. Originally Movable Type was free to download for a variety of uses, but the software license has evolved over time. In 2004, the product was released with a much more restrictive license (which allowed free use for only a single blog), creating an uproar within the Movable Type community and causing many users to migrate to WordPress. Since that time, Six Apart has revisited the licensing issue, and currently the software has a dual license. In 2007, the core software was made available under the general public license. However, the Pro and Enterprise versions of the software, with additional features, exist under a proprietary license. The commercial version of Movable Type also comes with technical support, which the open source version lacks. If you are choosing a version of Movable Type for your institution, it is important that you carefully examine all the licensing options to decide which one best fits your needs.

Movable Type is written in Perl and stores data within a MySQL, PostgreSQL, or SQLite database. Movable Type supports both static and dynamic page generation. Static pages are HTML files that are re-created when the static site content is changed. In contrast, dynamic pages are created on the fly when the browser requests them. Blog owners can choose to make their whole blog statically or dynamically generated, but most Movable Type blogs are made up of both dynamic and static pages. Dynamic pages are typically used for content that changes often, while static pages are typically used for content that isn't frequently updated.

Movable Type has many features in common with other blogging software like WordPress. Users can create blog posts, and assign categories and add tags to their blog posts. Comments can be submitted to Movable Type blogs, and the software includes a basic spam catching application. Additionally, the look and feel of blogs can be customized using templates and widgets or by selecting a design with StyleCatcher. Like WordPress, Movable Type allows users to extend functionality using plugins. One main feature differentiates Movable Type from WordPress. Moveable Type offers a Notifications functionality, which allows for email notifications to be sent to a list of email addresses when content is updated. This functionality is extremely helpful if your user base is more familiar and comfortable with email than with feeds.

Installing Movable Type

At the time of this writing, the current version of Movable Type was 5.01, released in January 2010. To install Movable Type, you need to download the install file from the Movable Type website (www.movabletype.org) on to your server. The easiest place to download the file is to your home directory on the server:

```
wget http://www.movabletype.org/downloads/
stable/MTOS-version.number-language.zip
```

Extract the Movable Type files:

```
unzip MTOS-version.number-language.zip
```

This will produce a folder called MTOS-version.number-language. This folder contains many files, the majority of which will live in your cgi-bin. Let's take a look at them by moving into the Movable Type folder and listing the files:

```
cd MTOS-version.number-language
ls -l
```

One folder in this directory (mt-static) will live in the web server root. Move mt-static to your web server root:

```
mv mt-static /path/to/webserver/root
```

In your cgi-bin, create a folder called mt:

```
mkdir /path/to/cgi-bin/mt
```

Move the rest of the Movable Type files to the mt folder you created in the cgi-bin directory:

```
mv * /path/to/cgi-bin/mt
```

Once you have done this, go to your.server.address/cgi-bin/mt/mt.cgi to start the setup process. You will be asked to input the web path to mt-static and the absolute server file path to mt-static (Figure 5.1).

Movable Type requires several pieces of software to function correctly, so the first thing the Movable Type setup does is check to see if you have all the necessary software. If all the necessary software is present the requirements screen will tell you so and will list optional packages that you can install to add functionality to Movable Type (Figure 5.2). If the necessary software (Perl modules) is not present, a

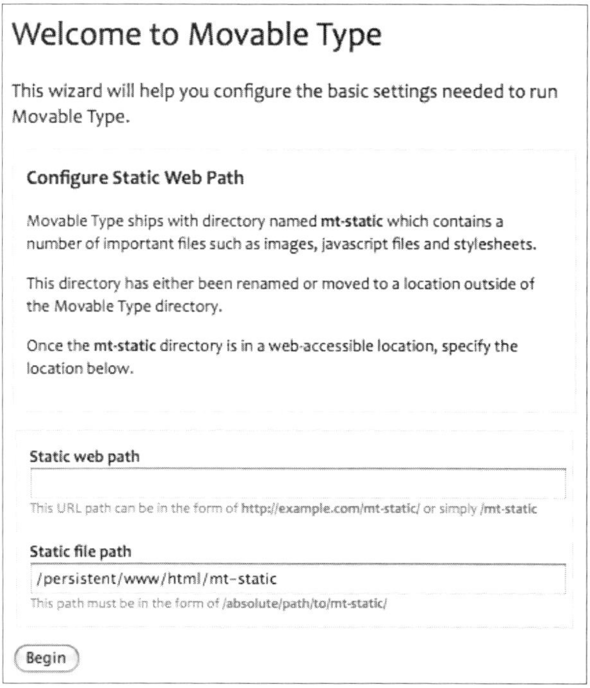
Welcome to Movable Type
This wizard will help you configure the basic settings needed to run Movable Type.
Configure Static Web Path
Movable Type ships with directory named mt-static which contains a number of important files such as images, javascript files and stylesheets.
This directory has either been renamed or moved to a location outside of the Movable Type directory.
Once the mt-static directory is in a web-accessible location, specify the location below.
Static web path
This URL path can be in the form of http://example.com/mt-static/ or simply /mt-static
Static file path
/persistent/www/html/mt-static
This path must be in the form of /absolute/path/to/mt-static/
Begin

Figure 5.1 Movable Type installation screen

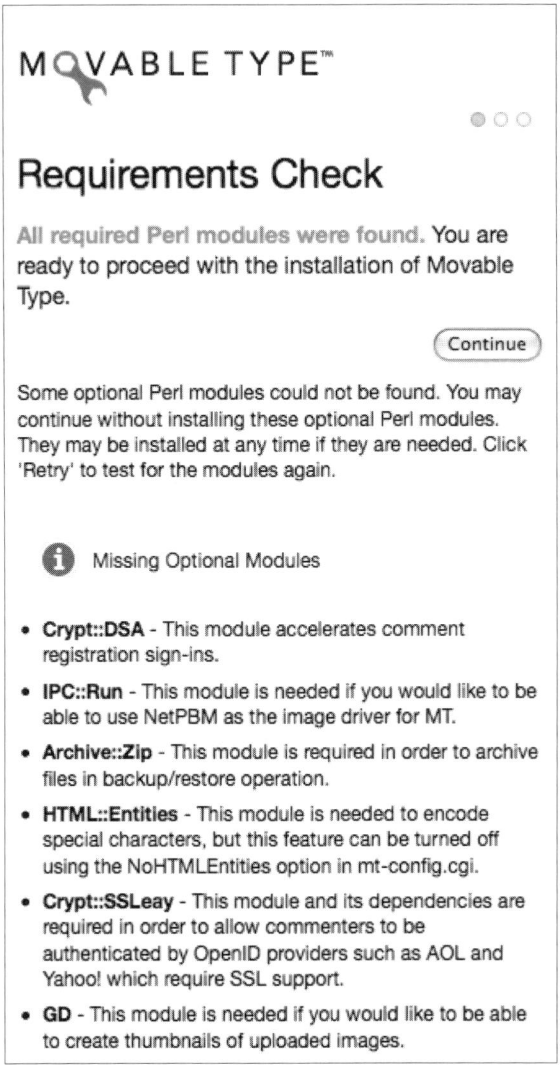
MOVABLE TYPE™
Requirements Check
All required Perl modules were found. You are ready to proceed with the installation of Movable Type.
Continue
Some optional Perl modules could not be found. You may continue without installing these optional Perl modules. They may be installed at any time if they are needed. Click 'Retry' to test for the modules again.
Missing Optional Modules
Crypt::DSA - This module accelerates comment registration sign-ins.
IPC::Run - This module is needed if you would like to be able to use NetPBM as the image driver for MT.
Archive::Zip - This module is required in order to archive files in backup/restore operation.
HTML::Entities - This module is needed to encode special characters, but this feature can be turned off using the NoHTMLEntities option in mt-config.cgi.
Crypt::SSLeay - This module and its dependencies are required in order to allow commenters to be authenticated by OpenID providers such as AOL and Yahoo! which require SSL support.
GD - This module is needed if you would like to be able to create thumbnails of uploaded images.

Figure 5.2 Requirements check

list of the necessary software will be generated and you will be asked to install this software.

Movable Type requires a database to function properly; you can use a MySQL, PostgreSQL, or SQLite database to store your data. At this point in the setup, you will need to enter information about your database, including the type of database (MySQL, PostgreSQL, or SQLite), the database name, username, and password (Figure 5.3).

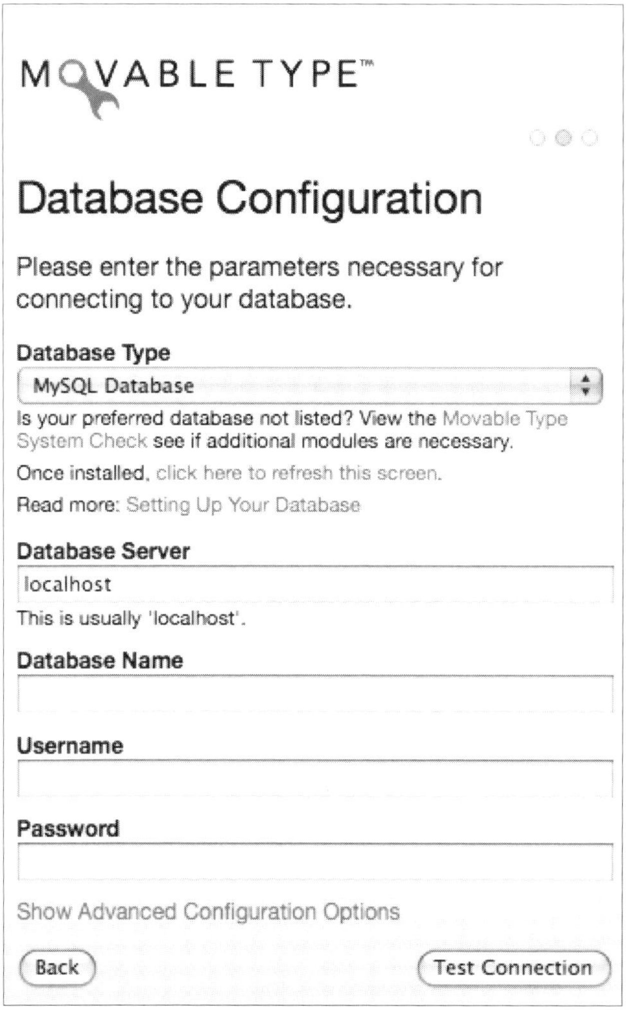
MOVABLE TYPE™
Database Configuration
Please enter the parameters necessary for connecting to your database.
Database Type
MySQL Database
Is your preferred database not listed? View the Movable Type System Check see if additional modules are necessary.
Once installed, click here to refresh this screen.
Read more: Setting Up Your Database
Database Server
localhost
This is usually 'localhost'.
Database Name
Username
Password
Show Advanced Configuration Options
Back
Test Connection

Figure 5.3 Movable Type database configuration screen

You need to have set up a database and user for Movable Type to use before you proceed through this section of the configuration. To set up the database and use in MySQL, first, log in to MySQL as the root user:

```
mysql -u root -p
```

Next, create a database for Movable Type to use:

```
create database_name;
```

Last, create a MySQL user for Movable Type to use and give it the appropriate permissions on the newly created Movable Type database:

```
GRANT ALL on database_name.* on username
identified by 'password' ;
```

Make sure you write down the name of the database, the username, and password, because this is the information you need to input into the database configuration screen. Once you have successfully done this you will be asked to set up a mail server. There are two options: sendmail or SMTP Server. Unless you know that sendmail is installed on your server, choose the SMTP Server option and input a valid SMTP server and email address. I use the SMTP server for the email account associated with my domain name.

The last thing Movable Type will do is create a configuration file with all the information you have just input. This can be done two ways: Either you can allow Movable Type to write the configuration to the server itself, or you can copy the configuration information into a text file named mt-config.cgi and upload this file to the server. I recommend the second option because it is more secure and doesn't require you to change file permissions on the server. To do this click on the link labeled "Show the mt-config.cgi file generated by the wizard" and copy the information. In the mt directory in your cgi-bin create a file named mt-config.cgi and paste into it the copied information. Return to the web browser, check the box labeled "I will create the mt-config.cgi file manually," and press Continue. You should see a message stating that you have successfully configured Movable Type (Figure 5.4).

Creating Your First Blog, User, and Post

Now you will need to create your first user for Movable Type. This should be your administrator account. Input a username, display name, email address, password, and password recovery phrase. You also will be asked to create your first blog. Input the blog name, blog URL, publishing path, and time zone. Remember that your publishing

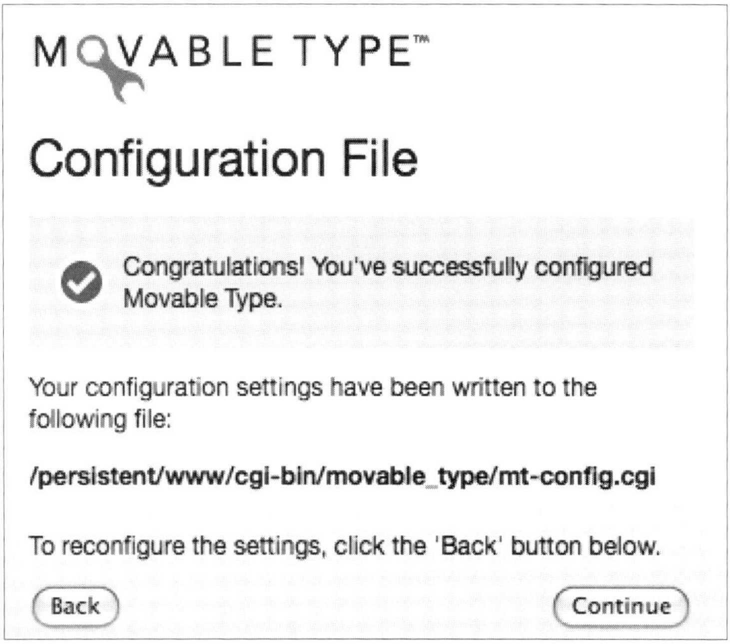
MOVABLE TYPE™
Configuration File
Congratulations! You've successfully configured Movable Type.
Your configuration settings have been written to the following file:
/persistent/www/cgi-bin/movable_type/mt-config.cgi
To reconfigure the settings, click the 'Back' button below.
Back
Continue

Figure 5.4 Movable Type installation complete

path must be a directory to which the web server has write access (Figure 5.5).

Once you've created your first blog, you will be redirected to a login screen, which you can use to log in and start posting to your blog. You can do this using the Write Entry link. Creating a post in Movable Type is extremely easy because the software includes a very simple and easy to use WYSIWYG editor for entering and formatting text. The interface has buttons for making lists, adding links, centering text, and adding images (Figure 5.6).

As with most blogging platforms, Movable Type posts can have tags or categories. Movable Type also allows you to add keywords to your posts. Once you have created your post and assigned tags, keywords, and categories, you can either publish it immediately or decide to publish it later at a specific date and time. The functionality of scheduling posts is very helpful if you want posts to come out at a specific time or if you like to pre-write content for your blog. Like

MOVABLE TYPE™
Create Your First Blog
In order to properly publish your blog, you must provide Movable Type with your blog's URL and the path on the filesystem where its files should be published.
Blog Name
Test Movable Type Blog
Blog URL
-47.compute-1.amazonaws.com/movabletype/test_movab
Publishing Path
/persistent/www/html/movabletype/test_movable_type_bl
Your 'Publishing Path' is the path on your web server's file system where Movable Type will publish all the files for your blog. Your web server must have write access to this directory.
Timezone
UTC-6 (Central Time)
Back
Finish install

Figure 5.5 Creating your first blog

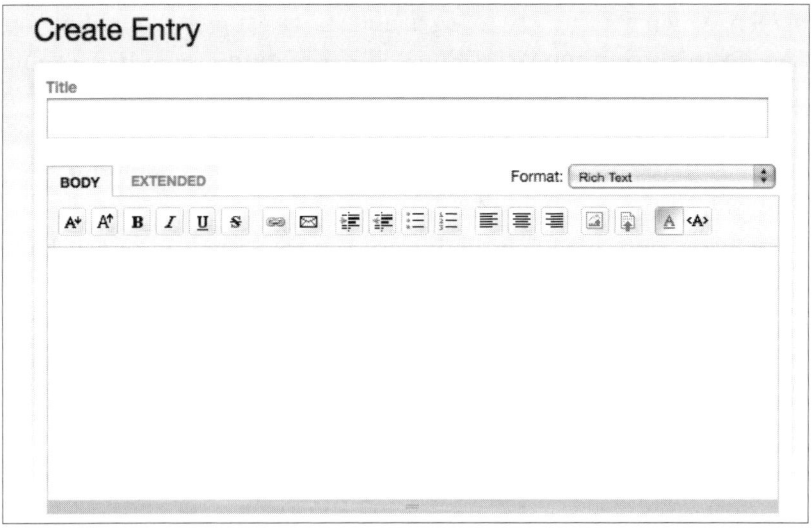
Create Entry
Title
BODY
EXTENDED
Format:
Rich Text

Figure 5.6 Creating an entry

WordPress, Movable Type also allows users to create static pages as part of their blog.

Media

One of the nice things about Movable Type is that it comes with a built-in asset management tool that you can use to keep track of your images, audio, and video. You can upload media ahead of time using the Create > Upload File link (Figure 5.7).

You can also add media files inline while creating posts or pages. When you click on the Image button, you are asked to choose an existing image or upload a new one. Choosing an existing image is as simple as selecting it from a list.

To upload a new image, click the Upload New Image link. Then use the Browse button to find the image you want to upload on your local computer. Remember to size your image appropriately before uploading it, or it won't fit properly into your post. Lastly, tell Movable Type where to upload the image. I like to keep all the images on my blog in a specific folder, so the path I'd recommend you select is Site Root/Images. Next you will be asked for some information about the

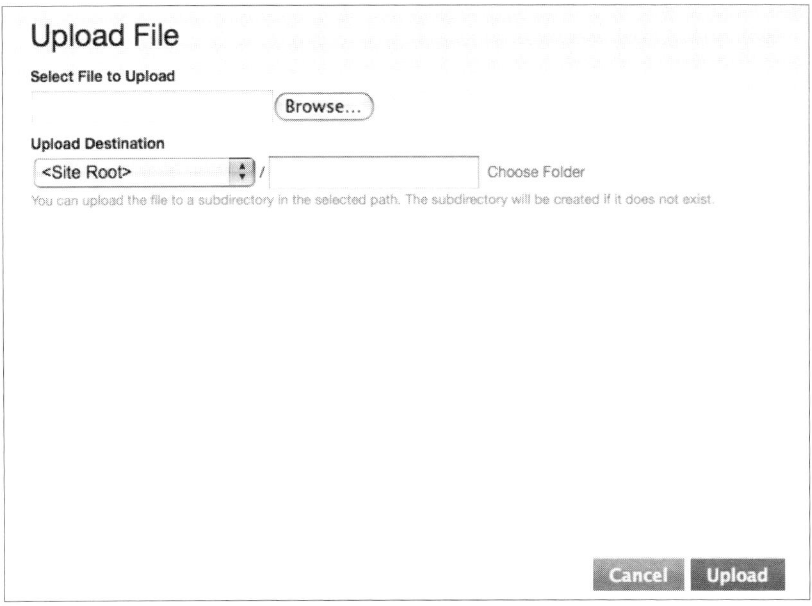

Figure 5.7 Uploading a file

image: name, description, tags, and how you want the image aligned. Input this information, click on Finish (Figure 5.8), and the image will be added to your entry.

Adding audio and video to Movable Type works very similarly. Simply use the Insert File button to add an audio or video file to your post or page.

Customizing Your Blog's Appearance

Customizing the appearance of your Movable Type blog can be done by using styles, templates, and widgets.

Styles allow you to select a basic look and feel for your blog. To choose a style, select Design > Styles. From the Styles screen, you can browse the Default Styles and the MT 4 Style Library to select a style for your blog. Once you choose a style, you need to choose a layout for that style and then select Apply the Design (Figure 5.9).

If you don't like the styles provided as part of the default Movable Type installation, you have two options. First, you can import a style from another source. Movable Type styles can be difficult to find, since the user community for Movable Type is much smaller than that for WordPress, and many Movable Type users are corporations or

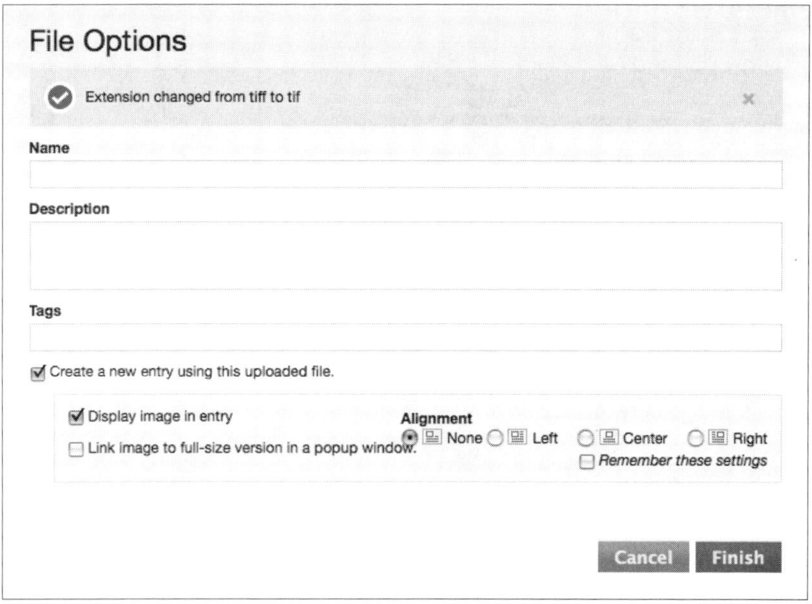

Figure 5.8 Adding file metadata

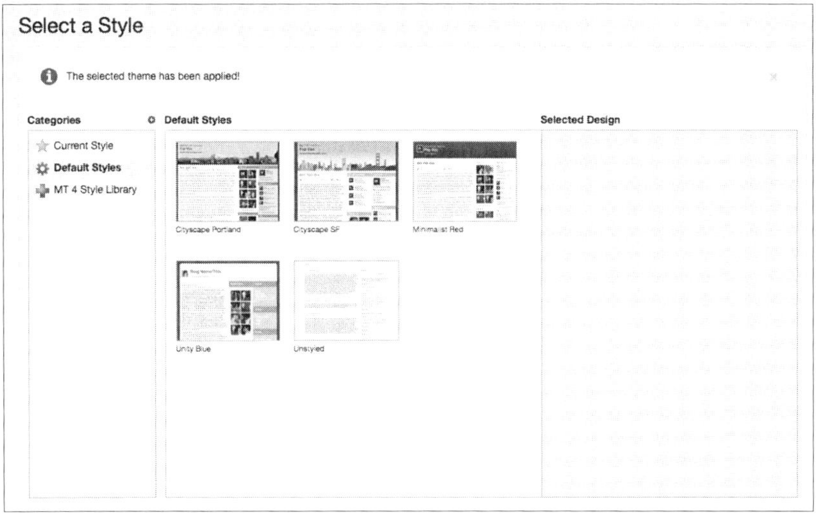

Figure 5.9 Selecting a style for your blog

organizations that aren't interested in publicly available styles. One possible source for Movable Type styles is CMR Movable-Type-Styles (github.com/mikert/Movable-Type-Styles). This site has a nice set of WordPress themes that have been converted to Movable Type. In order to get a new style, download the style (which will typically be a zip file). Extract the style, so that a folder is created. Place this folder in the mt-static/themes folder on your web server. Then you can select this particular style using the Movable Type style manager.

Lastly, you can build your own style. This process requires knowledge of HTML and CSS and shouldn't be undertaken lightly. Building your own Movable Type style also requires a strong knowledge of Movable Type templates. Templates are code that govern how specific types of content look in Movable Type. Typical templates include:

- Index
- Archive Index
- Category Entry Listing
- Monthly Entry Listing
- Entry
- Page

Templates can also include modules, which are repeatable code that can be used across templates. Typically modules include: Banner Header, Banner Footer, and Comments. The main challenge in developing your own Movable Type style is understanding what templates and/or modules need to be changed.

The last component to customizing the appearance of your blog is widgets. Widgets allow users to arrange and manage content on a page by dragging and dropping. Widgets in Movable Type are structured into sets, and each set of widgets appears within a given area of the page. By default, Movable Type comes with three widget sets: 2 Column Layout Sidebar; 3 Column Layout—Primary Sidebar; and 3 Column Layout—Secondary Sidebar. As you can probably guess, the 2 Column Layout Sidebar is used in the two-column style, while the 3 Column Layout Sidebars are used in the three-column layout. You can edit any of these widget sets to include or exclude particular widgets. The default set of widgets in Movable Type includes: Calendar, Category List, Creative Commons License, Monthly Archive List or Dropdown, Recent Comments, Recent Posts, Search Form, Subscribe to Feed, Tag Cloud, and Technorati Search. In addition, you can create your own widgets using Movable Type template tags and HTML.

You can also add widgets to areas of the page other than the sidebars. To do this, you will need to create a new widget set, then customize the Movable Type templates to insert the widget set code into the relevant template. So if you want to have a widget set in the footer of your blog, the first thing you need to do is create a new widget set (Figure 5.10).

You could name the new widget set Footer Widgets and then add the widgets you want to appear in the footer.

Next you need to edit the Banner Footer Template to add the line:

```
<$mt:WidgetSet name="WidgetSetName"$>
```

where WidgetSetName is the name of your widget set, in this case Footer Widget. The result would be the new widget set appearing in the footer (Figure 5.11).

Remember that after making changes to any of the design elements (styles, templates, or widgets), you need to republish your blog for the changes to take effect.

Like WordPress, Movable Type has a modular architecture, which allows functionality to be extended via plugins. Plugins for Movable

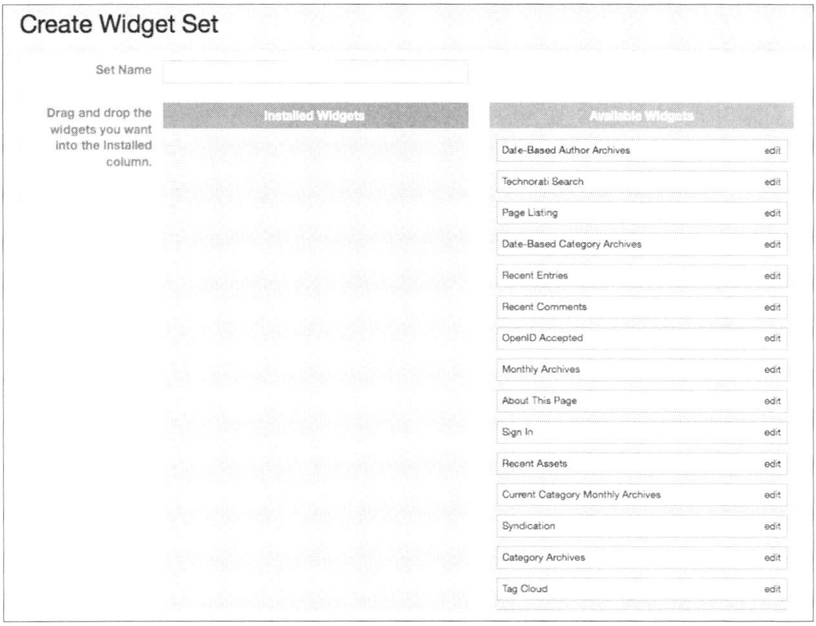

Figure 5.10 Creating a widget set

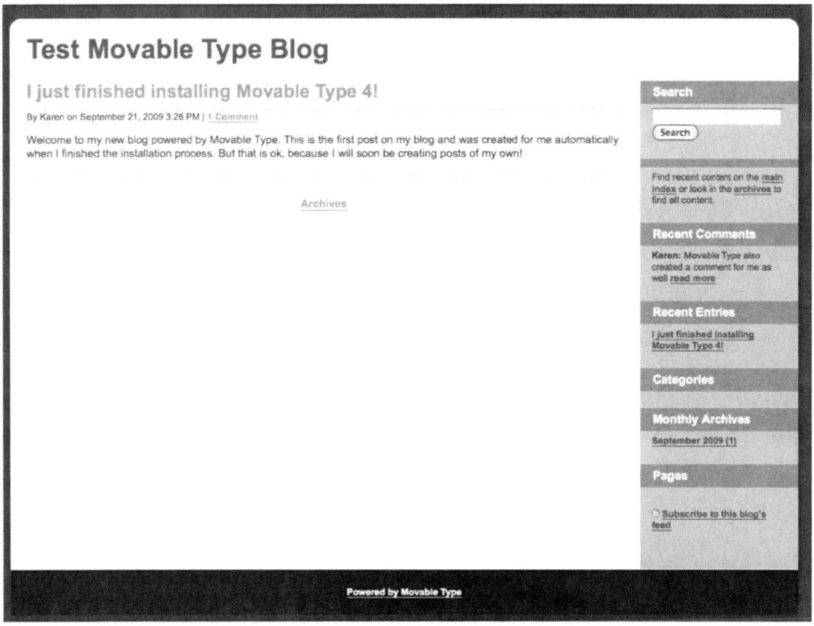

Figure 5.11 Example of widget set in footer

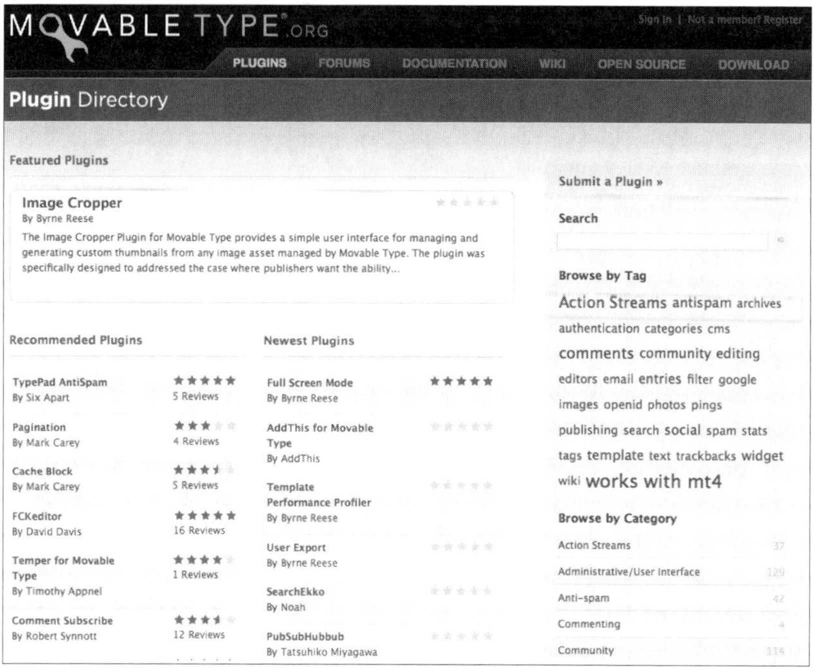

Figure 5.12 Movable Type community plugin directory

Type can be found by searching the Community Plugin Directory at plugins.movabletype.org (Figure 5.12).

There are a number of plugins that are helpful for library blogs. Comment Subscribe (plugins.movabletype.org/comment-subscribe) allows users to choose to be notified by email when others post follow up comments. iMT (plugins.movabletype.org/imt) creates an iPhone interface for Movable Type. Picnik Photo Editing (plugins.movabletype.org/picnik) allows you to edit images within Movable Type using Picnik and then update the image on your site. Sociotags (plugins.movabletype.org/sociotags) adds social tagging to Movable Type entries, allowing users to easily tag and bookmark posts. To install a plugin, download it to your home directory. Extract the plugin. View the contents of the folder created, which will be something like PluginName.Version. Check to see if it contains an mt-static folder. If it does, move the contents of the mt-static folder to your mt-static directory:

```
mv PluginName.Version/mt-static/*
/path/to/webserver/root/mt-static
```

Then remove the mt-static folder:

```
rm PluginName.Version/mt-static
```

Next move the rest of the files within the Plugin.Version directory into your Movable Type home directory (this is the mt directory in your cgi-bin).

```
mv PluginName.Version/* /path/to/cgi-bin/mt
```

Once you have done this, you should be able to activate the plugin within Movable Type. These instructions will only work for properly packaged plugins, and unfortunately many plugins are not packaged correctly. For more information about what properly packaged plugins should look like, consult the Movable Type document "The Basic Structure of a Plugin" (www.movabletype.org/documentation/developer/the-basic-structure-of-a-plugin.html).

User Community

MovableType.org houses the user community for Movable Type. It includes forums, documentation, a wiki, and the directory of Movable Type plugins. Looking at the community site, it would seem that the Movable Type community is less robust and active than that of WordPress; there are fewer plugins and styles, and forums appear less active. However, a core group of participants in the community are trying to keep things going. One very interesting recent development was the creation of a fork of Movable Type called Melody (open melody.org) in the summer of 2009. While this project intends to be backward compatible with Movable Type, the focus is much more on user community—something that seems somewhat lacking with Movable Type. An alpha version of Melody was released in April 2010 for testing and is worth watching to see if Melody supplants the open source version of Movable Type, runs in parallel, or fails completely. In any case, Melody may have a significant impact on the Movable Type user community in the near future.

Libraries Using Movable Type

Movable Type is used for a number of library blogs, most notably at the University of Minnesota, which uses Movable Type to support campus blogging via the UThink project (blog.lib.umn.edu). Other libraries that use Movable Type include Binghamton University Libraries, which uses Movable Type for its library news (library2.binghamton.edu/mt/librarynews/index.html); the Heartland (FL) Library Cooperative (www.myhlc.org), which uses Movable Type to power sites for its member libraries; and Orion Township (MI) Public Library Blog (www.orion.lib.mi.us/blogs/otplblog).

Movable Type or WordPress?

When choosing between Movable Type and WordPress, there are a couple of criteria to consider.

- First, what level of support does your library need and/or want? Six Apart offers a paid license for Movable Type that comes with support, whereas a library using WordPress would need to find a third-party company offering support. However, WordPress has a stronger user community in the U.S. than Movable Type and, as a result, may be better for libraries that want to be self-supporting and participate in a user community.
- Second, what programming languages are your staff familiar with? WordPress is written in PHP, while Movable Type is written primarily in Perl. If your library plans on customizing or extending either of these pieces of software, you'll likely want to choose the one that best fits the skills of your staff.

## CHAPTER 6

PmWiki

PmWiki is an open source program used for creating wikis that requires a web server (Apache or IIS) and PHP in order to run. While it doesn't need a database to store its data, it can be configured to store data in a database such as MySQL or SQLite using a plugin.

Installing PmWiki

In order to install PmWiki, download the basic installation package from the PmWiki website (www.pmwiki.org/wiki/PmWiki/Download). Unpack the install package archive, which will create a directory named pmwiki-2.2.4 (or something similar that represents the latest version of the software). Change the name of the directory to pmwiki (`mv pmwiki-2.2.4 pmwiki`), upload it to the web directory on your server, and then visit http://yourwebserver.com/pmwiki/pmwiki.php to do the initial setup of PmWiki. To do the rest of the basic setup of PmWiki, you will need to edit the local/config.php file. There are several basic variables in this file that you will want to set. These include:

- `$WikiTitle` (the wiki title)
- `$PageLogoUrl` (the logo for the icon that will appear in the top left-hand corner on every wiki page)
- `$DefaultPasswords[ 'admin' ]` (the administrative password)
- `$EnableUpload` (enables uploads)
- `$DefaultPasswords[ 'upload' ]` (the default password to upload files)
- `putenv("TZ=EST5EDT");` (variable to define the time zone)
- `$TimeFmt` (variable to define the appearance of times)

Clean URLs

If using PmWiki, you may want to set up clean URLs, which will remove the `?n=Group.Page` arguments that by default appear at the end of the URLs of PmWiki pages. This will make your wiki's URLs shorter, more readable, and more easily indexable. There are a number of ways in which this can be accomplished. The PmWiki Cookbook (www.pmwiki.org/wiki/Cookbook/Cookbook) outlines how to do this with URL rewriting, aliases, or an index file. The first two methods, URL rewriting and aliases, require that particular Apache modules be installed and that you have the access to create and edit either .htaccess files or the httpd.conf file. If you don't have either of these capabilities, then you will need to use the index file to simplify your URLs.

While all of these methods are described in detail in the PmWiki Cookbook, in this chapter we will only cover how to use an .htaccess file in Apache to create clean URLs. An .htaccess file allows for modification of some of the default settings of the web server, and many open source programs use this file in order to make the system function correctly. In the case of PmWiki, an .htaccess file can be used to allow PmWiki to be accessed via cleaner URLs, which are more typical of websites. The first step in this process is to create an .htaccess file. This file can be created on your local machine and uploaded to the server, or it can be created on the server itself using a text editor such as Pico or VI. In order to create clean URLs, your .htaccess file should be named .htaccess and contain the following lines:

```
# Use mod_rewrite to enable "Clean URLs"
for a PmWiki installation.
RewriteEngine On
# Define the rewrite base. This should
match the path in which you've installed
PmWiki in our case pmwiki
RewriteBase /pmwiki
# Send requests without parameters to
pmwiki.php.
RewriteRule ^$ pmwiki.php [L]
# Send requests for index.php to pmwiki.php.
RewriteRule ^index\.php$ pmwiki.php [L]
# Send requests to pmwiki.php, appending
the query string part.
RewriteRule ^([A-Z0-9\xa0-\xff].*)$
pmwiki.php?n=$1 [QSA,L]
```

Place the .htaccess file in the same directory as your pmwiki.php file—in this case, /pmwiki. Once you've done this, you'll be able to use URLs such as http://yourwebserver.com/pmwiki/Main/HomePage to access your wiki, instead of http://yourwebserver.com/pmwiki/pmwiki.php?n=Main.HomePage.

Authentication and Permissions

PmWiki allows for different types of authentication. By default, authentication is done via a single password shared by all PmWiki site editors. However, specific user accounts with particular permissions can be created as well. To do this you will need to edit the local/config.php file and add the following line:

```
include_once("$FarmD/scripts/authuser.php");
```

Once you have enabled identity-based authorizations, usernames and passwords can be created and stored locally within PmWiki or be drawn from an external service. If you are storing usernames and passwords locally, then they are kept within the AuthUser page. To add new usernames and passwords, go to www.yourwebsite/pmwiki/SiteAdmin/AuthUser and add usernames and passwords using the following syntax: `username: (:encrypt password:)`. If you want to draw usernames and passwords from an external source, there are two options: Apache .htpasswd files, or an LDAP server. More detailed technical instructions on setting up PmWiki to use these services for authentication are available on the PmWiki website (www.pmwiki.org/wiki/PmWiki/AuthUser).

In addition to these authentication methods, the add-on AuthCAS (www.pmwiki.org/wiki/Cookbook/AuthCAS) allows PmWiki to authenticate users using a CAS (Central Authentication Server). CAS is an application that helps to streamline authentication by providing a central server against which users are authenticated for various web-based applications. Each web-based application has to be configured separately to work with CAS. However, once this is done, there are two significant advantages for users. First, a user's username and password are the same across all systems. Second, once a user is logged into CAS, he or she is logged into all the systems that use CAS for authentication. The AuthCAS add-on allows PmWiki users to log in via CAS, potentially streamlining authentication.

Basic Features

Like most wikis, PmWiki uses a simple and easy-to-understand wiki syntax to allow users to format content. PmWiki also includes a toolbar that can assist novice users in creating simple text markup. The toolbar allows for simultaneous editing of content, letting two or more users edit the same page at the same time (Figure 6.1). The software keeps a history of edits to a page and allows pages to be restored to a previous version; files can be attached to a page, and revisions of attached files can be tracked as well. When users edit a page, they are able to add a summary of the changes being made, and PmWiki provides notifications via email or RSS feed when its pages change. Each page includes a printable version.

Pages within the wiki can be organized into groups and categories, allowing pages within the site to be divided into sections. The software also includes search functionality that allows users to search the full text of the wiki, as well as a variety of security and spam detection features. PmWiki lets you set individual user-based permissions and group permissions, which govern the ability to read and write pages as well as to upload files.

Figure 6.1 Example of PmWiki edit screen

Extending PmWiki

As with many pieces of open source software, the basic functionality of PmWiki can be extended. This is typically done via scripts, and the PmWiki website lists these in its Cookbook. Libraries using PmWiki may wish to consider several key add-ons. GMap (www.pmwiki.org/wiki/Cookbook/GMap) is an add-on that assists users with adding a Google Map to a wiki page. This could be used to create a map of branch libraries or show locations at which digital photos were taken. FlickrAlbum (www.pmwiki.org/wiki/Cookbook/FlickrAlbum) is an add-on that allows users to add albums from their Flickr account to their PmWiki pages. This add-on could be used to insert a set of screenshots, a gallery of digital images from an event, or digitized photos from special collections. SimplePieDisplay (www.pmwiki.org/wiki/Cookbook/SimplePieDisplay) allows users to add RSS feeds to their PmWiki pages. This feature is useful for an intranet site, letting you bring in content from an external source that you might want to monitor. For example, if you were creating a wiki for cataloging staff, you might bring in the RSS feed for OCLC service alerts to inform staff when downtime is expected or when the service is experiencing problems.

Skins

The look and feel of PmWiki can be highly customized via skins. There are a number of skins available for download on the PmWiki site (www.pmwiki.org/wiki/Cookbook/Skins), and you can preview screenshots of particular skins by visiting the SkinsGallery (www.pmwiki.org/wiki/Cookbook/SkinsGallery). Each skin in the gallery has its own page, which provides an overview of the skin, basic information, any special installation instructions, and a place for feedback about the skin. To install a new skin, download the skin from the SkinsGallery and unzip it. Next, upload the newly created folder to the skins folder within your PmWiki installation. To enable the skin for your site, open up the configuration file (local/config. php) and edit the skin variable `$Skin = 'skinname' ;` to match the name directory of your newly installed skin.

In addition to simply installing a new skin to customize a PmWiki site, it is also possible to modify an existing skin or create a completely new PmWiki skin. The Skin Guidelines (www.pmwiki.org/wiki/Cookbook/SkinGuidelines) and SkinTemplates (www.pmwiki.

org/wiki/PmWiki/SkinTemplates) pages on the PmWiki site provide an overview of how skins work and some basic information on how to create your own skin. Another option is to find an existing CSS-driven skin that closely resembles your desired layout and modify it. This typically means editing the skin's CSS file, which will be in the specific skin directory and will likely be named skinname.css.

Wiki Farms

PmWiki is typically used to run a single wiki. However, it can also be used to run multiple wikis using wiki farms. Before creating a wiki farm, a library should consider the following:

- Number of pages within each wiki
- Differences in settings between the wikis
- Users of the wikis
- Need for the wikis to look different

If your library needs to have wikis that have different settings—for example, different groups of editors, different designs, or different types of files to be uploaded—then running a wiki farm is likely your best option. The advantage of a wiki farm is that all the wikis run on the same code base and share the same components, but each can have its own settings. This structure allows upgrades to be performed easily, because only one directory of code has to be replaced—but each wiki can be unique and have its own users, look and feel, extensions, and administration. Wiki farms make upgrades and regular maintenance easier while providing flexibility. More information on creating wiki farms can be found on the PmWiki website (www.pmwiki.org/wiki/PmWiki/WikiFarms).

Often, though, a wiki farm is not necessary, because a single wiki can be divided into discrete sections. This means that all the content could conceivably live in a single wiki that is divided into sections and that different editors within the library maintain. If your library is considering creating several wikis that have the same group of users and the same settings, and contain few pages, creating a single wiki with several sections may be a better, more scalable option. The main disadvantage of wiki farms is that you cannot search across the content of the individual wikis within the farm. If you need this type of functionality, consider instead creating a single wiki and using

WikiGroup (www.pmwiki.org/wiki/PmWiki/WikiGroup) to separate sections of content.

User Community

PmWiki has a reasonable-sized user community. The PmWiki website has a wealth of documentation and an issue tracking system that allows users to submit bugs, feature requests, and documentation. Items in the issue tracking system can be searched and tracked as they move through the support process. Although there is no formal library-related PmWiki user group, several libraries currently use PmWiki, most often to create and organize their intranet content. One library using PmWiki for intranet content is Iowa State University Library. This wiki is password protected and not available to the public; however, an excellent article about the project entitled "From Zero to Wiki" can be found in the *Journal of Web Librarianship* (2007).[1] The University of Minnesota Libraries intranet (wiki.lib.umn.edu) uses PmWiki for its staff website and is a good publicly accessible example of PmWiki used as an intranet (Figure 6.2).

Several other libraries, including those at the University of Maryland and the University of Houston, use PmWiki to maintain specific types of internal documentation. The Information Technology Division (ITD) of University of Maryland Libraries, for instance, uses PmWiki to maintain its internal systems documentation (www.itd.umd.edu/pmwiki/pmwiki.php?n=Main.HomePage; Figure 6.3).

The University of Texas Libraries' acquisitions department uses PmWiki to record internal documentation. Its wiki contains detailed documentation for its electronic resources management and provides work tracking for its Verde and SFX software. The wiki, which was designed by Alisha Quagliana, takes advantage of PmWiki's page group feature to divide the documentation into sections (Figure 6.4).

At the University of Houston, PmWiki is used in the web services department for online systems documentation. PmWiki was chosen because of its simplicity. The software has a very limited set of system requirements, so it is easy both to install and to maintain.

Another innovative use for PmWiki in libraries is to host a wiki farm. McMaster University Library has a service called 2.0 Toolbox (blog.lib.mcmaster.ca), part of which is providing wikis for the campus (Figure 6.5). This service targets faculty who want to use wikis in

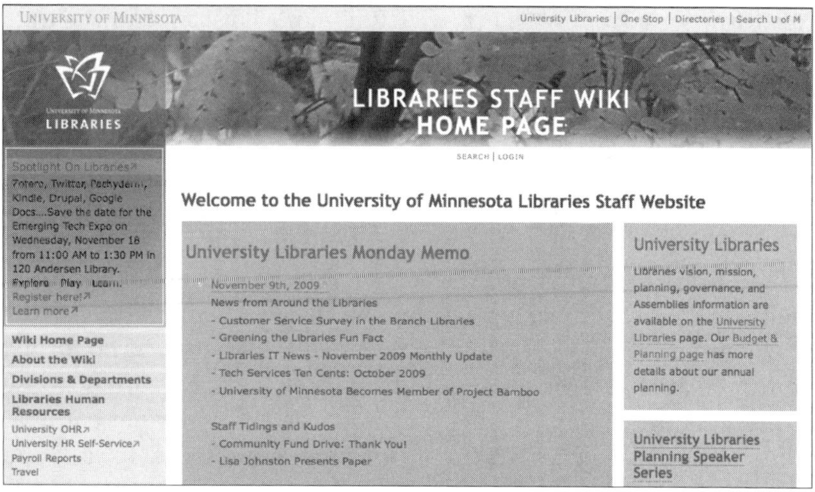

Figure 6.2 University of Minnesota Libraries staff website

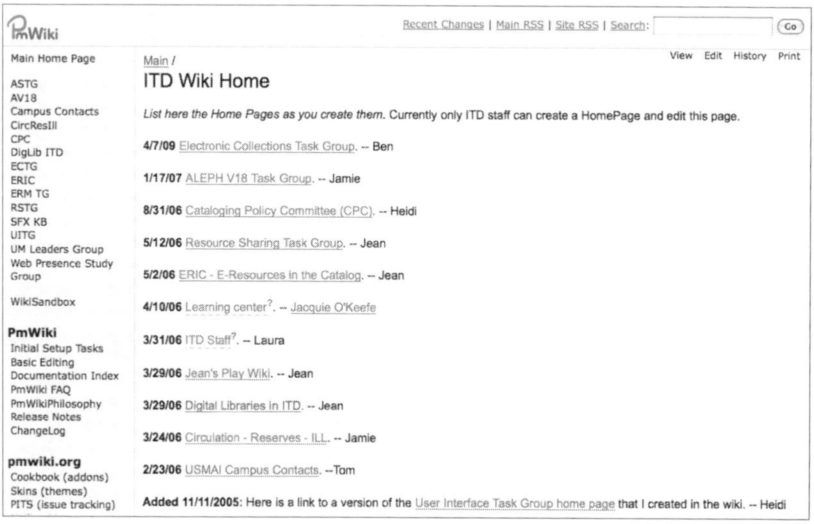

Figure 6.3 University of Maryland Libraries ITD Wiki

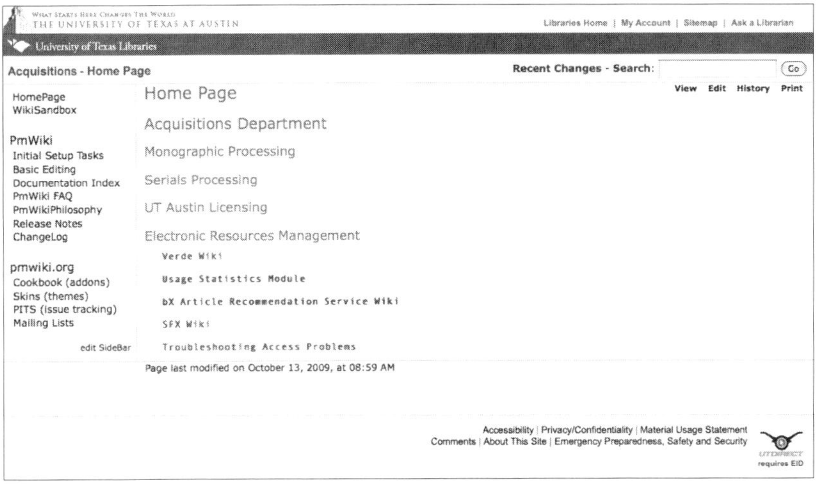

Figure 6.4 University of Texas Libraries PmWiki intranet

their courses, teaching, and research but also supports several non-faculty wikis. Typically these other wikis provide a workspace for working groups, teams, or departments, or contain internal library documentation.

PmWiki can be used for more than just intranets and documentation, though. The Forbes Library in Northampton, Massachusetts, uses PmWiki to create its Teen Lounge (www.forbeslibrary.org/teens). The library at University of South Carolina–Aiken uses PmWiki to edit and maintain the library website (library.usca.edu), and the South Carolina Library Association uses PmWiki to power its website (www.scla.org). The system is also flexible enough to be used to support digital library collections. The library at University of South Carolina–Aiken uses PmWiki to publish the Aiken County History Archive (library2.usca.edu/pmwiki.php; Figure 6.6).

Endnote

1. John Haupt, "From Zero to Wiki: Proposing and Implementing a Library Wiki," *Journal of Web Librarianship* 1, no. 1 (2007): 77–92.

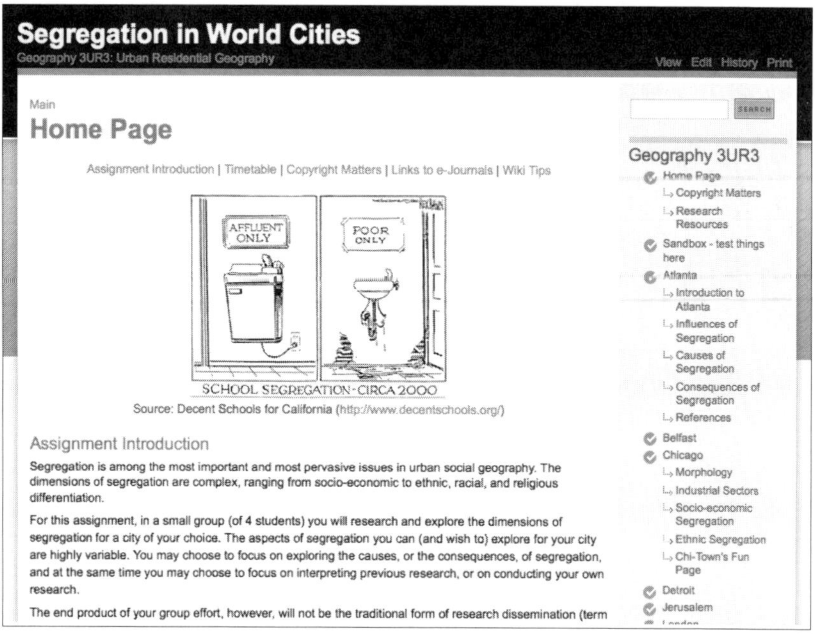

Segregation in World Cities
Geography 3UR3: Urban Residential Geography
View Edit History Print
Main
Home Page
Assignment Introduction | Timetable | Copyright Matters | Links to e-Journals | Wiki Tips
AFFLUENT ONLY
POOR ONLY
SCHOOL SEGREGATION-CIRCA 2000
Source: Decent Schools for California (http://www.decentschools.org/)
Assignment Introduction
Segregation is among the most important and most pervasive issues in urban social geography. The dimensions of segregation are complex, ranging from socio-economic to ethnic, racial, and religious differentiation.
For this assignment, in a small group (of 4 students) you will research and explore the dimensions of segregation for a city of your choice. The aspects of segregation you can (and wish to) explore for your city are highly variable. You may choose to focus on exploring the causes, or the consequences, of segregation, and at the same time you may choose to focus on interpreting previous research, or on conducting your own research.
The end product of your group effort, however, will not be the traditional form of research dissemination (term
SEARCH
Geography 3UR3
Home Page
Copyright Matters
Research Resources
Sandbox - test things here
Atlanta
Introduction to Atlanta
Influences of Segregation
Causes of Segregation
Consequences of Segregation
References
Belfast
Chicago
Morphology
Industrial Sectors
Socio-economic Segregation
Ethnic Segregation
Chi-Town's Fun Page
Detroit
Jerusalem

Figure 6.5 Example of a wiki powered by McMaster University Library 2.0 Toolbox

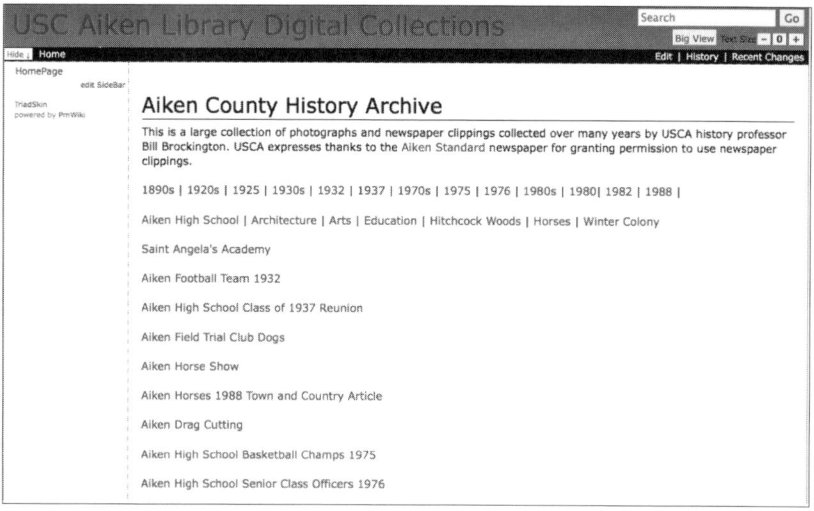

USC Aiken Library Digital Collections
Search
Go
Big View
Text Size
Hide
Home
Edit | History | Recent Changes
HomePage
edit SideBar
TriadSkin
powered by PmWiki
Aiken County History Archive
This is a large collection of photographs and newspaper clippings collected over many years by USCA history professor Bill Brockington. USCA expresses thanks to the Aiken Standard newspaper for granting permission to use newspaper clippings.
1890s | 1920s | 1925 | 1930s | 1932 | 1937 | 1970s | 1975 | 1976 | 1980s | 1980| 1982 | 1988 |
Aiken High School | Architecture | Arts | Education | Hitchcock Woods | Horses | Winter Colony
Saint Angela's Academy
Aiken Football Team 1932
Aiken High School Class of 1937 Reunion
Aiken Field Trial Club Dogs
Aiken Horse Show
Aiken Horses 1988 Town and Country Article
Aiken Drag Cutting
Aiken High School Basketball Champs 1975
Aiken High School Senior Class Officers 1976

Figure 6.6 Aiken County History Archive

## CHAPTER 7

MediaWiki

MediaWiki is another open source program used for creating wikis. It is used by a large number of websites—including Wikipedia, for which it was originally written. MediaWiki requires a web server (Apache or IIS), PHP, and database server (MySQL or PostgreSQL) in order to run. Starting with version 1.7, MediaWiki has required version 5.0 or higher of PHP to function.

Installing MediaWiki

To install MediaWiki, visit the download page on the MediaWiki website (www.mediawiki.org/wiki/Download) and download the latest version of the software (version 1.16.0 at the time this book went to press). The file will be in tar.gz format, so you will need to extract it. Mac users can do this natively; PC users should download 7-Zip (7-zip.org). When you extract the file it will create a folder named MediaWiki-1.16.0 (or whatever the current version is). I recommend that you rename the folder to MediaWiki. Then, upload this folder to your web server's root folder. In order for installation to work properly, the MediaWiki software needs to be able to read and write to the MediaWiki/config directory. To give the software the proper permissions, use the following at the Linux command line:

```
chmod -R o+w MediaWiki/config
```

Next, you need to create a database for MediaWiki to use to store its data. The following instructions detail how to set up MediaWiki to use MySQL as a datastore, assuming you have permissions to access MySQL from the command line on your server.

First, log in to MySQL using the root user:

```
mysql -u root -p
```

Second, create a database for MediaWiki to use:

```
create database wikidb;
```

Last, create a MySQL database user for MediaWiki to use and give it the appropriate permission:

```
grant index, create, select, insert,
update, delete, alter, lock tables on
wikidb.* to 'wikiuser'@'localhost'
identified by 'password';
```

Make sure you write down the name you gave the MediaWiki database as well as the username and password for the account you created for MediaWiki to access MySQL. You will need this information to complete the installation process.

Once you have created the MySQL database, visit the MediaWiki configuration webpage at http://your.website.net/MediaWiki/config. This page will present you with a form that will guide you through the basic installation process and ask you for some information, including the database name, database username, database password, database host, and database table prefix (Figure 7.1).

The database name, username, and password you should have already from creating your database. The database host is the hostname of the server on which your MediaWiki database is located. Most of the time this will be localhost, because your MySQL application and your MediaWiki installation will be on the same server. Database table prefix is a convention that is used for hosting multiple wikis. Since you are not hosting multiple wikis at this point, leave it blank. Fill in the other options and then press Submit. A setup script will create a LocalSettings.php file on your web server within the config directory.

The last thing you need to do is move this LocalSettings.php file from the config directory to the main wiki directory, in this case, your MediaWiki directory. Delete the config directory and change the permissions and ownership on the LocalSettings.php file so it is owned by the web server user and only readable and writable by this user. Once this is complete, installation is finished and MediaWiki is ready to use. Simply browse to it (http://your.server.net/MediaWiki) and begin editing. (For a more detailed installation guide, visit www.MediaWiki.org/wiki/Manual:Installation_guide.)

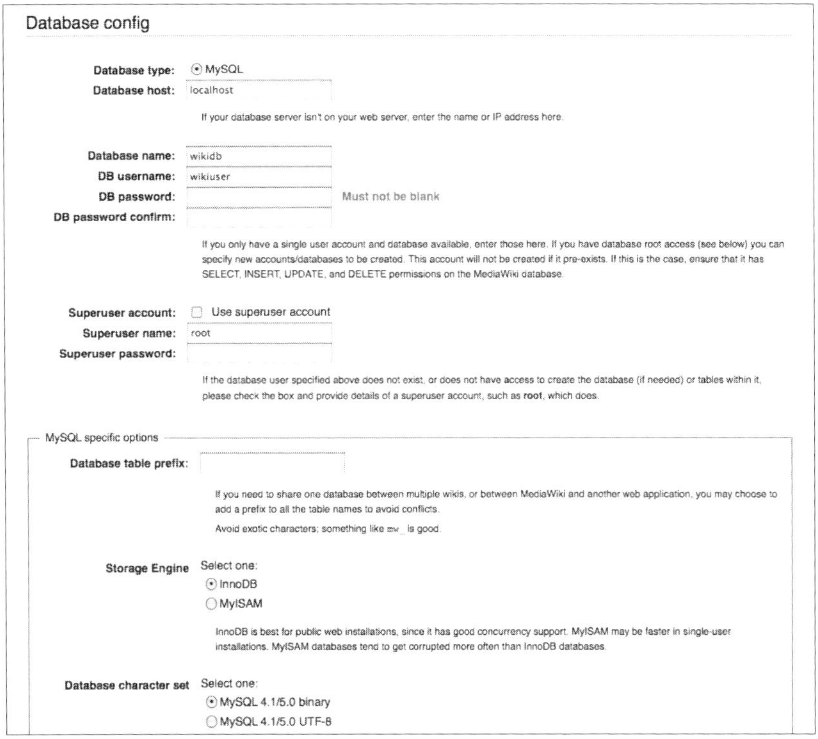
Database config
Database type: MySQL
Database host: localhost
If your database server isn't on your web server, enter the name or IP address here.
Database name: wikidb
DB username: wikiuser
DB password:
Must not be blank
DB password confirm:
If you only have a single user account and database available, enter those here. If you have database root access (see below) you can specify new accounts/databases to be created. This account will not be created if it pre-exists. If this is the case, ensure that it has SELECT, INSERT, UPDATE, and DELETE permissions on the MediaWiki database.
Superuser account: Use superuser account
Superuser name: root
Superuser password:
If the database user specified above does not exist, or does not have access to create the database (if needed) or tables within it, please check the box and provide details of a superuser account, such as root, which does.
MySQL specific options
Database table prefix:
If you need to share one database between multiple wikis, or between MediaWiki and another web application, you may choose to add a prefix to all the table names to avoid conflicts.
Avoid exotic characters; something like mw_ is good.
Storage Engine
Select one:
InnoDB
MyISAM
InnoDB is best for public web installations, since it has good concurrency support. MyISAM may be faster in single-user installations. MyISAM databases tend to get corrupted more often than InnoDB databases.
Database character set
Select one:
MySQL 4.1/5.0 binary
MySQL 4.1/5.0 UTF-8

Figure 7.1 MediaWiki installation screen database configuration

In addition to the basic settings put into place during installation, the LocalSettings.php file contains a variety of important configuration options, which should be set before you begin using your wiki. The most important of these are the following:

- `$wgSiteName` (name of website)
- `$wgLogo` (path to site logo that appears in the top left-hand corner)
- `$wgEnableUploads` (enable uploads)
- `$wgUploadDirectory` (place where files are uploaded to [local file system path])
- `$wgUploadPath` (place where files are uploaded to [URL path])

- `$wgFileExtensions` (file extensions for the types of files [jpg, png, gif, doc, ppt] that are allowed to be uploaded)

Authentication and Permissions

By default, MediaWiki uses an internal user list for authentication. MediaWiki can be configured to allow users to self-create accounts. However, you may choose to disable this option, as spammers often try to exploit this using automated account creation scripts. Administrators can add new accounts and assign accounts to permissions groups. The internal user list, though, isn't the only option for authentication. There are several extensions that provide other methods for authentication, including OpenID, CAS, LDAP, Shibboleth, and Kerberos. Once users have logged into the system, they belong to the default user group, which has rights to perform basic editing tasks within the wiki.

The default permission schema for MediaWiki is extremely open. Anyone can create a user account, and anyone who has a user account can create, edit, and move pages, as well as upload files. While this may work well for some libraries, other libraries may want to lock down their wikis more. If you want to have a greater control over permissions, you can either customize the permissions of existing user groups or create additional user groups and assign specific permissions to them. MediaWiki has very granular permissions options. You can set whether a particular user group can create or edit pages, upload files, move pages, create accounts, and much more. For a more detailed list of permissions, visit the MediaWiki user rights documentation (www.MediaWiki.org/wiki/Help:User_rights).

Editing

Once users are logged into MediaWiki and have the proper permissions, they can edit pages via wiki syntax. Basic wiki markup is very simplistic and allows users to perform formatting such as creating paragraphs of text, creating bulleted and numbered lists, linking to other pages within the wiki or other websites, or inserting images. MediaWiki provides basic inline help for users new to wiki markup (Figure 7.2).

In addition to the basic markup there is a whole variety of wiki markup that can be used to insert headers, media, tables, and

Admin my talk my preferences my watchlist my contributions log out
page discussion edit history delete move protect watch
Set $wgLogo to the URL path to your own logo image.
Editing Main Page
<big>'''MediaWiki has been successfully installed.'''</big>
Consult the [http://meta.wikimedia.org/wiki/Help:Contents User's Guide] for information on using the wiki software.
== Getting started ==
* [http://www.mediawiki.org/wiki/Manual:Configuration_settings Configuration settings list]
* [http://www.mediawiki.org/wiki/Manual:FAQ MediaWiki FAQ]
* [https://lists.wikimedia.org/mailman/listinfo/mediawiki-announce MediaWiki release mailing list]
navigation
Main Page
Community portal
Current events
Recent changes
Random page
Help
search
Go
Search
toolbox
What links here
Related changes
Special pages
Please note that all contributions to OSS Book Test Wiki are considered to be released under the Attribution-Noncommercial-Share Alike 3.0 Unported (see OSS Book Test Wiki:Copyrights for details). If you do not want your writing to be edited mercilessly and redistributed at will, then do not submit it here.
You are also promising us that you wrote this yourself, or copied it from a public domain or similar free resource. Do not submit copyrighted work without permission!
Summary:

Figure 7.2 Editing screen

mathematical formulas. Users can also insert HTML into the editor text box to format text. For those who might want to provide their users with an easier way to enter and edit text, it is also possible to install a WYSIWYG editor, a Word-like editing interface that allows users to format content easily within the page without having to know any markup language. The most popular WYSIWYG editor is FCKeditor, which can be added to MediaWiki via an extension (www.MediaWiki.org/wiki/Extension:FCKeditor_(Official)), which is currently in beta. Once installed, FCKeditor adds a toolbar that allows users to easily format their wiki content.

Several other extensions also add this type of functionality. Two examples are Wikiwyg (www.MediaWiki.org/wiki/Extension:Wikiwyg) and MeanEditor (www.MediaWiki.org/wiki/Extension:MeanEditor). However, the first is considered to be unstable and the second experimental, so libraries should seriously consider whether to add any of these extensions. An alternative would be to provide library staff with basic training in wiki markup and good help text.

Uploading Files

In addition to creating and editing pages, wiki editors can upload files to the wiki. The types of files that users can upload is controlled by the wiki administrator via the `$wgFileExtensions` variable in the LocalSettings.php file. Many wikis allow users to upload images, sound files, and videos. To upload a file, use the Upload link in the left-hand menu. Next, navigate to the file you want to upload from your computer to the wiki. Once you have selected the file, click the Upload File button (Figure 7.3).

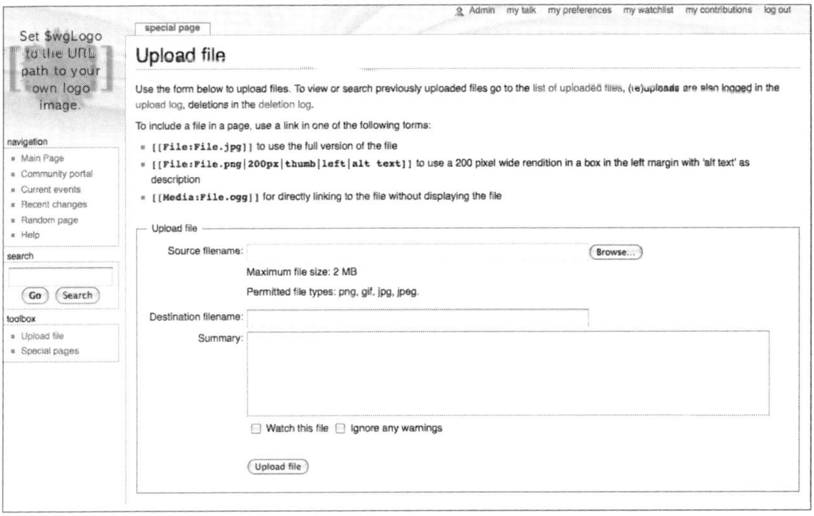
Admin my talk my preferences my watchlist my contributions log out
special page
Set $wgLogo to the URL path to your own logo image.
Upload file
Use the form below to upload files. To view or search previously uploaded files go to the list of uploaded files, (re)uploads are also logged in the upload log, deletions in the deletion log.
To include a file in a page, use a link in one of the following forms:
[[File:File.jpg]] to use the full version of the file
[[File:File.png|200px|thumb|left|alt text]] to use a 200 pixel wide rendition in a box in the left margin with 'alt text' as description
[[Media:File.ogg]] for directly linking to the file without displaying the file
navigation
Main Page
Community portal
Current events
Recent changes
Random page
Help
search
Go
Search
toolbox
Upload file
Special pages
Upload file
Source filename:
Browse...
Maximum file size: 2 MB
Permitted file types: png, gif, jpg, jpeg.
Destination filename:
Summary:
Watch this file
Ignore any warnings
Upload file

Figure 7.3 Uploading files

Each file uploaded to MediaWiki ends up with its own page and, as a result, can be easily linked to or embedded within any other page. So, for example, if I wanted to add the image I just uploaded to a wiki page, I would use the following wiki markup:

```
[[ Image:Wiki.png|This is Wiki’s logo]]
```

Media

There are many options that control how an image is added and displayed on a page in MediaWiki. The size of the image can be controlled, as well as its position on the page. Images can include captions and can serve as links. For specific details on these options, visit the MediaWiki images documentation (meta.wikimedia.org/wiki/Help:Images_and_other_uploaded_files).

MediaWiki also has the capability of creating image galleries from uploaded images. The basic syntax for this is as follows:

```
<gallery caption="Sample gallery"
widths="100px" heights="100px" perrow="3">
File:Drenthe-Position.png
File:Flevoland-Position.png
File:Friesland-Position.png
File:Gelderland-Position.png
File:Groningen-Position.png
File:Limburg-Position.png
</gallery>
```

This will create a gallery that looks like Figure 7.4.

Images aren't the only types of files that can be uploaded to MediaWiki. Video, sound, and various other files can be uploaded, and linking to other types of media files works very similarly to linking to images. To link to a sound file, the following wiki markup would be used:

```
[[media:Classical guitar scale.ogg|A sound
file]]
```

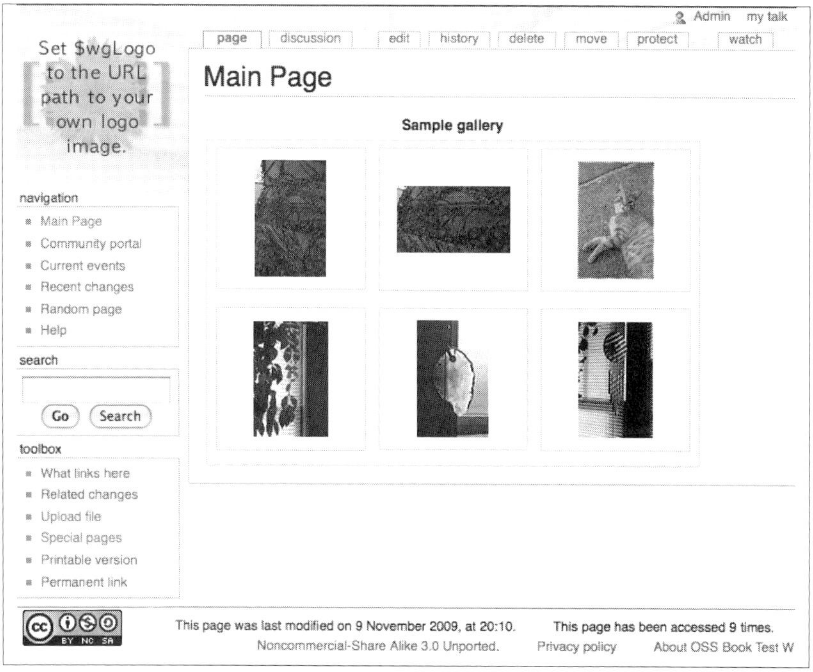

Figure 7.4 Gallery of images

This syntax will create the link "A sound file," which, when clicked, takes one to the classical guitar scale.ogg file. By default, MediaWiki doesn't come with the ability to play media files; one can simply link to these files. To play sound or video files inline, it is necessary to install an extension. Currently, there are several extensions for playing uploaded media, all of which are in beta. FlashMP3 (www.MediaWiki.org/wiki/Extension:FlashMP3) allows MP3 files to be played inline, and OggHandler (www.MediaWiki.org/wiki/Extension:OggHandler) allows ogg audio files to be played inline.

Extending MediaWiki

MediaWiki's functionality can be enhanced by installing extensions. Extensions are PHP code that add on new functionality. We've already mentioned several extensions, including those for adding WYSIWYG functionality and playing embedded media files. However, those are just a few of the possible types of extensions. Other MediaWiki extensions are available, such as reCAPTCHA (www.MediaWiki.org/wiki/Extension:ReCAPTCHA), which provides additional security features, and SimpleAntiSpam (www.MediaWiki.org/wiki/Extension:SimpleAntiSpam), which adds spam catching utilities.

Other MediaWiki extensions facilitate the incorporation of external content such as feeds, maps, or images. These include SimplePie (www.MediaWiki.org/wiki/Extension:SimplePie) and RSS Reader (www.MediaWiki.org/wiki/Extension:RSS_Reader), both of which are in beta and allow you to incorporate feeds into a wiki page. The GoogleMapExtension (www.MediaWiki.org/wiki/Extension:GoogleMapExtension) allows you to incorporate Google Maps into your wiki, and the Flickr extension (www.MediaWiki.org/wiki/Extension:Flickr) allows you to incorporate images from Flickr. These are just a few extensions that may be useful to libraries implementing MediaWiki; for a more complete list, visit the Extension Matrix (www.MediaWiki.org/wiki/Extension_Matrix).

Skins

Skins are used to customize the look and feel of your wiki. By default, MediaWiki comes with nine skins (Chick, Classic, Cologne Blue, Modern, MonoBook, MySkin, Nostalgia, Simple, and Vector). MediaWiki uses the MonoBook skin by default. However, you can choose to use another of the basic skins for your wiki, or you can add other skins from the gallery of user styles (www.MediaWiki.org/wiki/Gallery_of_user_styles) or other MediaWiki template sites (such as MediaWiki2u.com). Some of these skins are variations on one of the basic skins, but others are built entirely from scratch.

You can try out the other default skins by either changing the `$wgDefaultSkin` variable in your LocalSettings.php file or by customizing your skin in your personal MediaWiki account preferences.

If you want to install a new skin, you need to download it, unzip it, and then upload it to your wiki's skins directory. To activate the skin, edit your LocalSettings.php file to `$wgDefaultSkin = 'skin-name';`. This will make the newly installed skin the default for your wiki. You can also test the skin by adding it to the list of available skins in the preferences and then setting the skin as the default in your account preferences.

In addition to installing and testing other skins, you can customize an existing skin to make it fit your needs. Typically a skin is made up of the following files:

- SkinName.php
- SkinName.deps.php
- SkinName/main.css
- SkinName/IE60Fixes.css

If you are looking to change basic parts of a skin, such as the color or fonts, then editing the CSS file will more than likely get the job done. If you want to change the layout of the page, depending on the skin, you may need to edit both the CSS and the SkinName.php file. The SkinName.php file is a template file that creates the basic sections of the page such as the head, body, and footer. The body section of the template contains a variety of subsections, which are detailed in the Skinning section of the MediaWiki manual (www.MediaWiki.org/wiki/Manual:Skinning). If you don't want a particular section to appear, then you can comment it out or remove it from the template. However, take care when making these kinds of modifications if you are unfamiliar with the functions of MediaWiki, as you may make particular tools or features unavailable by commenting out particular sections. For those particularly interested in skinning MediaWiki, Richard Carter's *MediaWiki Skins Design* book (Packt Publishing) is an excellent resource that provides the necessary information for creating a custom skin.

Wiki Farms

Some libraries may want to run more than one wiki, and the best way to do this with MediaWiki is to create a wiki farm. (For more on wiki farms, see Chapter 6.) To create a wiki farm, you will need to download the basic MediaWiki installation package and upload it to your server. Then, create a directory for your first wiki and make symbolic links from the files in the basic MediaWiki directory to your first wiki's directory. (A symbolic link is a little like a shortcut in Windows; it allows you to create a pointer to a file/folder that actually lives somewhere else in the file system.)

Next, create directories for images and extensions, because these will be individual for each wiki. Lastly, proceed through the normal installation process. This should create a LocalSettings.php file within the directory for your first wiki. You can edit this file to customize it for the wiki that you have created.

To create the next wiki, simply create another directory and repeat the process. Each directory you create is a new wiki with its own folders for uploads and extensions. If you want to install a skin for a particular wiki, add the desired skin to the base MediaWiki directory, then edit the LocalSettings.php file of the wiki for which you want to use that skin to designate the skin for that wiki.

User Community

MediaWiki has a tremendous user community and support network, including extensive online documentation, a mailing list, IRC channel, and externally hosted forum (www.mwusers.com). In addition, there is a support desk and a system for requesting new features and tracking bugs. One of the best features of the MediaWiki website is that it provides links to various testing environments for MediaWiki, including a sandbox for seeing how the editor works, a site for testing administration tools, and a test wiki for wiki software developers to use to test new code. The software is extremely popular and is used by a variety of institutions and groups, from WordPress support documentation (codex.wordpress.org/Main_Page) to internal documentation at companies like Intel and Pfizer.

MediaWiki is also extremely popular in libraries. The Library Success wiki (libsuccess.org) runs on MediaWiki and lists more than 15 library wikis powered by MediaWiki. In addition, the wikis of the American Library Association (ALA) are all powered by MediaWiki (wikis.ala.org/readwriteconnect/index.php/ALA_wikis). These include the LITA Wiki (wikis.ala.org/lita/index.php), the ALA Conference Wiki (annual.ala.org/2010/index.php?title=Main_Page), and the ACRL wiki (wikis.ala.org/acrl/index.php). Many types of libraries use MediaWiki. In academic libraries, the software is often used to create subject guides or internal documentation; for example, Norwich Library (library2.norwich. edu/guide/index.php) uses MediaWiki for its research guide portal (Figure 7.5). What is great about the Norwich example is its unified appearance and portal homepage, which makes content easily findable and browsable.

A different approach to subject wikis is the Ohio University Libraries Biz Wiki (www.library.ohiou.edu/subjects/bizwiki/index.php) put together by Chad Boeninger (Figure 7.6). This wiki provides a comprehensive set of resources for business students. Unlike many other wikis, the Biz Wiki also makes excellent use of media and interactivity, as evidenced by the video on the wiki homepage and the embedded Meebo chat window. Both of these features make this wiki more interesting and engaging for students. In addition to the Biz Wiki, Ohio University Libraries has two other very interesting wikis: LitWiki (www.library.ohiou.edu/subjects/litwiki/index.php) and

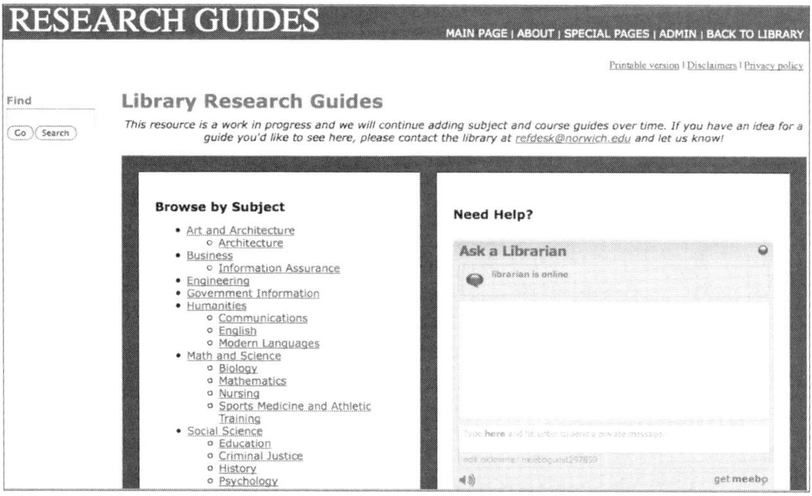

Figure 7.5 Norwich Library research guide portal

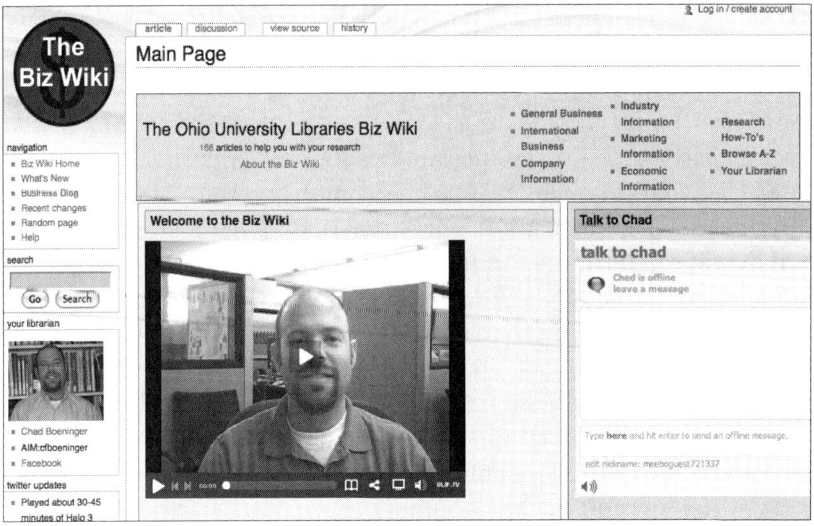

Figure 7.6 Biz Wiki

CommWiki (www.library.ohiou.edu/subjects/commwiki/index.php). These wikis employ some of the same tools and features as the Biz Wiki. The LitWiki is interesting because, unlike the other two wikis, its layout and design has been highly customized (Figure 7.7). The CommWiki differs in that incorporates news from the library's feed via a Google Gadget (Figure 7.8).

These three wikis from Ohio State University Libraries demonstrate just how versatile MediaWiki is and how much it can be customized to meet the needs of a library and its users. Wikis can also be used for internal documentation. For instance, the University of Connecticut Libraries use MediaWiki to power its staff wiki (wiki.lib.uconn.edu/index.php).

Public libraries are also using the MediaWiki software to create subject guides and area guides. The St. Joseph County (IN) Public Library has published an extensive set of subject guides using MediaWiki (www.libraryforlife.org/subjectguides/index.php; Figure 7.9). The Grand Rapids (MI) Public Library runs GRPLpedia (www.grpl.org/wiki/index.php), which is a wiki that provides information for various groups of GRPL users—adults, teens, children—as well as local history and special collection information (Figure 7.10). The wiki also includes a variety of information about library collections, including lists of new books and movies, and PDFs of guides to special collection materials. One feature of the New Releases page is that it incorporates book covers.

As you can see from these examples, MediaWiki is a very powerful tool that can give libraries the flexibility and functionality to create valuable content for library users. In addition, its strength as a tool for internal documentation can help libraries keep track of important internal policies and procedures. The software is fairly simple to install and can be extended and customized to meet the many different needs of libraries.

LOG IN / CREATE ACCOUNT
GO
SEARCH
LitWiki
Main Page
Research Guides
Film
Theater
Literature
Ask a Librarian
Welcome to Ohio University Library's LitWiki.
The LitWiki is a collection of film, theater and literature resources available through Ohio University Libraries, designed to assist researchers in finding the best resources for their projects or topics. The LitWiki contains links to databases and websites. Most resources will only be available to current members of the Ohio University community, as many of the resources are subscription databases. Any questions? Ask Lorraine Wochna, your bibliographer for film, theater and literature.
Try my blog: | AldenFYI to get the latest info on a variety of things
Latest News: Upcoming new entries to Litwiki:
Digital Media Center
Digital Video Collection
Prelinger Archives
Artstor
Project Muse
Literary Criticism Online

Figure 7.7 LitWiki

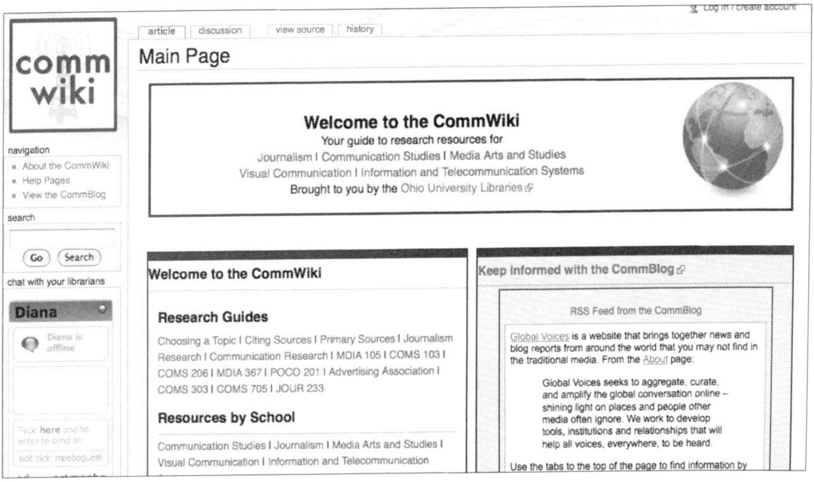
article
discussion
view source
history
comm wiki
Main Page
Welcome to the CommWiki
Your guide to research resources for
Journalism I Communication Studies I Media Arts and Studies
Visual Communication I Information and Telecommunication Systems
Brought to you by the Ohio University Libraries
navigation
About the CommWiki
Help Pages
View the CommBlog
search
Go
Search
chat with your librarians
Diana
Diana is offline
Welcome to the CommWiki
Research Guides
Choosing a Topic I Citing Sources I Primary Sources I Journalism Research I Communication Research I MDIA 105 I COMS 103 I COMS 206 I MDIA 367 I POCO 201 I Advertising Association I COMS 303 I COMS 705 I JOUR 233
Resources by School
Communication Studies I Journalism I Media Arts and Studies I Visual Communication I Information and Telecommunication
Keep informed with the CommBlog
RSS Feed from the CommBlog
Global Voices is a website that brings together news and blog reports from around the world that you may not find in the traditional media. From the About page:
Global Voices seeks to aggregate, curate, and amplify the global conversation online – shining light on places and people other media often ignore. We work to develop tools, institutions and relationships that will help all voices, everywhere, to be heard.
Use the tabs to the top of the page to find information by

Figure 7.8 CommWiki

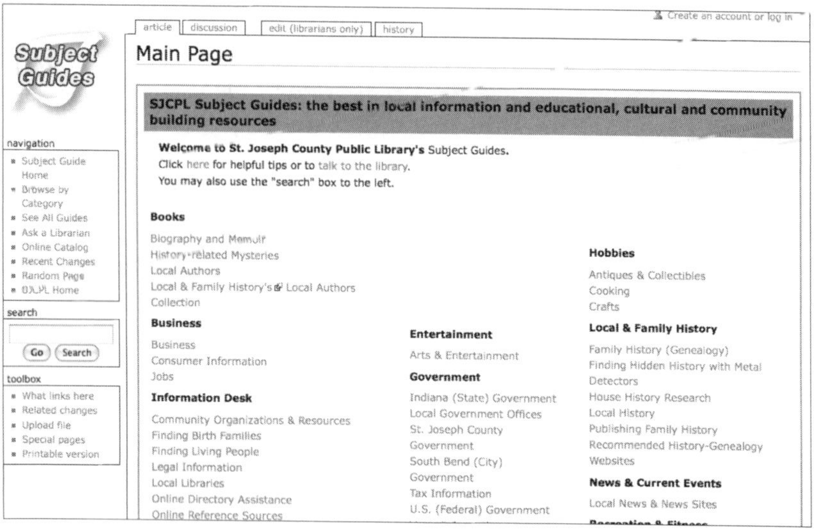

Figure 7.9 St. Joseph County Public Library subject guides

Figure 7.10 GRPLpedia from Grand Rapids Public Library

Part III

Content Management Systems

CHAPTER 8

WordPress as a CMS

Over the past few years, the use of content management systems to manage web content has become more popular. A content management system (CMS) is a web application that consists of a database that stores the website content, plus one or more web templates that control the layout of pages, including both the navigation features and the content. Once a user is logged into the CMS, he or she can add content to the site using a WYSIWYG editor. A CMS greatly simplifies website maintenance in several ways: by eliminating the need to maintain individual webpages, by allowing multiple users to add or create content, and by allowing users who do not know HTML code to add content to the site.

The next few chapters discuss three popular open source CMSs: WordPress, Joomla, and Drupal. Although WordPress was intended as a blogging platform (see Chapter 4), it can easily be used as a simple CMS and is very suitable for small- to medium-sized websites. The Joomla CMS is user-friendly and is suitable for medium-sized websites. The Drupal CMS is very flexible and powerful, and is capable of running multiple large websites. To aid in comparing the three systems, all three CMSs will be illustrated using the same sample site in the figures throughout these chapters: the Cortland (NY) Free Library website (www.flls.org/CortlandLib). This website was chosen as a good example of a site that may have outgrown the technology that drives it. The current website is comprised of static HTML pages, and the library is trying to incorporate several different Web 2.0 technologies into these HTML-based pages. The following three chapters will demonstrate how each of the three CMSs could simplify website maintenance and the integration of Web 2.0 features.

Earlier we discussed WordPress as an open source tool for blogging. In this chapter, we will cover how WordPress can be used as a CMS. WordPress has always provided its users with the ability to manage both blog posts and static page content, as well as a way to manage tools for managing different types of media. These features make WordPress akin to a simple CMS. While not as full featured as a true open source CMS like Drupal or Joomla (discussed in the next two chapters), WordPress provides basic CMS functionality that is appropriate for a small academic or public library site.

To get started with using WordPress as a CMS, you need to determine some basic information about your site. Most important here is your site architecture. What pages make up your site, and do they have subpages? What do you want your homepage to look like? What do you want your subpages to look like? Your sub-subpages? Once you have determined this, you can look for, download, and install a theme that matches your basic needs. One of the biggest theme repositories is the WordPress Themes Directory (wordpress.org/extend/themes).

When choosing a theme you should consider the following:

- What kind of banner do you want?
- Where do you want your site navigation to appear?
- What kinds of layouts do you want to use? One column, two column, three column?
- Do you want a fixed or scalable layout?

Once you have answered these questions, you can begin to look for an appropriate theme. Don't get caught up in details like colors and fonts! These characteristics can easily be changed, either via options offered in the theme itself or by changing the style sheet.

Creating a Customized Homepage

The first step in using WordPress as a CMS is creating a customized homepage. Any page that is part of your WordPress site can be designated as the site's homepage. This is done by choosing Settings > Reading from the WordPress Administrative panel. From this screen, you can change the front page display from your latest posts to a static page. There are two dropdown menus here: One allows you to choose which of your pages you want to be your homepage, and a second allows you to specify which page you want to contain your most recent posts. Once you've saved this change, that static page will appear as your homepage (Figure 8.1).

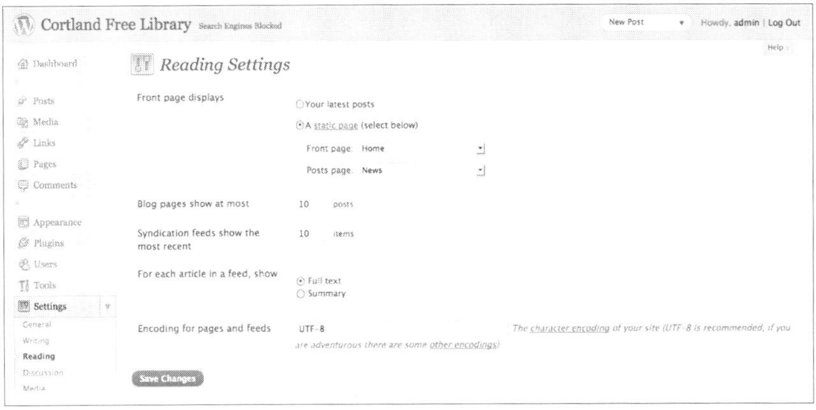

Figure 8.1 WordPress set as your homepage

Customizing Your Theme

If you are used to running WordPress as a blog, you'll recognize that the pages in your blog typically use the same layout—all the pages look the same. But what if you want the homepage of your site to have a three-column layout and the rest of the pages to have a two-column layout? This is where page templates come into play. Most WordPress themes include a standard template for pages: page.php. This file contains a mix of HTML and PHP code that tells the system what any page should look like.

The most basic theme is typically made up of the following files:

- index.php (governs the main look and feel of the site for both posts and pages, if you don't have a page.php file)
- style.css (style sheet for the theme)
- header.php (contains the header information, including the HTML HEAD section)
- footer.php (contains the footer information)
- sidebar.php (typically used to create the left- or right-hand navigation) [In the case of themes with a three-column layout, there are two sidebar files: sidebar.php and sidebar2.php, which create the content in the left and right columns respectively.]
- comments.php (governs how the comments look)

- comments-popup.php (governs how the popup comments look)

Each of these templates draws on other files to create the overall style of your WordPress site. If you want to customize the look and feel of your site, it is crucial that you understand these basic files that make up a theme.

Other files often included in a theme are:

- page.php
- archive.php
- single.php
- category.php
- tag.php

All of these except page.php govern how posts are displayed, whether it be a single post (single.php), posts from a particular category (category.php), or posts with a particular tag (tag.php). However, it isn't necessary to have all these templates if you want your post pages to look pretty much the same. If these special post templates aren't present, WordPress defaults back to the default template (index.php). In contrast, the template page.php only controls how pages are displayed. So if you want your static pages to look distinct from your posts, you will need to create this template.

What if you want different pages to have different layouts and designs? In this case, you need to be able to specify that a given page not use the default template. You can override the default template in a number of ways. First, you can create a template that matches the name of the page and use it to make that particular page look different. So, if you wanted a page named "About" to look different, then you would create a template named about.php. Second, when you create a new page on your WordPress site, you are able to specify which page template you want to use for that page (Figure 8.2).

So let's say your site has two levels of pages, and you want the first level of pages to have a three-column layout but the second level of pages to have a two-column layout. You could structure your default page template (page.php) to be a three-column layout and then create a two-column layout template (let's call it subpages.php) to use with those second-level pages you want to have two columns. For each of your subpages, you would simply need to

Template
Links
Some themes have custom templates you can use for certain pages that might have additional features or custom layouts. If so, you'll see them above.

Figure 8.2 Setting a page template

choose the subpages.php template from the Page Template drop-down when you create a page.

A more efficient way to control the layout and design of pages is with conditional tags. Conditional tags check to see if the content being rendered matches a specific set of criteria. There are several criteria that can be checked, but two of the most important when dealing with Pages are `is_front_page()` and `is_page()`. While there is no conditional tag for checking to see if a page is a subpage, the following PHP code will do the trick:

```
<?php
// Get $post if you're inside a function
global $post;

if (is_page() && $post->post_parent ) {
  // This is a subpage
} else {
  // This is not a subpage
} ?>
```

By incorporating conditional tags into your default page template, you can control how your pages appear based on the criteria described here. This method saves a great deal of time when you want a large group of pages to look different from the default template.

Sidebars

Most WordPress sites have at least two columns, one for the body, which contains the content, and one for navigation. The style of a site's navigation pane is controlled by sidebar.php. You have a few options when it comes to customizing this navigation portion of your site. You can edit sidebar.php directly, you can use widgets if your theme is widget compatible, or you can do a little of both. Widgets are snippets of content that can be placed in the sidebar portion of your site. You can control what widgets display via the Presentation Administration panel of your WordPress site. Simply click on the Appearance tab, then on Widgets. From here you will see a standard set of widgets you can drag and drop to appear in the sidebar. WordPress comes with a default set of widgets, including Archives, Calendar, Categories, Links, Meta, Pages, Recent Comments, Recent Posts, RSS, Search, Tag Cloud, and Text.

In addition to the default widgets, you can download and install a number of widgets from the WordPress website (wordpress.org/extend/plugins/tags/widget). Two that are highly recommended are Flexi Pages Widget (wordpress.org/extend/plugins/flexi-pages-widget) and Category Posts Widget (wordpress.org/extend/plugins/category-posts). Flexi Pages Widget allows you to display a list of pages in your sidebar, and Category Posts Widget allows you to display the posts from a particular category (or categories) in the sidebar. Both of these widgets can be invaluable when creating websites in WordPress.

The Widgets web-based interface is an incredibly user-friendly way to customize your site. However, the default setup for most WordPress themes is that the widgets you select display uniformly across your site. This typically means that, if you want your post archives to appear only on post-related content and not on pages, you can't use widgets.

There are two ways around this. The first is to use the conditional tags discussed earlier to customize your sidebar.php, so that certain content displays in the sidebar only on certain pages. Let's say you want a block of information containing the library's hours to appear only on the left sidebar of the homepage. You could wrap this element in a conditional tag so it is displayed only on the homepage; the code would look like this:

```
<?php
if (is_front_page()) {
  <h3>Hours</h3>
  <p>M - Th<br/>
  10:00 am - 9:00 pm </p>
  <p>Friday<br/>
```

```
    10:00 am - 5:00 pm
    </p>
    <p>Saturday<br/>
    10:00 am - 5:00 pm
    </p>
    noon - 5:00 pm </p>
}
?>
```

There are, however, some major problems with this approach. First, you have to be able to use conditional tags effectively in your theme. This is a hurdle that can be overcome by spending the time to create a good theme. However, there is also a second issue. Site content that may need to be regularly updated by non-web staff may become part of the theme itself. This is not something you want to have happen, because the whole point of a CMS is to let staff be responsible for updating content without having to know about coding. Therefore, a good alternative approach is to use the Widget Logic plugin (wordpress.org/extend/plugins/widget-logic), which allows you to control which widgets display in a conditional way (Figure 8.3).

With the Widget Logic plugin, you can choose to have certain content appear in the sidebar of certain pages. The plugin uses conditional tags to accomplish this. So if you want the hours to appear only on the homepage, then you would insert the conditional tag `is_front_page()` into the Widget Logic box. Similarly, the conditional tag `is_page(3)` would make a given widget only appear on page id 3. Widget Logic is an extremely powerful way to control the look and feel of your website without having to spend time learning how to customize theme files extensively.

Template Tags

In some cases it may be necessary to customize the theme for a website. The key to customizing a WordPress theme is to understand the files that make up the theme and the template tags used in those files. We previously discussed the various files that make up a theme; now we are going to spend some time discussing template tags, which generate content within a theme. The most important tag in any WordPress template is the Loop. Without the Loop, the content for

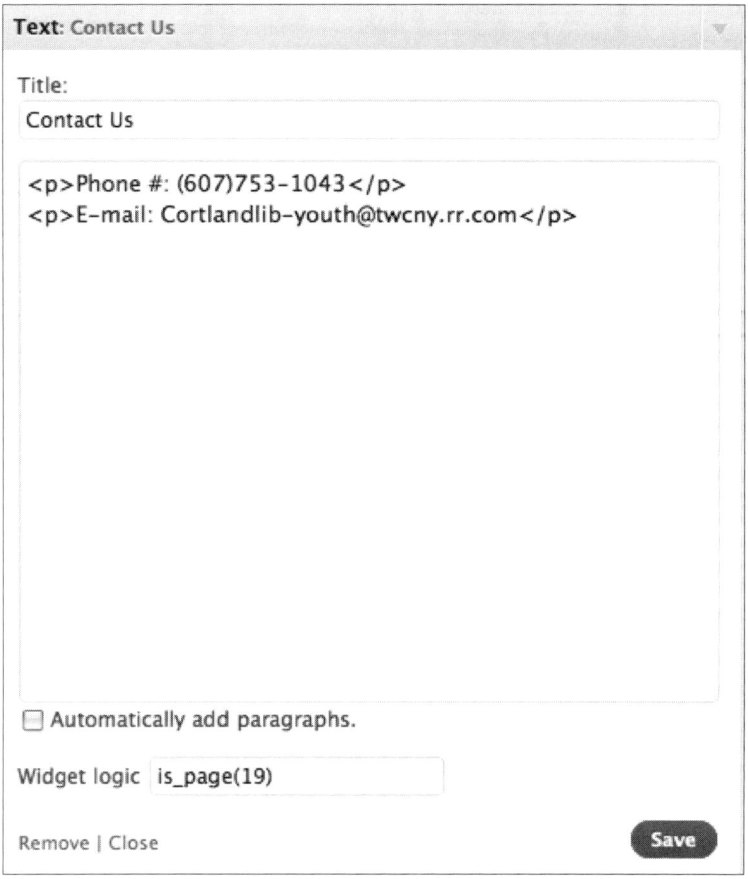

Figure 8.3 Setting Widget Logic

the post/page will not display. The Loop starts with the following syntax:

```
<?php if ( have_posts() ) : while (
have_posts() ) : the_post(); ?>
and ends with this syntax
<?php endwhile; else: ?>
 <p>Sorry, no posts matched your
criteria.</p>

<!— REALLY stop The Loop. —>
 <?php endif; ?>
```

The Loop typically contains the following tags: `the_title()`, `the_content()`, `the_permalink()`, `the_time()`, `the_author()`, `the_category()`, `the_tags()`, and `the_meta()`. These tags are pretty self-explanatory: `the_title()` displays the post title, `the_content()` displays the body of the post/page, `the_permalink()` displays a permanent link to the page/post, `the_time()` displays when the page/post was updated, and so on. One tag that can be slightly confusing is `the_meta()`. This tag displays any custom fields that exist for the post/page. We will talk in more detail about custom fields a bit later.

In addition to these main tags that are used to make the post/page content display, there are some other template tags worth noting. These include `wp_list_authors`, which lists all the authors of a given WordPress website; `wp_list_categories`, which lists all the categories that are part of a WordPress website, with links to posts within those categories; and `wp_list_bookmarks()`, which lists all the links included in a WordPress website's blogroll. These tags can be very helpful in designing the sidebars of your WordPress website. More information about template tags is available via the WordPress Codex (codex.wordpress.org/Template_Tags).

Plugins of Interest to Libraries

In addition to customizing your WordPress website via themes and template tags, you can also use plugins to customize and extend its functionality. There are lots of plugins available for WordPress, and you can find them all at wordpress.org/extend/plugins. While many of these are geared toward bloggers, there are a few of particular interest to libraries using WordPress as a CMS. Two especially useful plugins are Google Maps for WordPress (wordpress.org/extend/plugins/google-maps-for-wordpress) and OpenBook Book Data (wordpress.org/extend/plugins/openbook-book-data). Google Maps for WordPress allows users to embed a Google Map in a post or page. This is particularly useful if you want to include a Google Map of your library's location in an About or Directions page (Figure 8.4).

The OpenBook Book Data plugin allows users to input an ISBN into a post or page and have a book jacket and basic information about the book appear on the post/page. This plugin is helpful for libraries that are posting book reviews as part of their website (Figure 8.5).

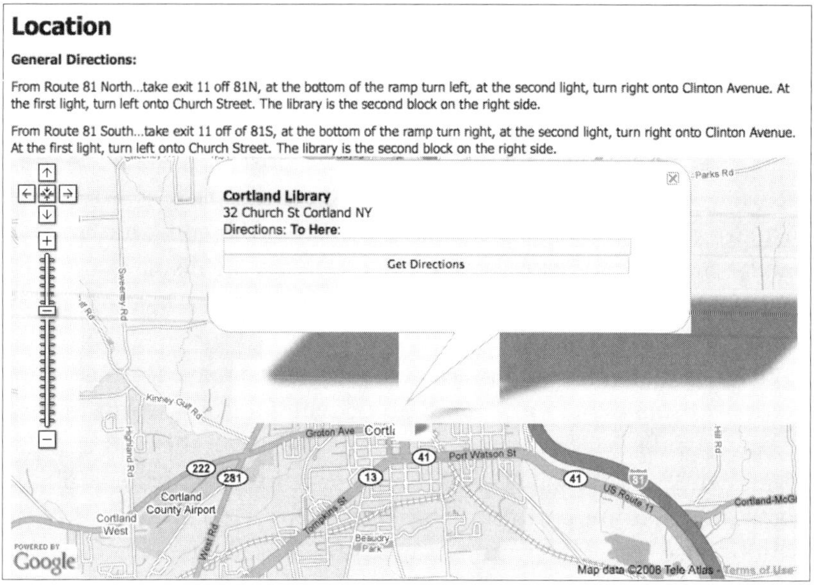
Location
General Directions:
From Route 81 North...take exit 11 off 81N, at the bottom of the ramp turn left, at the second light, turn right onto Clinton Avenue. At the first light, turn left onto Church Street. The library is the second block on the right side.
From Route 81 South...take exit 11 off of 81S, at the bottom of the ramp turn right, at the second light, turn right onto Clinton Avenue. At the first light, turn left onto Church Street. The library is the second block on the right side.
Cortland Library
32 Church St Cortland NY
Directions: To Here:
Get Directions
Parks Rd
Sweeney Rd
Kinney Gulf Rd
Groton Ave
Port Watson St
Highland Rd
Hill Rd
222
281
13
41
41
81
Cortland County Airport
Cortland West
US Route 11
Tompkins St
West Rd
Beaudry Park
Cortland-McGr
POWERED BY
Google
Map data ©2008 Tele Atlas - Terms of Use

Figure 8.4 Map embedded via Google Map plugin

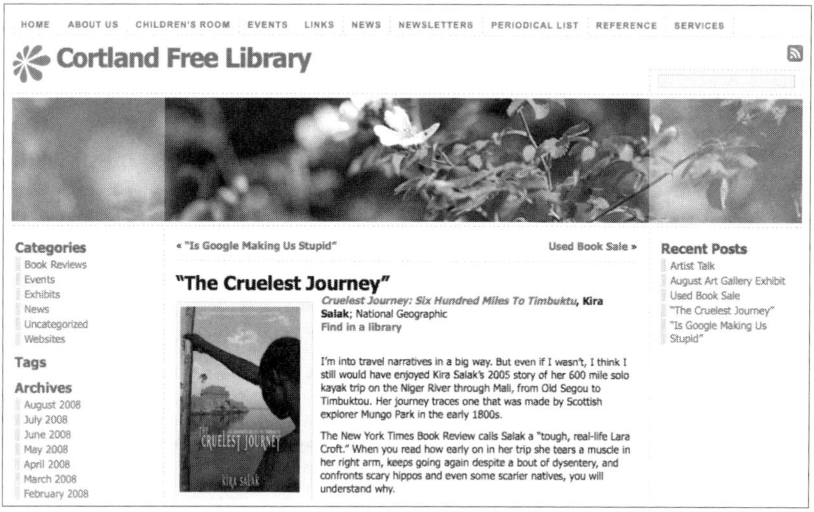
HOME
ABOUT US
CHILDREN'S ROOM
EVENTS
LINKS
NEWS
NEWSLETTERS
PERIODICAL LIST
REFERENCE
SERVICES
Cortland Free Library
Categories
Book Reviews
Events
Exhibits
News
Uncategorized
Websites
Tags
Archives
August 2008
July 2008
June 2008
May 2008
April 2008
March 2008
February 2008
« "Is Google Making Us Stupid"
Used Book Sale »
"The Cruelest Journey"
Cruelest Journey: Six Hundred Miles To Timbuktu, Kira Salak; National Geographic
Find in a library
I'm into travel narratives in a big way. But even if I wasn't, I think I still would have enjoyed Kira Salak's 2005 story of her 600 mile solo kayak trip on the Niger River through Mali, from Old Segou to Timbuktou. Her journey traces one that was made by Scottish explorer Mungo Park in the early 1800s.
The New York Times Book Review calls Salak a "tough, real-life Lara Croft." When you read how early on in her trip she tears a muscle in her right arm, keeps going again despite a bout of dysentery, and confronts scary hippos and even some scarier natives, you will understand why.
Recent Posts
Artist Talk
August Art Gallery Exhibit
Used Book Sale
"The Cruelest Journey"
"Is Google Making Us Stupid"

Figure 8.5 Book information embedded via OpenBook Book Data plugin

Another plugin that is helpful in creating library websites in WordPress is Inlinefeed (wordpress.org/extend/plugins/inlinefeed). This plugin allows you to embed an RSS or Atom feed in a post or page and can be used, for instance, to add a list of new books to a page if your catalog provides a feed of new titles (Figure 8.6).

Libraries can also use the Inlinefeed plugin to add local and national news to a webpage or to add a feed of the library's photos from Flickr. Adding a feed is fairly simple: Just type the URL for the feed into the Inlinefeed shortcode. A shortcode is a simplified tag specific to WordPress that allows users to add dynamic content to a WordPress post or page. Shortcodes can embed files or create objects, draw in data from another website, and perform a variety of other tasks that would normally require lots of complicated, ugly code (Figure 8.7).

Many libraries maintain lists of links for their users. While you can create such a list as a static page, WordPress offers a better way to manage this content through the Manage Links functionality and the Blogroll Links plugin (wordpress.org/extend/plugins/blogroll-links). Using the Manage Links functionality, you can create links and add them to categories. Next, you create the page on which you want a set of links to be displayed. Using the Blogroll Links plugin, add the shortcode for the particular set of links you want to display. As you can see in Figure 8.8, links can be included in an existing page with text. Once the page is saved, the shortcode is transformed into the actual links (Figure 8.9).

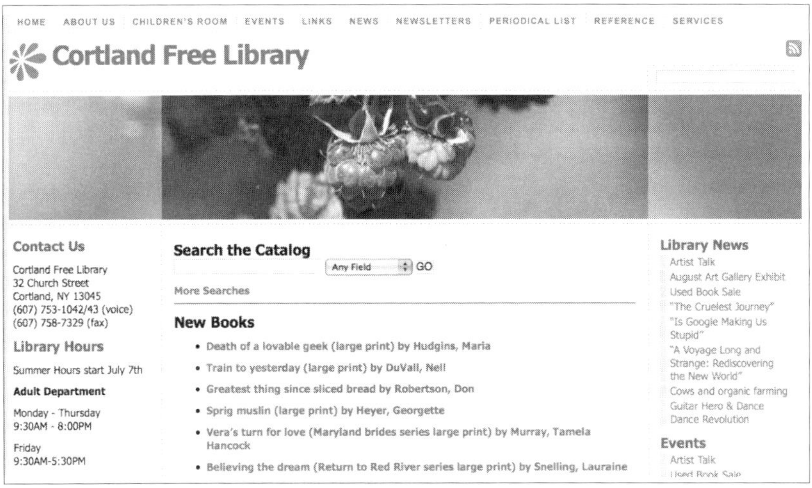

Figure 8.6 Feed embedded via Inlinefeed plugin

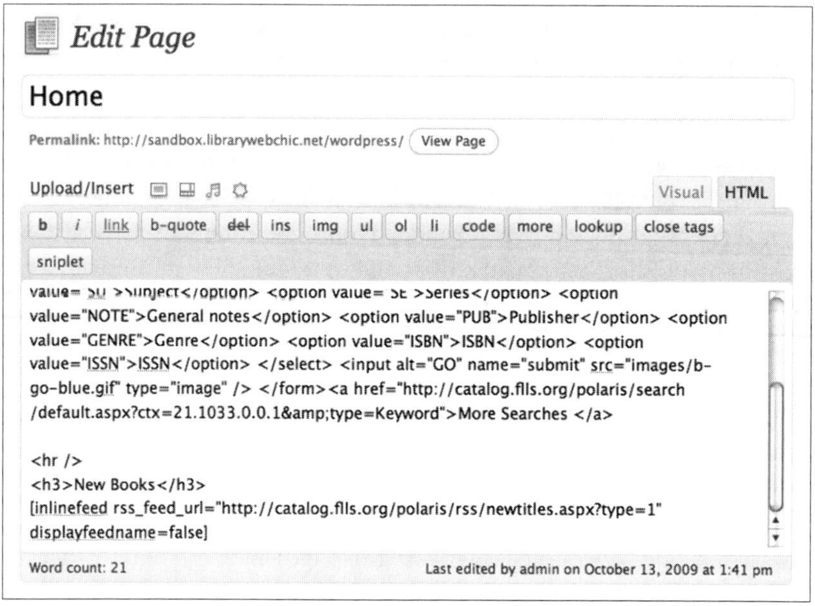
Edit Page
Home
Permalink: http://sandbox.librarywebchic.net/wordpress/ View Page
Upload/Insert
Visual HTML
b i link b-quote del ins img ul ol li code more lookup close tags
sniplet
value="NOTE">General notes</option> <option value="PUB">Publisher</option> <option
value="GENRE">Genre</option> <option value="ISBN">ISBN</option> <option
value="ISSN">ISSN</option> </select> <input alt="GO" name="submit" src="images/b-
go-blue.gif" type="image" /> </form><a href="http://catalog.flls.org/polaris/search
/default.aspx?ctx=21.1033.0.0.1&type=Keyword">More Searches </a>
<hr />
<h3>New Books</h3>
[inlinefeed rss_feed_url="http://catalog.flls.org/polaris/rss/newtitles.aspx?type=1"
displayfeedname=false]
Word count: 21
Last edited by admin on October 13, 2009 at 1:41 pm

Figure 8.7 Shortcode for embedding feed

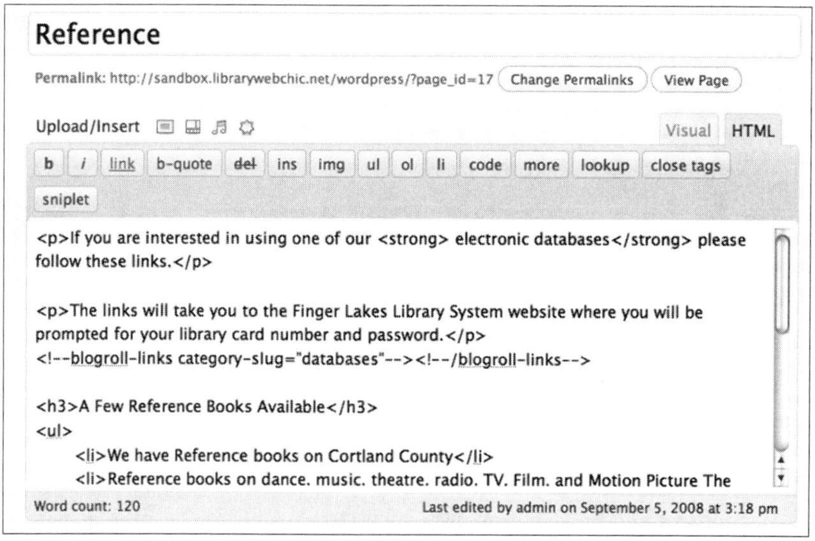
Reference
Permalink: http://sandbox.librarywebchic.net/wordpress/?page_id=17 Change Permalinks View Page
Upload/Insert
Visual HTML
b i link b-quote del ins img ul ol li code more lookup close tags
sniplet
<p>If you are interested in using one of our <strong> electronic databases</strong> please
follow these links.</p>
<p>The links will take you to the Finger Lakes Library System website where you will be
prompted for your library card number and password.</p>
<!--blogroll-links category-slug="databases"--><!--/blogroll-links-->
<h3>A Few Reference Books Available</h3>
<ul>
<li>We have Reference books on Cortland County</li>
<li>Reference books on dance. music. theatre. radio. TV. Film. and Motion Picture The
Word count: 120
Last edited by admin on September 5, 2008 at 3:18 pm

Figure 8.8 Shortcode for embedding links

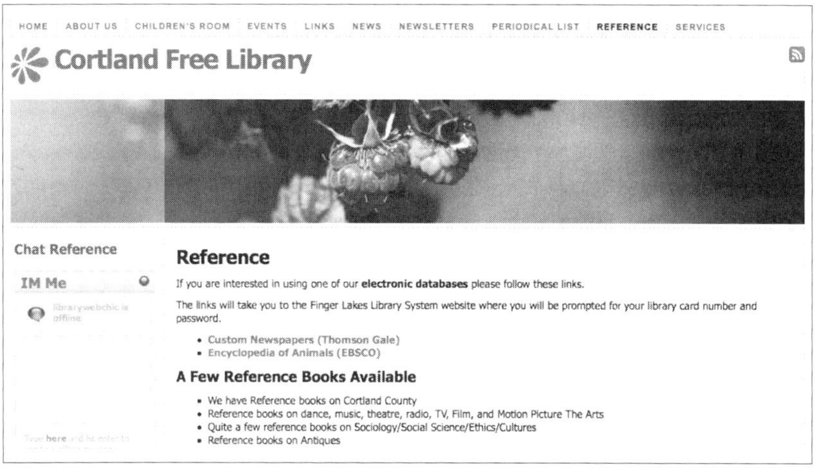
HOME ABOUT US CHILDREN'S ROOM EVENTS LINKS NEWS NEWSLETTERS PERIODICAL LIST REFERENCE SERVICES
Cortland Free Library
Chat Reference
IM Me
Reference
If you are interested in using one of our electronic databases please follow these links.
The links will take you to the Finger Lakes Library System website where you will be prompted for your library card number and password.
Custom Newspapers (Thomson Gale)
Encyclopedia of Animals (EBSCO)
A Few Reference Books Available
We have Reference books on Cortland County
Reference books on dance, music, theatre, radio, TV, Film, and Motion Picture The Arts
Quite a few reference books on Sociology/Social Science/Ethics/Cultures
Reference books on Antiques

Figure 8.9 Links embedded via plugin

Advanced Techniques and Tricks for Using WordPress as a CMS

Some libraries may want to include media content on their website, and WordPress is well suited to managing this type of content. We discussed the Media Manager feature of WordPress in Chapter 4. In addition to this basic media management functionality, WordPress can be used to create photo galleries. To create a photo gallery, first upload the photos you want to include to the page on which you want the gallery to display (Figure 8.10). Use the Media Management tool to put the photos in the order you want them to appear. Next, insert the `[gallery]` shortcode into your page and save the page (Figure 8.11). Once you have done this, thumbnails of the uploaded photos will appear, each linked to a full-size version of the photo (Figure 8.12).

This is a very effective but simple way to create a gallery in WordPress. If this doesn't meet your needs, however, or if you want a slideshow of your photos, install the NextGEN Gallery plugin (wordpress.org/extend/plugins/nextgen-gallery), which can be used to create both galleries and slideshows. Additional features include JavaScript effects and a widget for displaying random pictures in a sidebar.

Many library websites include a calendar of library events. The best plugin to accomplish this is the Events Calendar plugin (wordpress.org/extend/plugins/events-calendar), which allows you to create posts, assign them to a particular category of your choosing, and have them displayed as part of an Events Calendar. The key to making the

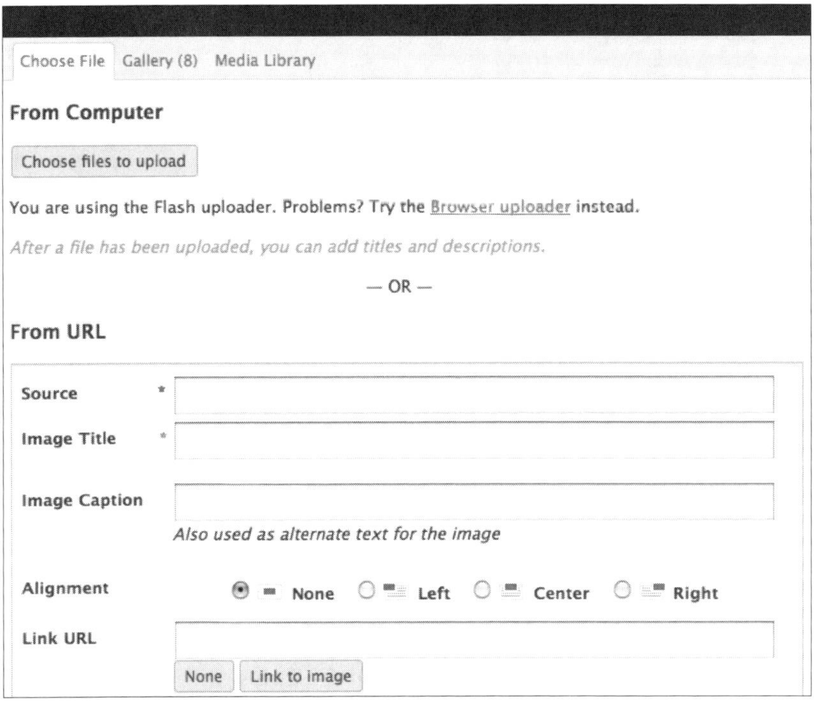

Figure 8.10 Uploading images for a gallery

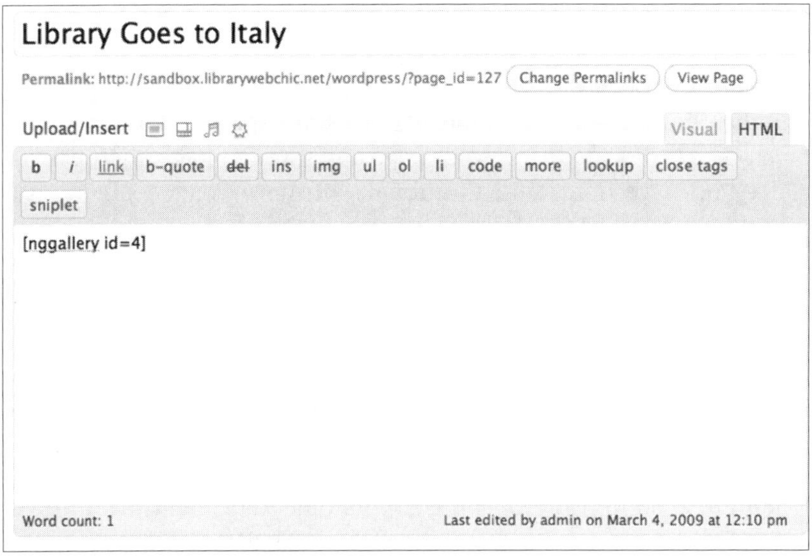

Figure 8.11 Gallery shortcode within a page

Figure 8.12 Example gallery

calendar work is to configure the Events Calendar plugin settings correctly (Figure 8.13). The plugin adds fields to the Edit Post screen that allow you to input start date/time and end date/time (Figure 8.14).

The plugin also adds two new widgets: the Events Calendar Widget and the Upcoming Events Widget. The Events Calendar Widget allows you to see a calendar that you can navigate to see events on a particular date (Figure 8.15). The Upcoming Events Widget allows you to create a list of upcoming events (Figure 8.16).

Lastly, to create a page that displays all the events, create a new page in WordPress and call it Events. Next, you need to install and activate the Sniplets plugin (wordpress.org/extend/plugins/sniplets). Then go to Tools > Sniplets and create a Sniplet called Event List. In the content, put:

```
<?php ec3_get_events(5); ?>
```

Insert the code `[ sniplet Event List]` into the Events page. You should then see your upcoming events displayed in this page (Figure 8.17).

Libraries Using WordPress as a CMS

Many libraries use WordPress for their blogs, and a number of public libraries use WordPress as a CMS, including:

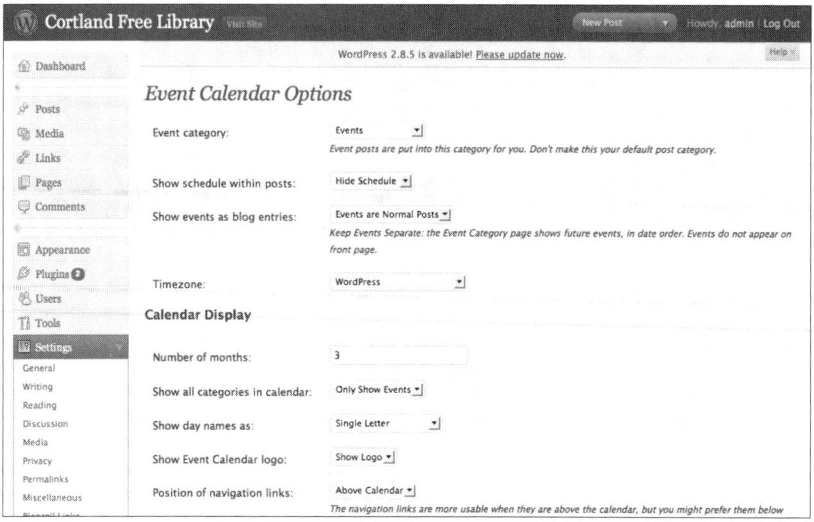

Figure 8.13 Events Calendar plugin settings

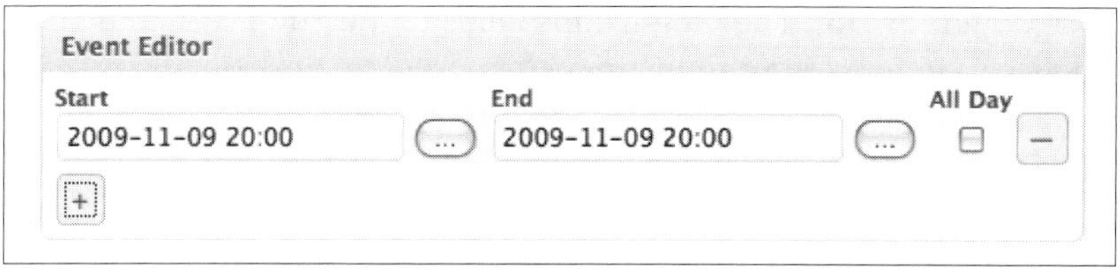

Figure 8.14 Event field in post

- Atchison (KS) Public Library (www.atchisonlibrary.org)
- Dartmouth (MA) Public Libraries (www.dartmouth publiclibraries.org)
- Park County (CO) Library (parkcountylibrary.org)
- Patagonia (AZ) Public Library (www.patagoniapublic library.org)
- Stevens Memorial Library (www.stevensmemlib.org)

Several state library organizations are assisting public libraries with installing and configuring WordPress as the platform for their library websites. The most significant of these is the Kansas State Library's My Kansas Library on the Web (www.mykansaslibrary.org), which supports more than 140 libraries' WordPress websites.

Figure 8.15 Example of an Events Calendar Widget

Figure 8.16 Example of an Upcoming Events Widget

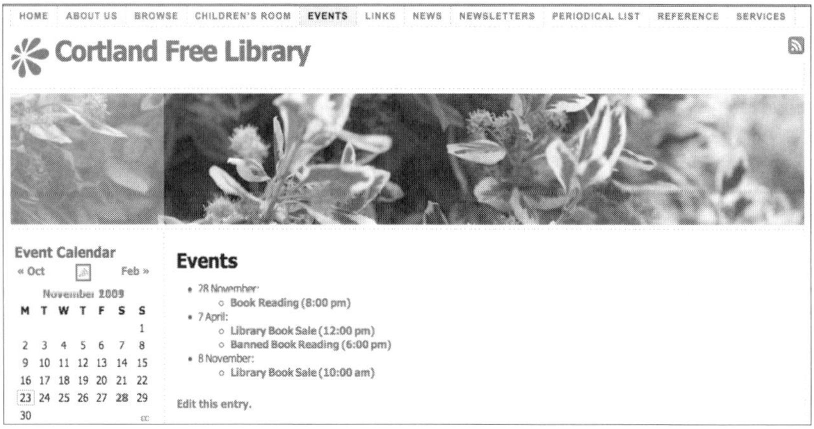

Figure 8.17 Example of an Events page

WordPress is also used as a CMS by a few college and university libraries, including:

- California State University–East Bay (library.csueastbay.edu)
- Brigham Young University Library departments, divisions, and other niches (lib.byu.edu/sites/sc)
- Millsaps College Library (library.millsaps.edu)

A major advantage to WordPress as a CMS is that it is simple and easy to use. There are lots of plugins available to extend WordPress's basic functionality, and it is easy to create new themes or modify existing themes to meet your needs. Probably the biggest advantage of WordPress, though, is its large user base. This means there is a good support network to draw upon.

The biggest disadvantage of WordPress is that you can't easily create custom content types with different types of fields. For instance, events and contact info are difficult to manage. Additionally, customizing the display of groups of page/posts requires knowledge of PHP. If your website has special types of content, or you wish to configure custom displays of content, then a more flexible CMS such as Joomla or Drupal might be a better choice.

CHAPTER 9

Joomla

Joomla is a development fork of Mambo, an award-winning CMS that began development in 2000, offering both an open source product, Mambo Open Source, and a commercial product, Mambo CMS. In August 2005, several of the Mambo developers broke away from the Mambo project and formed their own group, OpenSourceMatters. They released Joomla version 1.0 shortly after, and Joomla went on to receive several awards of its own in 2006 and 2007. It has an active community base, in a multitude of languages.

Installing Joomla

Joomla itself is easy to install but requires Apache, PHP, and MySQL to first be installed on the server or desktop. Before installing Joomla, you must also first create a MySQL database for it to use.

Download the most recent version of Joomla at www.joomla.org. Unpack the Joomla zip file into your web directory and then access the directory in your browser. The Joomla installation will walk you through the steps of configuring access to the MySQL database, FTP access, and the administrator username and password. During the install, you will also have the opportunity to install sample data. If this is your first time using Joomla, it is recommended that you install the sample data, as then you will have a fully configured site to learn on (Figure 9.1).

Basic Configuration

Once you have logged into the administrator part of Joomla, you will see the Joomla control panel. The control panel gives you easy access to managing content, users, and site parameters. The control panel also gives you quick access to statistics about logged-in users, popular content, and recently added content. Especially valuable features

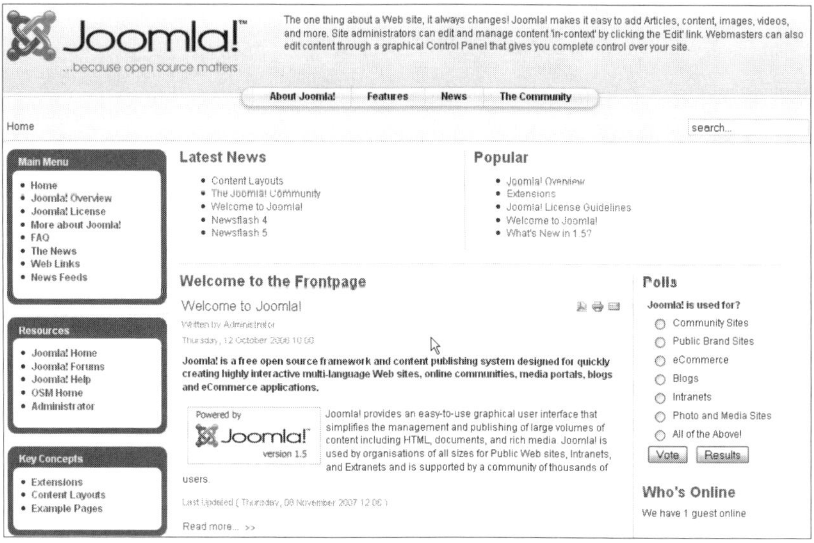

Figure 9.1 Joomla installation screen

include the mouseover help and the area specific help. For example, if you find you need help while you are adding an article, clicking on the Help button on that screen will give you context-sensitive help on adding and configuring articles (Figure 9.2).

Before adding content or users, you will first want to set the global configuration parameters for your site. Click on the Global Configuration button to enter this section. You will see that the configuration of your site is divided into three tabs: Site, System, and

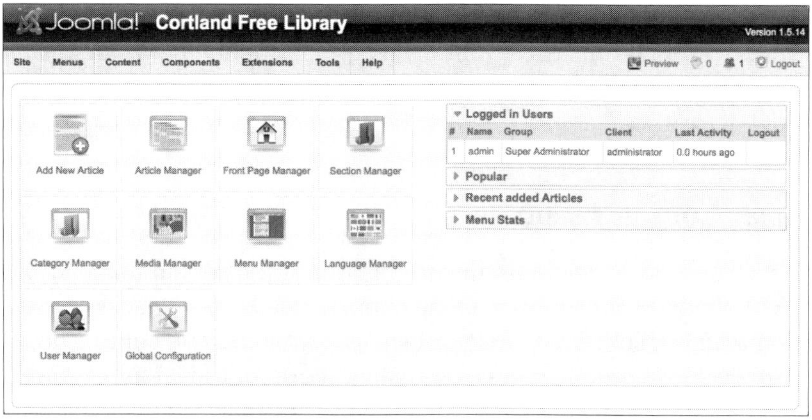

Figure 9.2 Joomla administrator screen

Server. The Site section gives you the opportunity to change the FTP access, site metadata, the default WYSIWYG editor, and the search engine optimization (SEO) options. Turning on the options for Search Engine Friendly URLs and Add Suffix to URLs will provide your site with page URLs that will help search engines crawl your site and will make data collected by an outside web analyzer easier to understand.

The System panel contains several important settings, including user registration, what media types can be uploaded, and session time-out. The most important settings for a new Joomla site are the user registration settings, which allow you to restrict new user accounts until your site is complete and secure. Once you allow user registration, you can permit registered users to create, publish, and edit content. The Server panel gives access to FTP, time zone, database, and mail server settings.

Understanding the Joomla Site Structure

Before entering content into a Joomla site, you need to plan your content to fit within the Joomla system. Joomla has a two-level site structure. At the top level are sections. For a library site, the Joomla sections might be something like Tools, Services, About, and News. Each section can hold multiple categories, which is Joomla's second organization level. For example, the Tools section might hold the categories Find Books, Find Articles, and so on. Joomla articles will hold the majority of your content. Each article is assigned to a category within a section. As an article can only be assigned to one category/section, it may be tempting to leave your articles uncategorized. However, it is recommended that you categorize your articles, as it will be easier to locate them later.

Creating sections and categories within Joomla is easy. Start by creating the sections within the Section Manager. Minimal information is required, and the default settings are fine for most purposes. For each section, enter the section name, chose whether to publish it, and set the access level (public, registered users, or special users). For example, if you are creating an intranet within your Joomla site, the section name might be Intranet and the access level limited to registered users. The process of creating a new category is almost identical to creating a section, with the exception that you must assign a section to each category. While creating both sections and categories, you have the opportunity to enter data into the Description field. The

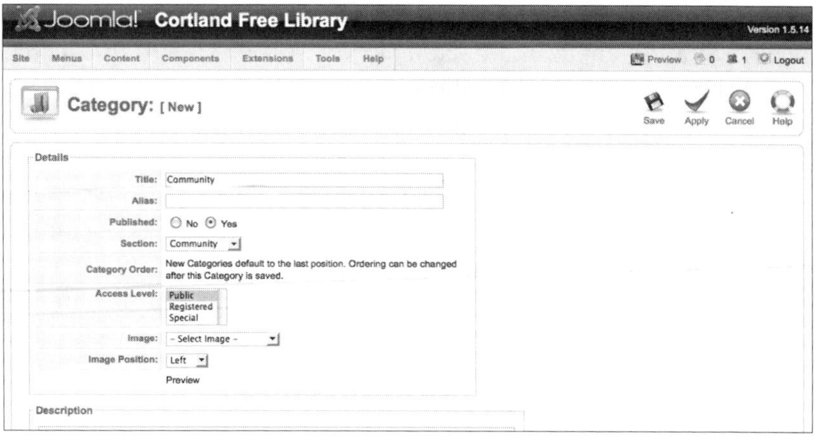

Figure 9.3 Joomla categories

data that you enter here should be considered a form of content, as you can create links directly to sections and categories (Figure 9.3).

The Article Manager is used to create, sort, archive, and delete articles. Before creating any articles, you will want to configure the global parameters within the article manager (Figure 9.4).

These parameters allow you to hide or show certain information about each article created. For example, you may wish to hide author names, creation date, and the number of hits each article received, but opt to show the date that the page was last modified and provide links to print or email the article content. If your Joomla install is an intranet, you may also wish to configure the articles to be viewable only by registered viewers. As you start to create articles, you can override these global parameters on an article-by-article basis.

To create a new article, click on the New icon. Enter a title, select a section and category to assign the article to, and you are ready to enter content (Figure 9.5).

Article content is entered into the WYSIWYG editor. The Joomla 1.5 install comes with two WYSIWYG editors, TinyMCE and XStandard Lite. TinyMCE is the default editor. It has close-to-word-processor functionality and includes the ability to upload images and to edit the html directly. The other editor available, XStandard Lite, adds better CSS and XHTML compatibility. However, XStandard Lite requires software to be installed on each computer. Article content may also be added as straight HTML code by selecting the No Editor option in the site's global parameters.

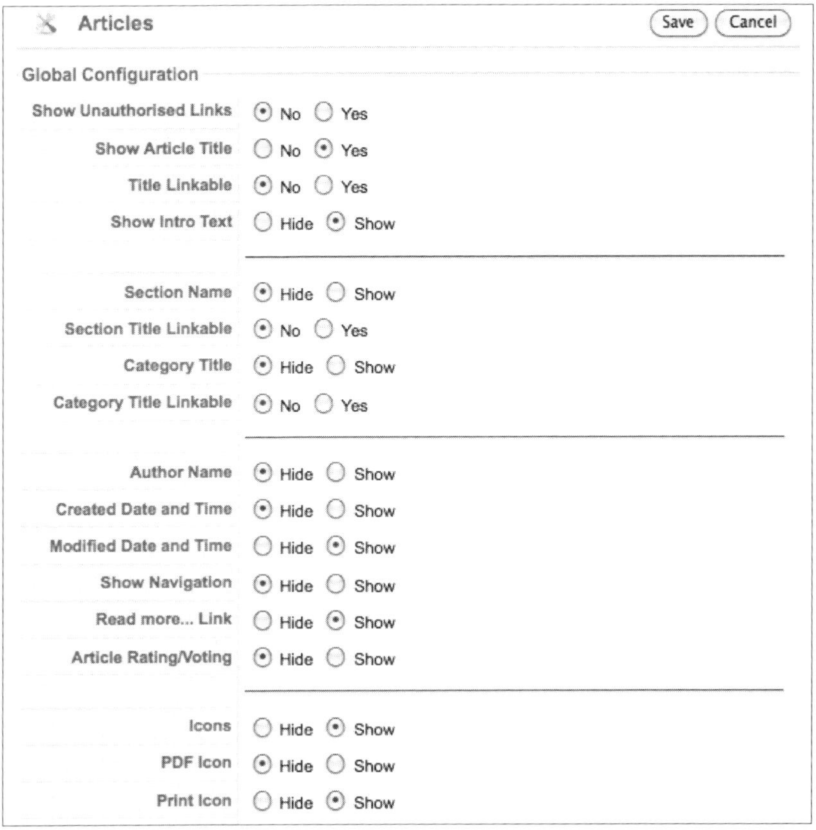

Figure 9.4 Global article parameters

After entering your article content, you have many options that you can customize for each article. The basic article parameters allow you to send the article to the front page of the site, choose when the article is available for viewing, and set the access level of the article (i.e., the article may be set to "registered" if it is to be viewed only by logged-in users). The advanced article parameters allow you to override the global article parameters you set earlier. The metadata area allows you to add a description and keywords for your article content. Search engines sometimes use the description underneath the page title in a search results listing. Keyword metadata was formerly used by search engines for page ranking; however, some sites abused the use of keywords and most search engines have since changed their ranking algorithms. However, article keywords are still useful within

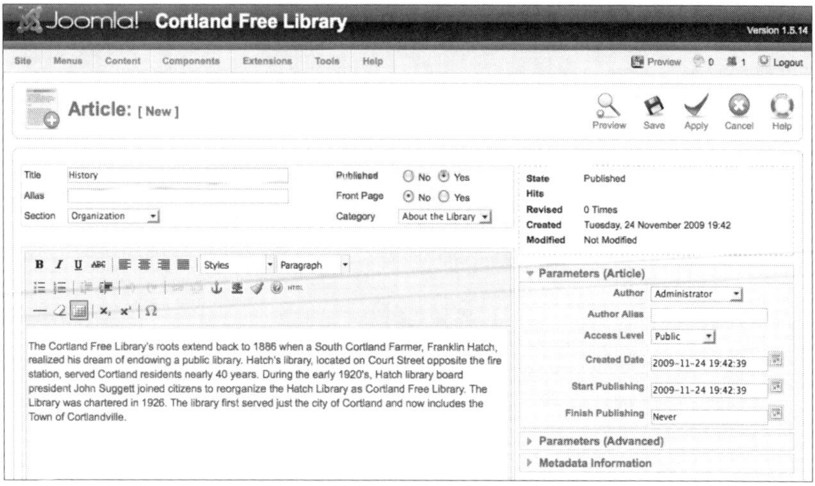

Figure 9.5 Article creation screen

your Joomla site, as they are indexed and used in the Related Items module discussed later in this chapter.

Customizing Your Joomla Site

Templates or themes control the design of your Joomla site. Joomla templates are very flexible in that you can often change certain features, such as color schemes and where content and navigation panes display, from the Joomla administrator panel. One thing to keep in mind, though, is that templates created for Joomla 1.0x may not work on Joomla 1.5x—and vice versa. Free Joomla templates are easy to find on the web at sites such as www.siteground.com/joomla-hosting/joomla-templates.htm. As the template that you choose will affect everything from where content and menus can be placed to whether your site is XHTML compliant, here are a few things to consider:

- Do you want a two-column or three-column layout?
- In case you need to edit the template, are you more comfortable with a table- or CSS-driven layout?
- Where do you want your navigation to appear?

Best of Joomla (www.bestofjoomla.com) hosts both free and commercial templates, and allows you to filter the template results by desired features. It is also possible to either create a Joomla template from scratch or to use a "sandbox," or starter, version of a Joomla template. Two good sandbox templates can be found at www.bulletprooftemplates.com/forum and at www.howtojoomla.net/content/view/84/6.

The basic file structure of a Joomla template is as follows:

```
/templatename
  /css
    /template_css.css
    /index.html (blank file)
  /images
    /index.html (blank file)
    /... (all of your template images)
  /index.php
  /templateDetails.xml
  /template_thumbnail.png
```

Index.php is the file that your site will use to pull in and display your content. TemplateDetails.xml contains the metadata about the template, the location and names of the files used in the template, locations and names of the cascading style sheets used in the template, and which module positions are available for this template. Modules are a type of Joomla extension, and each template can dictate where a module type will appear on your site

Joomla makes it easy to install and activate new templates. Once you have found and downloaded a template that you wish to try, log in to the Joomla Administrator panel and choose Install/Uninstall from the Extensions menu. You can install the template as a zipped file, from a directory on your server, or from a download link URL. Select the method you wish to use and click Upload, and Joomla will unpack and install the template into the template directory on your server or localhost. To activate the template, choose Template Manager from the Extensions menu, select the template you wish to activate, and then click Default in the upper right menu. You can then click Preview from the upper right menu to see your new template. The template manager also allows you to change parameters such as headers, color schema, and fixed versus fluid width layouts. While in the template manager, click on the name of a template and you will be taken to a screen that allows you to edit that template. You also have the option of editing the HTML and CSS of the template from within Joomla itself. While on the Edit Template screen, you can preview a template by clicking on Preview. This feature not only gives you a good idea of how your content will be laid out in a certain template, it also shows you where the various modules will be positioned (Figure 9.6).

Keep in mind that if you make changes to the templates that come pre-installed with Joomla, those changes will be overwritten when you update Joomla.

It is also possible to assign multiple templates to your Joomla site. For example, if you wish to have a separate design for an intranet section of your Joomla site, you would enter the Template Manager and select the template that you wish to assign to your intranet section. Click down to the Menu Assignment section of the page, and select the pages on your site that you wish to have the new template. Save your changes, and when you refresh your site, that section will have the new design.

Modules, Components, and Plugins

Joomla packages all nonarticle content and user interactive content within modules, components, and plugins, which are known collectively as Joomla "widgets," in that these are usually small sidebar sections, such as a navigation menu or a poll. By default, modules usually allow for only limited user interaction, but custom modules can be created that

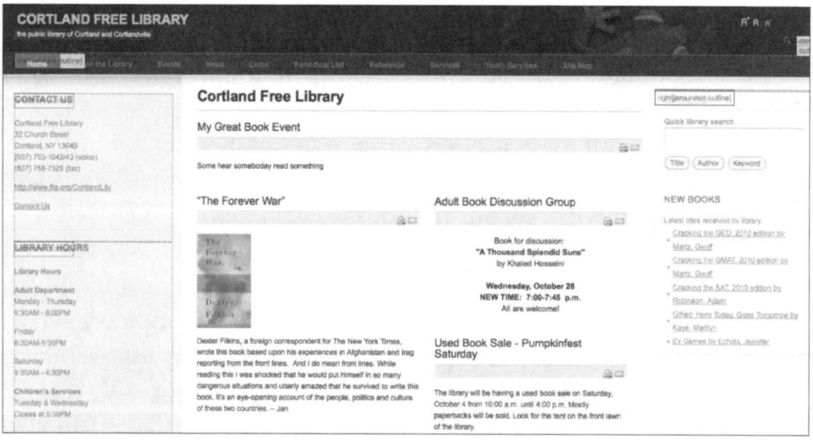
CORTLAND FREE LIBRARY
CONTACT US
LIBRARY HOURS
Cortland Free Library
My Great Book Event
Some hear somebody read something
"The Forever War"
Dexter Filkins, a foreign correspondent for The New York Times, wrote this book based upon his experiences in Afghanistan and Iraq reporting from the front lines. And I do mean front lines. While reading this I was shocked that he would put himself in so many dangerous situations and utterly amazed that he survived to write this book. It's an eye-opening account of the people, politics and culture of these two countries. – Jan
Adult Book Discussion Group
Book for discussion:
"A Thousand Splendid Suns"
by Khaled Hosseini
Wednesday, October 28
NEW TIME: 7:00-7:45 p.m.
All are welcome!
Used Book Sale - Pumpkinfest Saturday
The library will be having a used book sale on Saturday, October 4 from 10:00 a.m. until 4:00 p.m. Mostly paperbacks will be sold. Look for the tent on the front lawn of the library.
Quick library search
Title
Author
Keyword
NEW BOOKS

Figure 9.6 Joomla template content areas

allow for more user interaction. Where a module is positioned on a Joomla site usually depends on the template and is found within the templateDetals.xml file. You can see what modules are available in your current template either by looking at the templateDetails.xml file or by adding ?tp=1 to the end of your Joomla site URL.

Components are more flexible than modules and appear in the "content" position of your site. Popular Joomla components add capabilities such as forums and multimedia. Plugins are the most complex of the Joomla extensions and override Joomla's basic functionality. There are a number of extensions installed by default during the setup of your Joomla site. While there are a number of third-party extensions available, which have been created by the Joomla community, it is strongly recommended that you learn the basic Joomla functionality before you install third-party extensions. The most frequent mistake new Joomla users make is to install an extension to add some functionality that is already present.

Menus

Menus are one of the most frequently used Joomla modules. By default, new articles in Joomla are featured on the homepage chronologically, so in its simplest form, Joomla functions as a blog. To convert your Joomla site from a blog to website, you'll need to give users access to content organized by topic. To do this you need to create navigation for your site by building menus in the Menu Manager in the Administrator panel (Figure 9.7).

To create a new menu, click New from within the Menu Manager. Enter a unique name and a title for your new menu, and save it. Once you have created your menu, you can start adding navigation links by clicking on the Edit Menu Items icon. For each menu item, you have several content and layout type options. For example, you can link to a single article, category, or section. If you have extensions installed, you may be able to link to the extensions modules. While there are built-in layouts available, you can also change the layout by editing the PHP file associated with the menu item. You will find the files in \template name\html\com_content\ of your template directory.

After you have created a menu in the Menu Manager, the next step is to create a module for that menu. All content outside of the main content panel is positioned using modules, so to have a menu appear

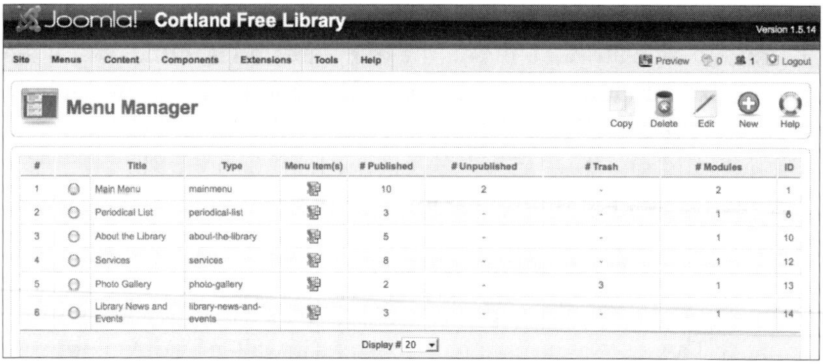

Figure 9.7 Menu Manager

on your site, you need to create and enable a corresponding module (Figure 9.8).

Joomla's menu system adds flexibility to your Joomla site. You have control over where a menu appears on a page, what pages menus appear on, and what CSS classes apply to the menu.

Customizing Your Front Page

In Joomla, the look and feel of your homepage is very flexible. By default, the Home link on the main menu links to the front page component. Published articles that are sent to the front page appear as blog posts. You can customize the layout of new articles by editing the Home link in the Menu Manager (Figure 9.9).

You can also customize your front page by having Home link to an article with static content, or you can customize what is shown on the homepage with the following code:

```
<?php if($_REQUEST['view']=="frontpage")
{?>
Have the HTML code for the homepage layout
<? }
else{?>
Have HTML code for the rest of the pages
<?php } ?>
```

This code allows you to place specific content on the front page, such as a welcome statement. You may also wish to change the template

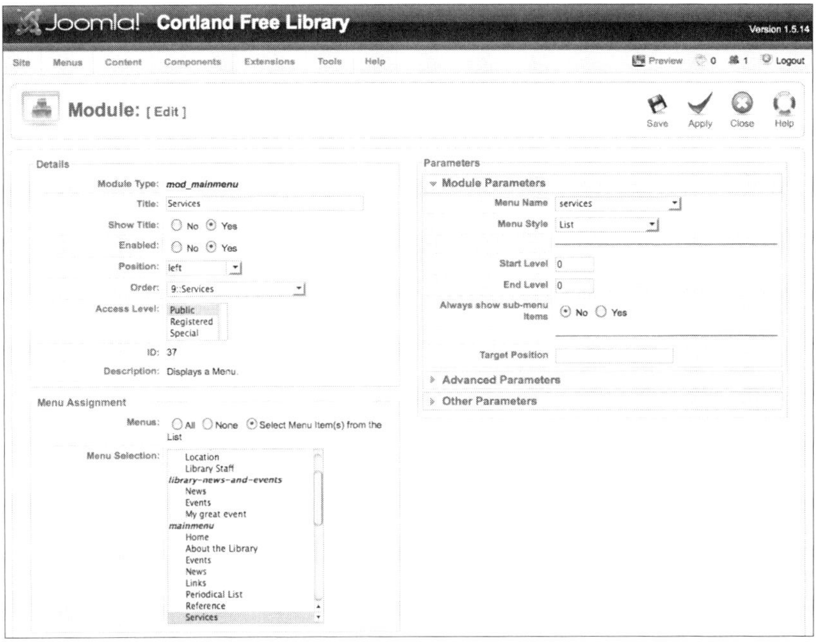

Figure 9.8 Menu Module

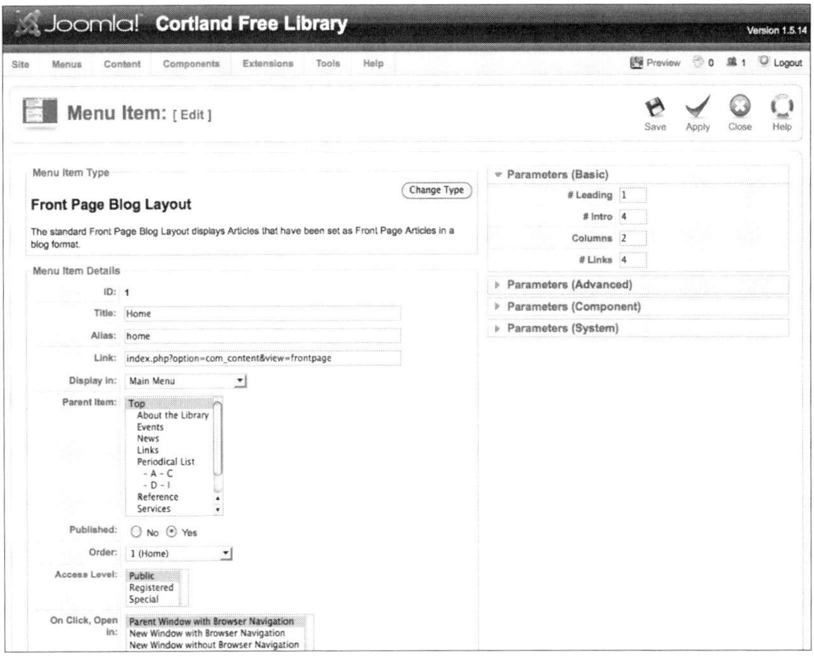

Figure 9.9 Front page menu item

code to customize the appearance of breadcrumbs on your homepage. If you have enabled the breadcrumb module, you can hide the breadcrumbs on the front page by placing the following code in your template's index.php file:

```
<?php if( JRequest::getVar( 'view' ) ==
'frontpage' ) { ?>
  <p> </p>
<?php } else { ?>
  <p>You are here: <jdoc:include type="
  module" name="breadcrumbs" /></p>
<?php } ?>
```

Joomla Modules of Interest to Libraries

The default Joomla installation has several pre-installed modules that will be of interest to libraries. For example, there are modules to display RSS feeds, create context-specific RSS feeds, and display links to related content (Figure 9.10).

Joomla has the ability to create context-specific RSS feeds. When you place the module Syndicate on any of your pages, Joomla creates an RSS feed for content added to that page. You may wish to place the

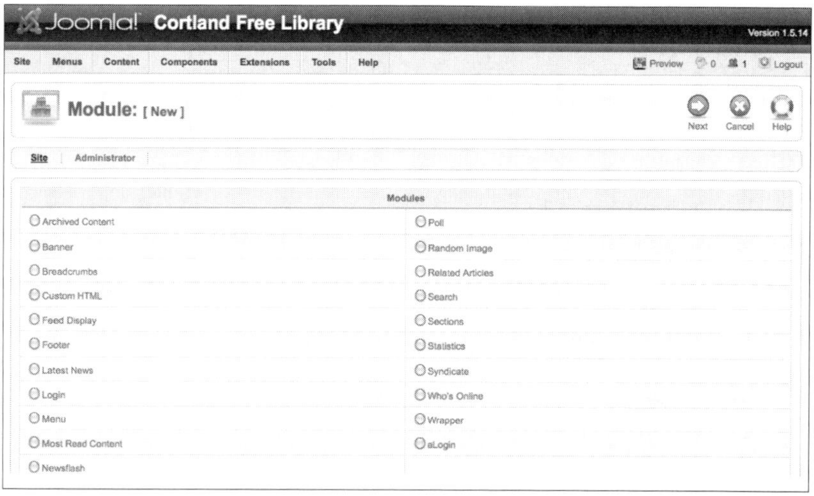

Figure 9.10 Joomla modules

Syndicate module on your events page, for example, to push new event information to your patrons as it is updated.

The module Feed Display allows you to pull in and display external RSS feeds. For example, if your catalog has an RSS feed for its new books, you can display a list of new books using this module. Within the Feed Display module, you can choose how many feeds to display, whether to link to the original source, and whether to display the contents of each item or post.

You can also create modules with HTML code using the Custom HTML module. Before creating a custom HTML module, you need to turn off the WYSIWYG editor in the global configuration panel; otherwise the WYSIWYG editor will strip out part of the html code. One way in which this module is useful for library sites is that it allows you to create a catalog search module. By inserting the HTML code for your catalog's search form, you create a module for a catalog search box that can be placed anywhere you like on your site (Figure 9.11).

If you have added metadata keywords as you created each article, you will want to make use of the Related Items module. This module searches the keywords you have added to articles and will display a list of links to articles with related content. The Related Items module creates a way for library patrons to stumble upon information that they may not have noticed otherwise.

```
<form name="formMain" method="post" action="default.aspx" id="formMain">
<input type="hidden" name="__VIEWSTATE" id="__VIEWSTATE" value="" />

    <script language="javascript">
      <!--
      function set_sessionOrgID(varNewOrgID)
      {
          var strURLTemplate = "http://catalog.flls.org/polaris/default.aspx?ctx=__orgid__.1033.0.0.3";
              var strURL = strURLTemplate.replace("__orgid__", varNewOrgID);
              location.replace(strURL);
      }
      //-->
    </script>
<?xml version="1.0" encoding="utf-16"?>

<script language="javascript">

String.prototype.trim = function() { return this.replace(/^\s*|\s*$/g,''); }

function ProcessInput(e)
{
    if (window.event) // IE
        keyNum = e.keyCode;
    else if (e.which) // Netscape/Firefox/Opera
        keyNum = e.which;

        if (keyNum == 13)
        {
            e.returnValue = false;
            e.cancelBubble = true;
            DoKeywordSearch('KW');
            return false;
        }
```

Figure 9.11 Custom catalog module

Third-Party Joomla Extensions

One of the Joomla's greatest strengths lies in the numerous third-party extensions available at extensions.joomla.org. The functionality of the default Joomla installation can be expanded considerably by Joomla extensions: modules, components, and plugins. An extension may often consist of some combination of these three. For example, an extension might consist of a component that creates a directory of links, a module that creates navigation for that directory, and another module to display a list of newly added links.

The extensions NinjaXplorer, SecureForm, JoomlaPack, and JCE are back-end additions to Joomla that simplify and/or improve existing Joomla functionality. NinjaXplorer, a Joomla component developed by Ninja Forge (ninjaforge.com), is a file system explorer that allows you to edit, upload, delete, and download Joomla files. One handy feature of NinjaXplorer is the ability to set permissions on files. Occasionally a Joomla extension does not work properly due to the read/write access on the files associated with the plugin. Ninja Xplorer makes it very easy to edit these permissions (Figure 9.12).

Web form spam is a common plague on websites these days. If you want your patrons to be able to leave feedback for your library or log in and leave comments, you will need a way to block spam and bots. While there are many spam blocking systems, the CAPTCHA system is very popular and is available through Joomla extensions. One such extension is SecureForm from Alikonweb (www.alikonweb.it), which can be used to block contact form spam and registration bots. Most CAPTCHA systems have accessibility issues, but SecureForm offers the user the option to hear the CAPTCHA. SecureForm's login module requires CAPTCHA input before a user can register, log in, or request a password reset (Figure 9.13).

There are four files that need to be installed in order to get SecureForm up and running: the SecureForm plugin, the AUserManager component, the AContact component, and the ALogin module. By default, Joomla uses JavaScript cloaking to obscure email addresses that appear in any article. This feature, however, does not help with contact form spam. SecureForm's AContact component will add the CAPTCHA plugin to each contact form.

Backing up your Joomla installation is made easy with the JoomlaPack extension (www.joomlapack.net). Akeeba Backup extension (formerly know as JoomlaPack) can back up your entire installation or just the MySQL databases. If you choose to back up your entire

Figure 9.12 Using NinjaXplorer to edit permissions

Figure 9.13 SecureForm login screen

site, Akeeba Backup creates a zip file that, when unpacked and accessed in a browser, can re-create your Joomla installation for you. This extension is handy if you need to move to a new server and is also useful for creating backup sites, development sites, or training sites.

The Joomla content editor (JCE) extension is an alternative to the TinyMCE and XStandard Lite WYSIWYG editors that are installed with Joomla. XStandard Lite is a standards-compliant WYSIWYG editor that generates clean XHTML markup, and it has several enhancements over TinyMCE, such as accessibility compliant code. However, one problem with XStandard Lite as packaged for Joomla is that the editor only functions if the XStandard Lite package is installed on each user's computer. The JCE editor has better image editing and uploading features, has a "paste from Word" feature that cleans up Microsoft Office code, and offers a spell-check feature. Also, a useful feature of JCE for web developers is the syntax highlighted code view.

Joomla Extensions of Interest to Libraries

Although not specifically written for libraries, there are several Joomla extensions of particular interest for library websites. Xmap (joomla.vargas.co.cr) creates a site map based on your menu structure. Xmap will create dynamic site maps if your menus link to sections and categories (i.e., as you add articles to categories, Xmap will automatically add them to the site map). One way to make a quick site map is to create an unpublished menu of your site sections.

Adding an interactive Google map to your site makes it easy for your patrons to get directions to your library. The Plugin Googlemaps extension (joomlacode.org/gf/project/mambot_google1) is an easy-to-install, highly customizable Joomla extension that provides this function. Plugin Googlemaps allows you to specify the size of the map, the zoom level of the map, and whether the map includes pictures or the option to get directions.

Many library websites include photo galleries of library spaces, library events, and their community. There are many good photo gallery extensions available for Joomla. The Atlantic City Free Public Library, for example, uses the extension JoomGallery (www.en.joomgallery.net) to create slideshows of library events and photos from their archives (www.acfpl.org/index.php?option=com_joomgallery&Itemid=974). JoomGallery provides the ability to create categories and subcategories of images and to place images within multiple categories (Figure 9.14).

Although it is relatively easy to embed Flickr slideshows into a Joomla site, the extension MorfeoShow (morfeoshow.joomlaitalia.com) adds the ability to display a slideshow from a Flickr user or a slideshow based on Flickr tags. MorfeoShow has several gallery and slideshow options, including the ability to show a gallery as an interactive pile of Polaroids. The extension Phoca Gallery (www.phoca.cz/phocagallery) supports gallery themes and YouTube videos. Both of these photo gallery extensions feature customizable gallery layouts, batch uploading via zipped files, and integration with other Joomla extensions.

The basic Joomla installation comes with a Web Links component, which allows you to create a listing of web links organized by category. This component, though, does not allow for the creation of subcategories or for listing a link in multiple categories. Joomla extensions have been created to overcome these limitations, for example, AlphaContent (www.alphaplug.com), Sobi2 (www.sigsiu.net/sobi2.html), and Mosets Tree (www.mosets.com). AlphaContent not only adds considerable functionality to Joomla's web links component but also improves the contacts listing. AlphaContent can display

Figure 9.14 Atlantic City Free Public Library photo gallery

web links and contacts as a directory tree arranged by category. The Cumberland County (NJ) Library (www.clueslibs.org) uses AlphaContent to display its online resources (Figure 9.15).

AlphaContent is limited, however, by its inability to put links into more than one category. The Sigsiu online business index 2 (Sobi2) deserves a mention here, as it provides the functionality to add a web resource to more than one category. However, as it was designed to list business contacts, considerable tweaking is required in both the Sobi2 control panel and the Sobi2 template. Mosets Tree is a commercial directory listing extension for Joomla with considerable functionality. A demonstration of the capabilities of Mosets Tree can be seen at the Joomla extensions website (extensions.joomla.org). The Atlantic City Free Public Library (www.acfpl.org/index.php?option=com_mtree&Itemid=96) is using Mosets Tree to power its directory of internet resources (Figure 9.16).

An events calendar is a common feature of many library websites. JEvents (www.jevents.net) features multiple event categories, layout

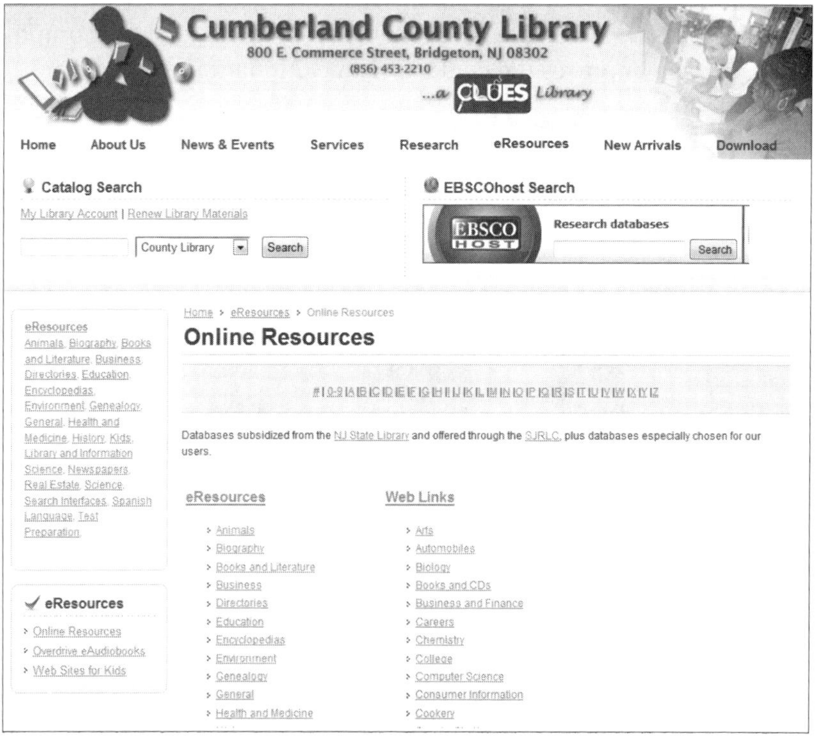

Figure 9.15 Cumberland County Library databases by subject

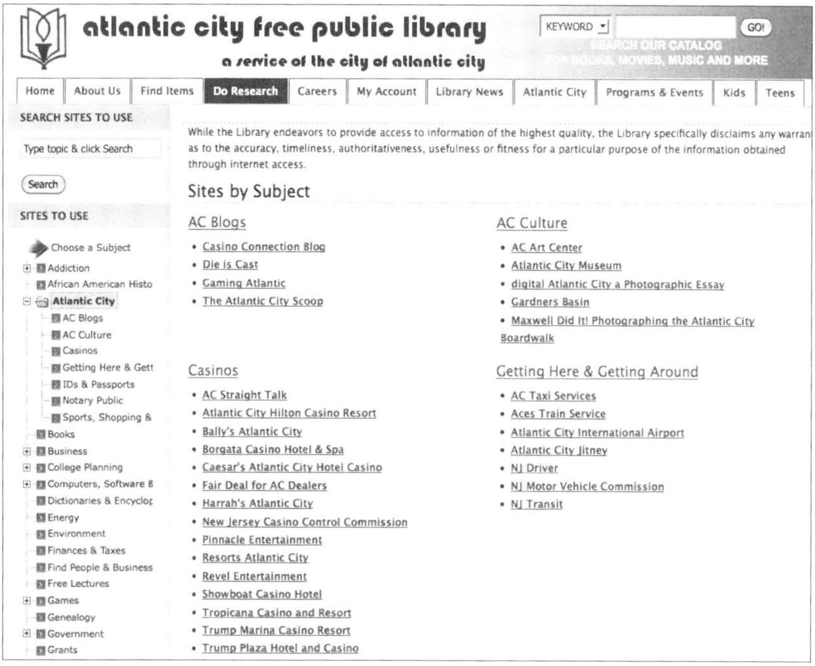

Figure 9.16 Atlantic City Free Public Library Mosets Tree directory

customization, and "mini-calendar" modules. The DeKalb County (GA) Public Library (www.dekalblibrary.org/eventscalendar) uses JEvents to display events sortable by branch library and event type (Figure 9.17).

Libraries Using Joomla

It's useful to look at what other libraries are doing to get ideas for how Joomla can be used to create library websites. Here are a few to get you started.

Public libraries:

- Atlantic City Free Public Library (www.acfpl.org)
- DeKalb County Public Library (www.dekalblibrary.org)
- Indian Prairie Public Library (www.indianprairielibrary.org)

Figure 9.17 The DeKalb County Public Library events calendar

- South Carolina State Library (www.statelibrary.sc.gov)
- Tyngsborough (MA) Public Library (www.tynglib.org)
- Whatcom (WA) Public Library (www.wcls.org)

Academic libraries:

- Health Sciences Library, Stony Brook University (www.hsclib.sunysb.edu)
- Lucy Scribner Library, Skidmore College (lib.skidmore.edu/library)
- Lupton Library, University of Tennessee at Chattanooga (www.lib.utc.edu/library-home/index.php)

Like any tool, Joomla as a content management system has its strengths and weaknesses. Joomla is second only to Drupal in terms of number of users, and, due to its popularity, Joomla has a very active community. Its discussion forums are "newbie" friendly and contain user guides to help with installing and troubleshooting Joomla. Templates and extensions for Joomla are easy to find and install. Joomla is very well suited for medium-sized websites and intranets. Each Joomla install only supports one website, so libraries that have multiple branch websites may find themselves maintaining multiple Joomla installations. A large site with a complex architecture would require a large time investment to restructure the site. For libraries wishing to create numerous subject guides containing database and internet links, Joomla lacks an easy solution.

## CHAPTER 10

Drupal

Drupal is a PHP-based open source content management system which, like Joomla, uses a database to store information. It can be run on Apache or IIS and uses MySQL or PostgreSQL for its database. Drupal comes with lots of pre-installed functionality, which can be enabled or disabled via modules; Drupal users can also add more functionality by downloading, installing, and enabling additional modules.

Installing Drupal

Drupal is extremely easy to install. This walk through assumes that you have installed Apache, PHP, and MySQL before beginning the installation process. If you want to know more details about installing Drupal using a different web server or database, please consult the Drupal handbook (drupal.org/getting-started/install). Once you have installed these prerequisites, you need to create a database for Drupal in MySQL and a MySQL user for Drupal to access that database. This is done by executing the following two commands in MySQL:

```
CREATE database database_name;
GRANT SELECT, INSERT, UPDATE, DELETE,
CREATE, DROP, INDEX, ALTER ON
database_name.* TO 'username'@' localhost'
IDENTIFIED BY 'password';
```

Next, download the Drupal files from the Drupal website (drupal.org) and upload them to the root of your web server. Drupal version 6.17 is the most recent version at the time of this writing. Make a copy of default.settings.php named settings.php, and make sure the web server has write permissions to this file:

```
cp default.settings.php settings.php
chmod a+w settings.php
```

You can then configure Drupal by visiting the base URL of your website. First, you will be asked to choose a language you want to install Drupal under (Figure 10.1). Next you will be asked to choose the type of database you are using (MySQL) and input the name, username, and password for the database that you just created (Figure 10.2). Last, you will be asked to add the first user account and provide basic website settings including the site name and default email address (Figure 10.3).

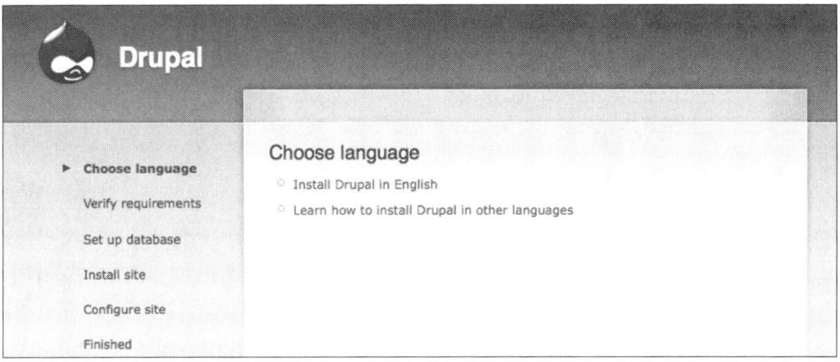

Figure 10.1 Drupal installation: Selecting a language

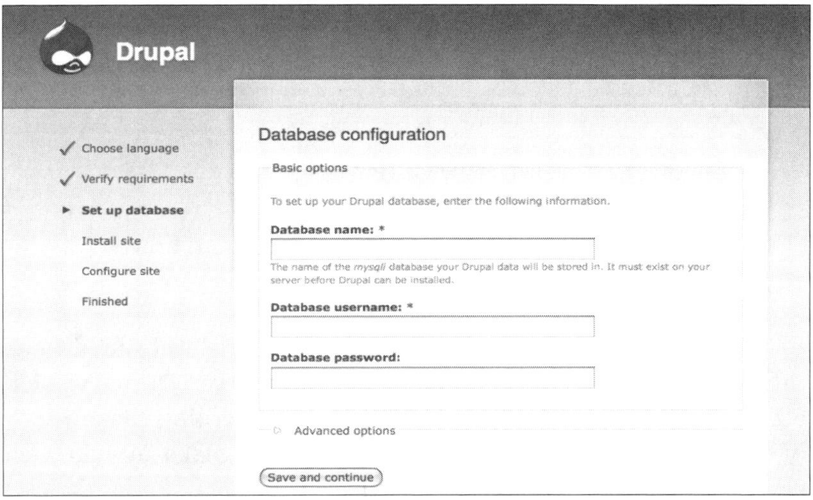

Figure 10.2 Drupal installation: Database configuration

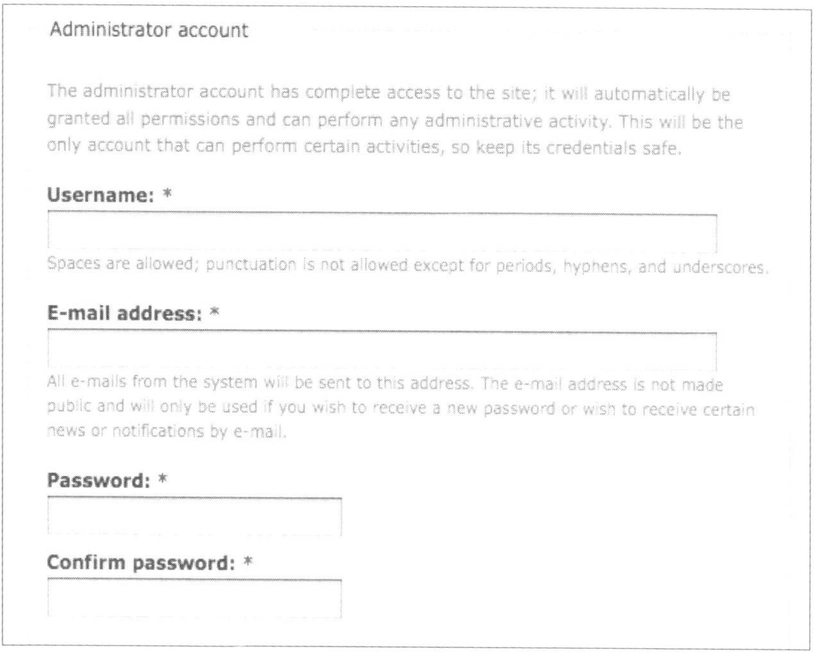
Administrator account
The administrator account has complete access to the site; it will automatically be granted all permissions and can perform any administrative activity. This will be the only account that can perform certain activities, so keep its credentials safe.
Username: *
Spaces are allowed; punctuation is not allowed except for periods, hyphens, and underscores.
E-mail address: *
All e-mails from the system will be sent to this address. The e-mail address is not made public and will only be used if you wish to receive a new password or wish to receive certain news or notifications by e-mail.
Password: *
Confirm password: *

Figure 10.3 Drupal installation: Creating an administrator account

After you have completed the web-based portion of the Drupal install, go back into your server and create a directory for file storage in the sites/default folder. Give the web server write permissions to this folder:

```
mkdir files
chmod o+w files
```

Once you have completed these steps, your Drupal website is ready to use.

Basic Configuration

By default, Drupal displays the most recent nodes added as its homepage. Drupal treats all content, regardless of what it is—a news story, event, or page—as nodes. If you want your most recent content to be your homepage, then no changes are necessary. However, if you want a specific page to be your site's home, then you will need to change the default front page. This is done by going to Administer > Site

Configuration > Site Information and changing the Default Front Page field to the node you want as your homepage. Any node that is part of your Drupal site can be can be made into the site's homepage. On the Site Information screen, you can also set other information about your site, such as the site name, slogan, and default email address.

In order to keep your Drupal site up-to-date and performing well, you should configure a regular cron job to run to perform scheduled maintenance. This can be done in a number of ways, but the simplest is to edit the crontab file to set the Drupal cron script to run at regular intervals. At the command line, type `crontab -e`. This will open up crontab and allow you to edit it. You can then add one of the following lines:

```
45 * * * * /usr/bin/wget -O - -q -t 1
http://yourserver.com/cron.php
45 * * * * curl --silent --compressed
http://yourserver.com/cron.php
```

Either of these lines will run the appropriate script—but in different ways. The first line uses the wget program to access the script, while the second runs the script using curl. You will need to make sure that the program you intend to use (wget or curl) is installed on your server and that you have input the correct path to it. Determine the path by typing `whereis wget` into the command line.

Content Types

By default, Drupal comes with several built-in content types enabled, including stories and pages. Stories are short pieces of content, similar to blog posts, that display the date created and the author's name. Pages are longer bits of content that are more static in nature and typically do not display the date created or the author's name. Additional content types can be added in two ways: by enabling additional default modules, or by installing other modules from the Drupal module directory (drupal.org/project/ Modules). Examples of content types that can be added include Blog, Book, Forum, Poll, Image, Event, and Web Form.

Building a Custom Content Type

Sometimes Drupal doesn't have a content type that meets your needs. In such a case, Drupal allows you to create custom content types. Using the Content Construction Kit (CCK; drupal.org/handbook/modules/cck) module, you can add different fields to your content type so that the data within it is structured appropriately. For example, a custom content type to keep track of information about library databases might contain fields for the database name, description, URL, and whether the database has full text. The first step in creating a new content type is to go to Administer > Content Management > Content Types and select the Add Content Type tab (Figure 10.4).

You will be asked to input basic information about your content type, such as its name, type, and description. You will also want to change the name of the Body field label to Description and then save your new content type. Next, select the Manage Fields link in order to add the new fields to the Library Database content type. First, add a field for the database URL. Next, add a field for whether the database contains full text. Last, add a field that will allow you to select what subjects a database is associated with. Once you have created the new content type, you will want it to display within the website. The best way to do this is by using CCK, Views, and Contemplate, which are described in the next section.

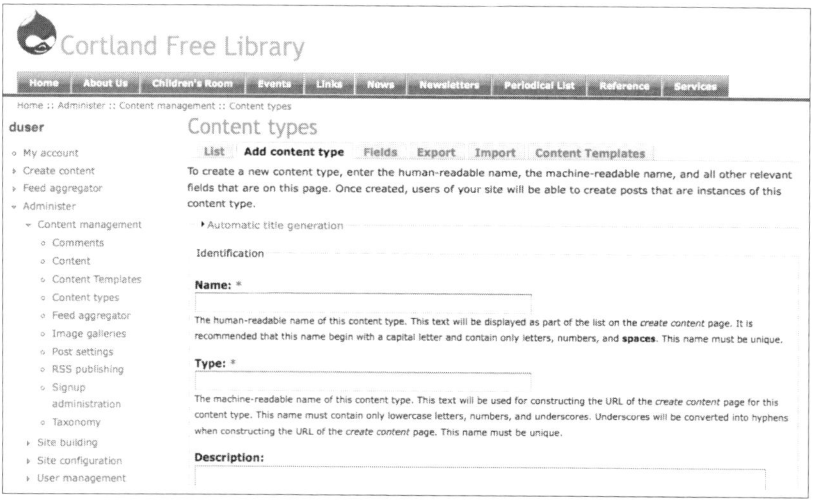

Cortland Free Library
Home
About Us
Children's Room
Events
Links
News
Newsletters
Periodical List
Reference
Services
Home :: Administer :: Content management :: Content types
duser
My account
Create content
Feed aggregator
Administer
Content management
Comments
Content
Content Templates
Content types
Feed aggregator
Image galleries
Post settings
RSS publishing
Signup administration
Taxonomy
Site building
Site configuration
User management
Content types
List
Add content type
Fields
Export
Import
Content Templates
To create a new content type, enter the human-readable name, the machine-readable name, and all other relevant fields that are on this page. Once created, users of your site will be able to create posts that are instances of this content type.
Automatic title generation
Identification
Name: *
The human-readable name of this content type. This text will be displayed as part of the list on the create content page. It is recommended that this name begin with a capital letter and contain only letters, numbers, and spaces. This name must be unique.
Type: *
The machine-readable name of this content type. This text will be used for constructing the URL of the create content page for this content type. This name must contain only lowercase letters, numbers, and underscores. Underscores will be converted into hyphens when constructing the URL of the create content page. This name must be unique.
Description:

Figure 10.4 Adding a content type

Modules

Modules are plugins for Drupal that extend, build on, or enhance Drupal's core functionality. These modules are not part of the core Drupal code and therefore may or may not be updated with each new release of Drupal. Additionally, the quality of the code can vary a great deal depending on the skill of the module developers and the time they have to work on the module.

Every Drupal site should have several key modules. Some of these add new content types (Figure 10.5) while others extend Drupal's functionality in other ways. Three modules that are essential are CCK, Views, and Contemplate. CCK, described in the previous section, allows users to add custom fields to a content type. Views (drupal.org/project/views) provides a flexible method for Drupal users to create and format lists of content. Contemplate (drupal.org/project/contemplate) allows users to format and style the custom fields within a given content type. Using these modules in combination, you can create custom content types and then format and display them to meet your needs. While the displays of particular content types can be customized using the Drupal theming system, the Contemplate module provides a more simplified way to make these customizations. To create a new template for a particular content type, select Administer > Content Template and then choose the content type you want to customize.

If you want to alter the main display of this particular type of node, choose Body. This will bring up a form where you can enter HTML and PHP code to format the fields in this content type. The

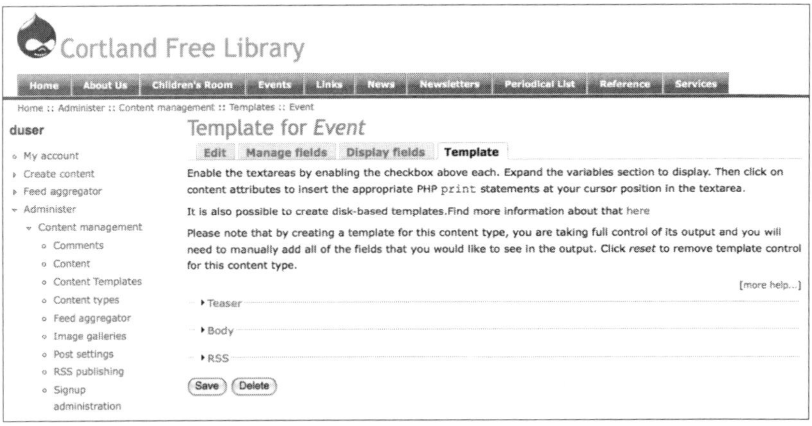
Cortland Free Library
Home
About Us
Children's Room
Events
Links
News
Newsletters
Periodical List
Reference
Services
Home :: Administer :: Content management :: Templates :: Event
duser
My account
Create content
Feed aggregator
Administer
Content management
Comments
Content
Content Templates
Content types
Feed aggregator
Image galleries
Post settings
RSS publishing
Signup administration
Template for Event
Edit
Manage fields
Display fields
Template
Enable the textareas by enabling the checkbox above each. Expand the variables section to display. Then click on content attributes to insert the appropriate PHP print statements at your cursor position in the textarea.
It is also possible to create disk-based templates.Find more information about that here
Please note that by creating a template for this content type, you are taking full control of its output and you will need to manually add all of the fields that you would like to see in the output. Click reset to remove template control for this content type.
[more help...]
Teaser
Body
RSS
Save
Delete

Figure 10.5 Adding a content template

Contemplate module provides a list of body variables, which contains all the fields available for display. Following is an example template used to format an Event node.

```
<div class="field field-type-text field-
field-location">
  <div class="field-items">
  <?php if ($node->event[ 'start_date_
format'] == $node->event[ 'end_date_
format']) {?>
  <div class="field-item"><div
class="field-label-inline-first">
Date/Time: </div> <?php print $node-
>event[ 'start_date_format']?> <?php print
$node->event[ 'start_time_format']?> - <?php
print $node->event[ 'end_time_format']?>
 </div>
<?php } else {?>
  <div class="field-item"><div
class="field-label-inline-first">Date/Time:
</div><?php print $node-
>event[ 'start_date_format']?> <?php $node-
>event[ 'start_time_format'] ?>
?>
     -
    <?php print $node->event[ 'end_date_
format']?> <?php $node-
>event[ 'end_time_format'] ?>
<?php }?>
  </div>
</div>
<div class="field field-type-text field-
field-location">
  <div class="field-items">
      <div class="field-item"><div
class="field-label-inline-
first">Location:</div><?php print $node-
>field_location[ 0][ 'view'] ?></div>
  </div>
</div>
```

```
<div class="field field-type-text field-
field-body">
  <div class="field-items">
  <div class="field-item"><?php print
$node->content[ 'body' ][ '#value' ]?></div>
</div>
</div>
<?php print $node-
>content[ 'signup' ][ '#valuc' ]?>
```

In addition to these three essential modules, there are several other modules that can make Drupal more usable for content creators and editors. WYSIWYG (drupal.org/project/wysiwyg) adds a graphical Word-like editor to easily allow users to add content. Image (drupal.org/project/image) adds the ability to upload images to Drupal and create galleries. Contact Forms (drupal.org/project/contact_forms) creates more efficient and usable contact forms. MultiBlock (drupal.org/project/multiblock) allows you to create multiple instances of blocks, or snippets of content, which can be added to different regions of your Drupal site. Token (drupal.org/project/token) allows you to place small bits of text into larger documents via simple placeholders.

Event (drupal.org/project/event) allows Drupal users to create event nodes and display these in a variety of event calendars. While this module is still not quite ready for production in Drupal 6, it is worth checking out if events are a significant portion of your library website. An important complementary module to Event is the Signup module (drupal.org/project/signup), which allows users to "sign up" for a particular node. In the case of events, this means users can sign up to attend an event, and Drupal content editors can configure a sign-up to only allow a specific number of people to register. In addition, editors can send a mass email to people who have signed up and keep track of who actually attended. Using these modules in concert, libraries can manage their events and track patron attendance.

In addition to these modules, there are several others that are of interest to libraries. The Book Post module (drupal.org/project/book post) allows users to post information about books by entering an ISBN into a post. The module uses the ISBN to retrieve the book cover image and basic information (author, title) about the book. The MARC module (drupal.org/project/marc) allows the user to import MARC records as nodes and can be used for creating a book review site or library catalog. Bibliography Module (drupal.org/project/biblio) allows users to manage and display lists of scholarly publications. OAI-PMH Module (drupal.org/project/oai2) provides a way to harvest data from the Bibliography Module via the OAI-PMH interface.

Customizing Your Drupal Site

The next step you should take in configuring your Drupal site is to choose a theme. There are many themes available for download; the key is finding one that meets your needs. Consider the following:

- What kind of banner do you want?
- Where do you want your site navigation to appear?
- What kinds of layouts do you want to use? One column, two column, three column?
- Do you want a fixed or scalable layout?

Once you have determined these things, you can begin to look for an appropriate theme. Colors and fonts can easily be changed either via options in the theme itself or by changing the style sheet, so don't get caught up in these minor details.

Drupal themes can be downloaded and installed from a variety of sites, including the main Drupal Themes page (drupal.org/project/Themes) and Sooper Themes (alldrupalthemes.com). Make sure to download a theme that matches the version of Drupal you are running. To install a new theme, follow these steps:

- Download the theme you want to install to your local computer.
- Extract the theme.
- Upload the theme to your server. You should put the folder into sites/all/themes.
- Enable the theme.

Once you have installed the theme, you can make it the default. This is done by going to Administer > Site Building > Themes and choosing the new theme you have installed. This makes the theme available to users. Many themes allow you to customize certain aspects of the display via the Theme control panel. For example, you can choose to enable or disable the display of certain page elements such as the logo, mission statement, and search box, or you can choose the image you want to use for your logo. Some themes allow you to control the color scheme of the site.

Once you have a theme in place, you need to decide how your content will be laid out on the page. This is done using blocks, which are snippets of content that can be added to particular regions of your Drupal site. By default, Drupal comes with a set of default blocks, including all menus, "powered by Drupal," recent comments, a search form, syndicate, who's online, who's new, and user login. In addition to these basic blocks, you can add more blocks by enabling modules or installing new modules. For example, enabling the Poll module makes available a Most Recent Poll block, and adding the Image modules adds two blocks: Latest Image and Random Image. You can also add your own unique block using the Add a Block tab, which brings up a screen where you can create your block (Figure 10.6).

HTML or PHP can be input into a custom block. The Drupal website also has a selection of block snippets that can help you customize your site.

Typically each theme has several regions, or blocks, into which content can be inserted. In the case of the Z Classic theme there are six regions: header, left sidebar, content top, right sidebar, content bottom, and closure. Most Drupal themes contain at least five regions: header, left sidebar, content, right sidebar, and footer. Some themes, like AD Blueprint (drupal.org/project/ad_blueprint), provide many blocks in order to give designers as much flexibility as possible. A key

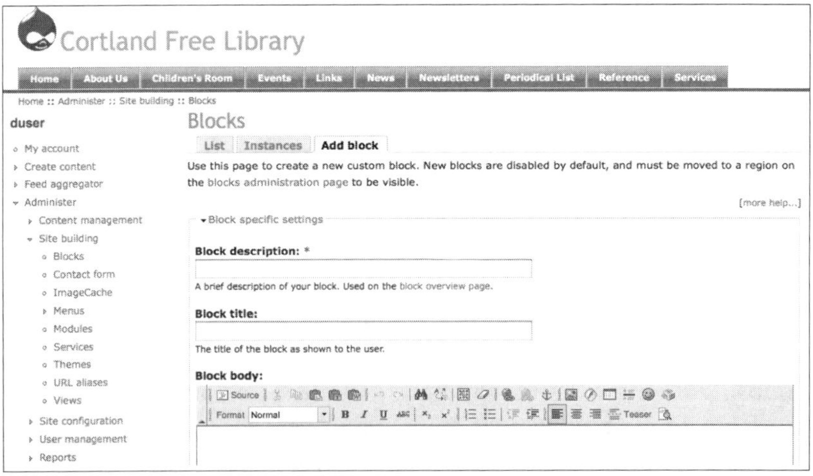

Figure 10.6 Adding a custom block

concept to remember with blocks is that if a block is empty, it collapses. So, for example, if the right sidebar block is empty, the main content will take up that space (Figure 10.7).

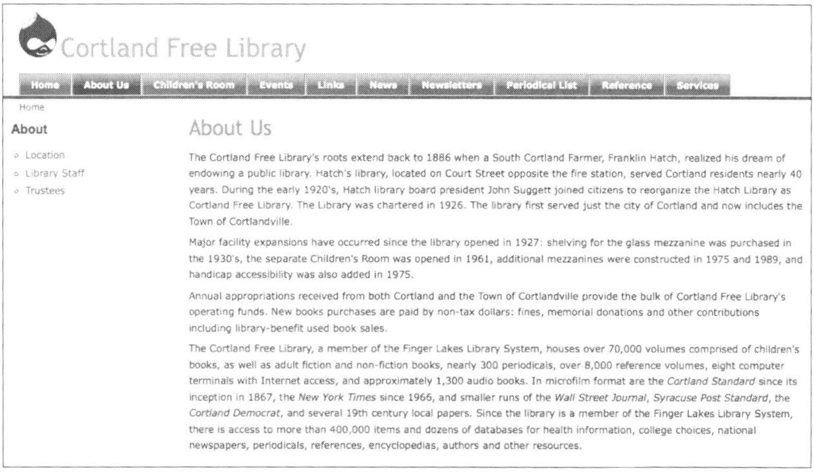
Cortland Free Library
Home
About Us
Children's Room
Events
Links
News
Newsletters
Periodical List
Reference
Services
Home
About
Location
Library Staff
Trustees
About Us
The Cortland Free Library's roots extend back to 1886 when a South Cortland Farmer, Franklin Hatch, realized his dream of endowing a public library. Hatch's library, located on Court Street opposite the fire station, served Cortland residents nearly 40 years. During the early 1920's, Hatch library board president John Suggett joined citizens to reorganize the Hatch Library as Cortland Free Library. The Library was chartered in 1926. The library first served just the city of Cortland and now includes the Town of Cortlandville.
Major facility expansions have occurred since the library opened in 1927: shelving for the glass mezzanine was purchased in the 1930's, the separate Children's Room was opened in 1961, additional mezzanines were constructed in 1975 and 1989, and handicap accessibility was also added in 1975.
Annual appropriations received from both Cortland and the Town of Cortlandville provide the bulk of Cortland Free Library's operating funds. New books purchases are paid by non-tax dollars: fines, memorial donations and other contributions including library-benefit used book sales.
The Cortland Free Library, a member of the Finger Lakes Library System, houses over 70,000 volumes comprised of children's books, as well as adult fiction and non-fiction books, nearly 300 periodicals, over 8,000 reference volumes, eight computer terminals with Internet access, and approximately 1,300 audio books. In microfilm format are the *Cortland Standard* since its inception in 1867, the *New York Times* since 1966, and smaller runs of the *Wall Street Journal*, *Syracuse Post Standard*, the *Cortland Democrat*, and several 19th century local papers. Since the library is a member of the Finger Lakes Library System, there is access to more than 400,000 items and dozens of databases for health information, college choices, national newspapers, periodicals, references, encyclopedias, authors and other resources.

Figure 10.7 Example of right sidebar

You can use PHP to make a given block appear on all pages or only on certain pages by including or excluding pages you want the block to appear on. In addition, PHP can be used to make a block appear only under certain conditions. For example, you might choose to have a certain block appear only on particular content types. Following is the code that will make a block only appear on pages.

```
<?php
$match = FALSE;
$types = array('story' => 1);
if (arg(0) == 'node' && is_numeric(arg(1)))
{
  $nid = arg(1);
  $node = node_load(array('nid' => $nid));
  $type = $node->type;
  if (isset($types[ $type] )) {
    $match = TRUE;
  }
}
return $match;
?>
```

Menus

Menus are sets of links to pages within your Drupal site or on external sites. Drupal comes with three menus by default: Administration, Primary Links, and Secondary Links. The Administration menu represents the links that make up the back-end editor portion of the Drupal site. This menu is changed as new modules are added and should not typically be customized. The Primary Links and Secondary Links menus are used for links that are part of the public website. Most themes use these two menus and position them in specific regions on the screen. For example, in the Zen Classic theme, the Primary Links menu creates the tabs at the top of the site. In addition to these two default menus, Drupal allows you to create as many other menus as you would like. All the menus that you create are available as blocks, which you can position on pages within the site or add to a customized theme.

Drupal menus can be hierarchical and have many layers and levels. So, for example, you might have a menu that looks something like this:

- Search
- About
  - Policies
  - Contact Us
- Services
  - Interlibrary Loan
  - Instruction

Drupal allows you to determine which sections of the menu should be expanded, or open, and which should be contracted, or closed. In our example menu just given, we could choose to have the About section be expanded to always show the subpages but have the Services section contracted to show only the top level link, unless the user was on one of the subpages within that section.

To create a new menu or edit an existing one, go to Administer > Site Building > Menus. To add a new menu, select the Add a Menu tab; you will then be asked to give it a machine-readable name, a title, and a description. It is helpful to create a menu name that makes sense, as this is the label under which the menu will appear in the Blocks page. In addition, adding a menu description will help you keep track of how a given menu is used within your Drupal site.

To edit an existing menu, click on the menu name. You will see a list of all the items currently in the menu, and from here you can use the Add Item tab to add a new item to the menu. When you add a new item, you will be asked to give it a name and enter a path: either to a node within your Drupal site (node/5) or to an external page via a full URL (www.librarywebchic.net). Once you have added an item to a menu, you have a number of options. You can click on a particular menu item to edit it, you can drag and drop a menu item to change its position in the list, or you can drag and drop it to nest it under an existing menu item.

Taxonomies

Drupal's taxonomies functionality allows users to categorize content using both tags and administrator-defined terms. Terms within Drupal are organized into vocabularies. So, for example, you might have a Tags vocabulary, which allows your users to enter a set of terms as free text. You might also have a Subjects vocabulary, which is a controlled hierarchy of terms that users may choose to assign to a piece of content. In addition, Drupal taxonomies allow for a single term or multiple terms to be assigned to a piece of content from a particular vocabulary so for example, you could choose to assign two terms from the Subjects vocabulary—say, Anthropology and Sociology—to the same piece of content. Taxonomies also allow you to define related terms for a given term. This feature functions similarly to a "see also" reference within an index. Vocabularies in the taxonomies can be affiliated with certain content types and can be required or optional. As a result, when users create content of a particular type, they'll see a list of the vocabulary terms that go with it. Users can then categorize the content they are creating using the vocabularies affiliated with that content type.

Taxonomies are probably one of Drupal's most powerful features, but they are also one of its most confusing. Typically, taxonomies are used to segment site content. Each term within a vocabulary has its own URL, which takes the following form: taxonomy/term/1. When this URL is visited, all the nodes that are assigned this taxonomy term will be listed. Using this technique, you could list all of the nodes that were assigned a specific term, such as Anthropology. In addition, the taxonomy functionality allows you to create URLs that represent a collection of multiple taxonomy terms, using the syntax taxonomy/term/1+3, or the intersection of two terms (1 and 3), using the syntax taxonomy/term/1,3. Drupal also creates feeds for each taxonomy term or combination of terms, which can be accessed using the syntax taxonomy/term/1/0/feed.

Some Drupal users utilize taxonomies to drive their site menus rather than using the standard menu functionality of Drupal. There are two modules, the Taxonomy Menu (drupal.org/project/taxonomy_menu) or DHTML Menu (drupal.org/project/dhtml_menu), that can help with creating menus from taxonomies. However, this approach takes a great deal of planning, forethought, and organization. It works very well for content that is highly structured, such as a list of databases, each of which has assigned subjects. Using the taxonomy module, you can create a menu that lists all the terms in the Subject vocabulary and then link to a list of the databases assigned to each specific term.

Many modules make use of Drupal's built-in taxonomy functionality to create features within the module. Two examples are the Forum module and the Image module. The Forum module creates threaded discussion space within Drupal, using taxonomy terms to create topic threads. The Image module has a feature that allows users to create galleries of images by creating an Image Gallery vocabulary, with each "gallery" added as a specific term. By assigning images to a term, you are then able to create galleries. While this approach works, it isn't always intuitive to Drupal users. If you choose to use taxonomies as part of your site, make sure you plan them out carefully and that labels and other user interface elements are sufficiently clear to allow site editors to easily add terms.

Libraries Using Drupal

There is a significant group of Drupal users within the library community. The Drupal4Lib mailing list provides a forum for library Drupal users to converse and ask each other questions. The list is open for anyone to subscribe, and the list archives are available on the web (listserv.uic.edu/archives/drupal4lib.html). In addition to this list, the Drupalib website is a space for Drupal-related library announcements, such as new libraries adopting Drupal, new library-related modules created, updates to library-related Drupal modules, and information about library Drupal gatherings (drupalib.inter operating.info). In the summer of 2009, a Drupal4Lib LITA Interest Group was founded. Another source for library-related Drupal information is the Drupal Libraries Group (groups.drupal.org/libraries). This site includes lots of information about library-related modules, gatherings of Drupal library users, presentations about Drupal in libraries, and code snippets.

The Drupal Libraries Group website also provides an extensive list of libraries currently using Drupal (groups.drupal.org/node/13473), which is worth checking out. Some library implementations of Drupal of note include:

- Darien (CT) Library (www.darienlibrary.org)
- University of Michigan Library (www.lib.umich.edu)
- McMaster University Library (library.mcmaster.ca)

Much of the Darien Library site features the Story content type, which is used to highlight the latest news and information for that particular area in the library. The library homepage, in particular, highlights the latest stories that have been posted, including announcements, events, and news (Figure 10.8). The site makes extensive use of taxonomies to facilitate the division of the website into sections. This use of taxonomies can be seen within the Teens section of the Darien site (Figure 10.9).

In addition to the basic portions of the site being Drupal-driven, Darien Library's site also includes an implementation of SOPAC, the Social OPAC. (For more information about SOPAC, see Chapter 15.) Using SOPAC, Darien Library is able to integrate library catalog content into its website and bring Web 2.0 social features to library content (Figure 10.10).

The University of Michigan Library website is also powered by Drupal. This website uses the CCK, Views, Solr, and Organic Groups modules. Using the Solr module, the library is able to index the node content within its Drupal website and then combine this index with the VuFind Solr index of its library catalog, Solr indexes of non-Drupal files on its web server, and an index of external content, such as LibGuides, to create a single search of library content. This structure enables the site to return search results in a unified way to library users (Figure 10.11).

In addition, the University of Michigan Library uses the Organic Groups module (drupal.org/project/og) to associate staff with service

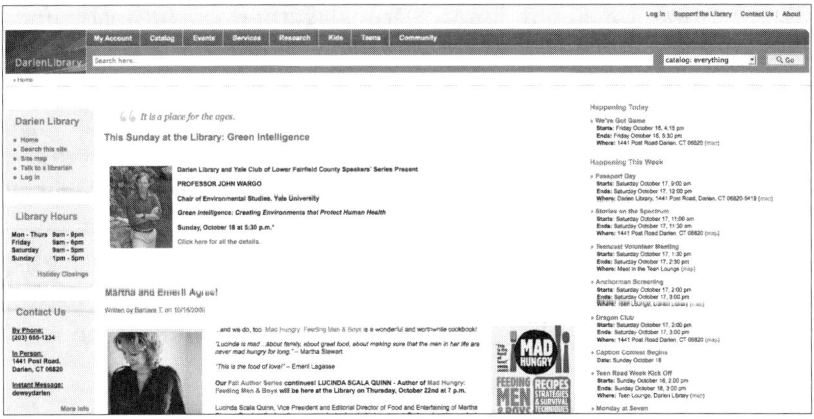

Figure 10.8 Darien Library homepage

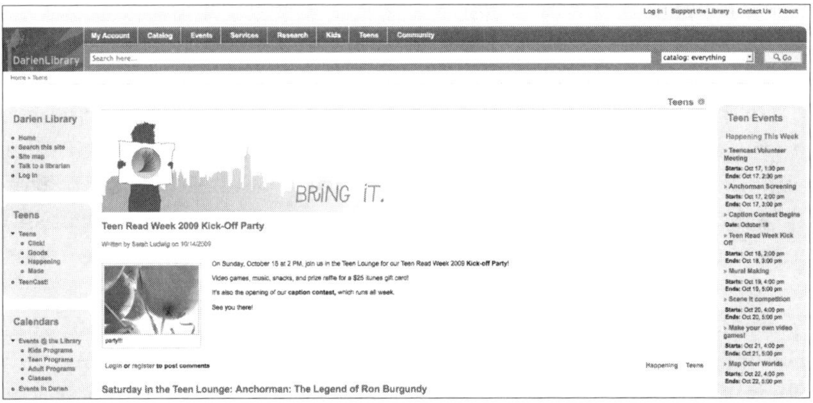

Figure 10.9 Darien Library Teens page

points, departments, and committees with an external presence and then give these staff permissions to edit and update content. Organic Groups are especially appropriate for this purpose because many of these "groups" span multiple divisions in the traditional organizational structure of the University of Michigan Library. Using Organic Groups allows the correct people to have permissions to update content and allows the website to be structured around the users' mental models rather than the organizational management structure of the libraries (Figure 10.12).

One of the most admirable things about the University of Michigan Library site is the design, which doesn't have a typical

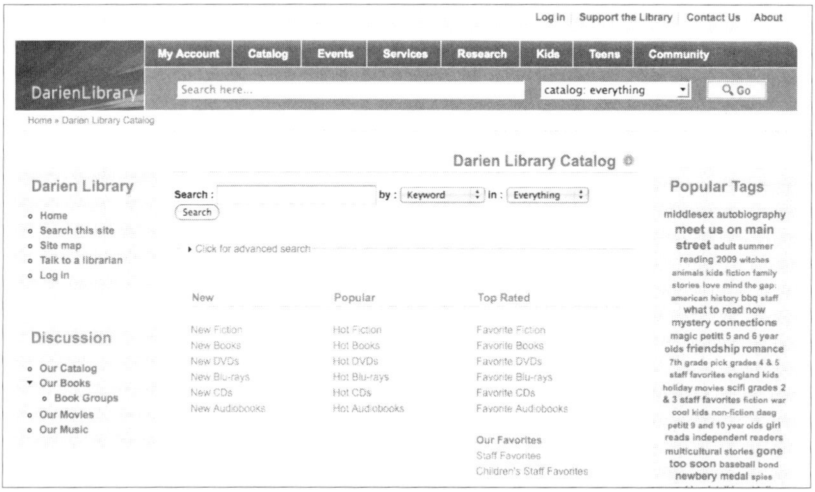

Figure 10.10 Darien Library SOPAC

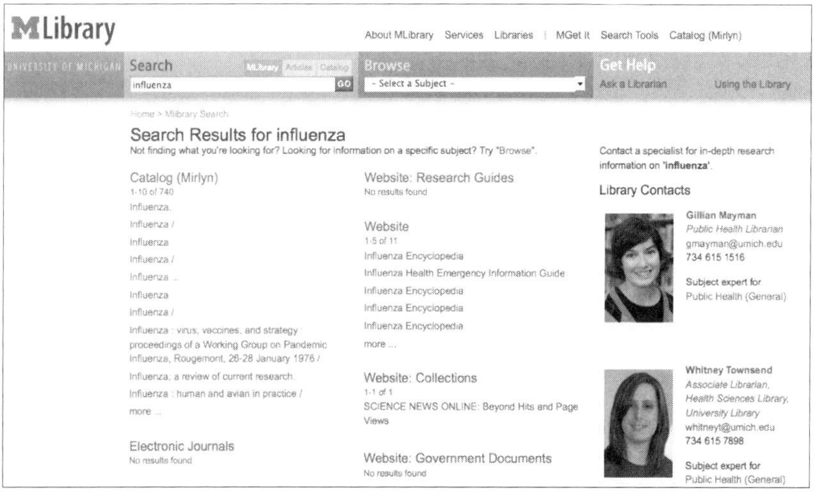

Figure 10.11 University of Michigan Library search results

"Drupal-like" look. By taking advantage of Drupal's custom content type option, University of Michigan Library has been able to create templates that are flexible and allow library staff to easily customize and update content. The pages for the individual libraries are particularly good (Figure 10.13), as are the pages that represent particular services (Figure 10.14), because they incorporate lots of different types of structured content.

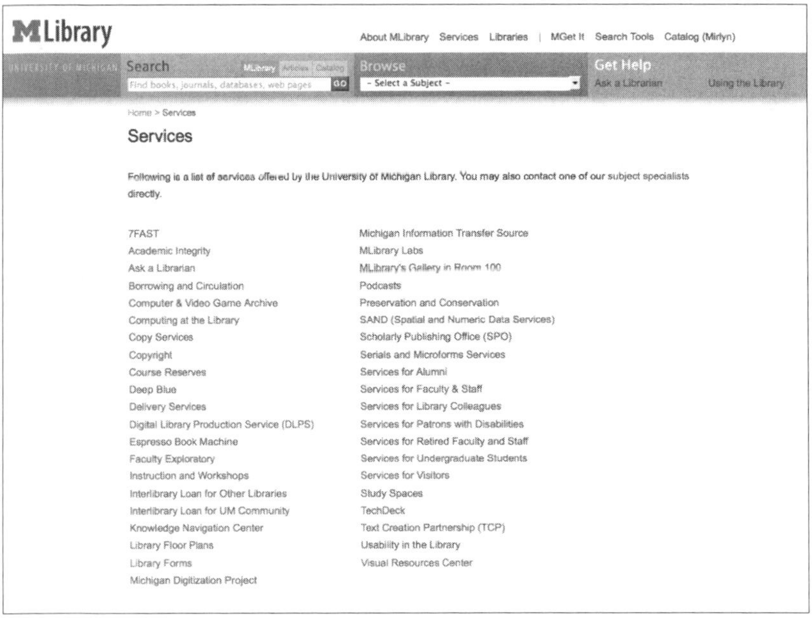

Figure 10.12 University of Michigan Library Services page

The University of Michigan Library website demonstrates both Drupal's power and its flexibility as a content management system. The staff there have been able to highly customize Drupal to meet their needs and create a unique look for their site.

The McMaster University Library website is another example of a Drupal library site that uses a number of interesting Drupal modules: The library's list of databases (title, subject) is created using CCK and Views, and its Subject Guide pages are also created via a combination of CCK and Views (Figure 10.15). Additionally, the Drupal Frequently Asked Questions module (drupal.org/project/faq) powers the FAQ page of its Help section (Figure 10.16).

The McMaster University Library website features attractive mouseover dropdown menus created using Nice Menus (Figure 10.17; drupal.org/project/nice_menus) and uses the Event module (drupal. org/project/event) to power the site's Event Calendar. The site also makes extensive use of the Webform module (drupal.org/project/webform) to create a variety of online forms, from the Contact Us form to the Request a Library Class form (Figure 10.18).

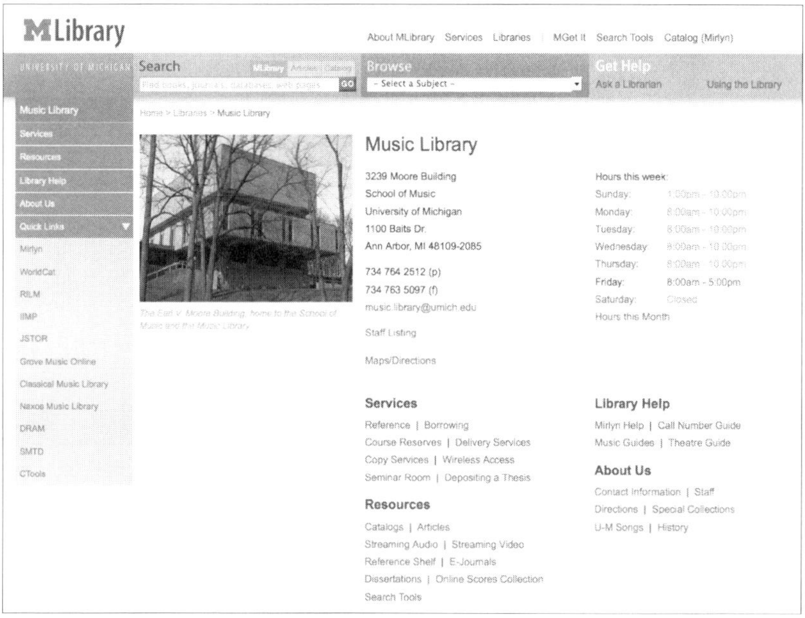

Figure 10.13 University of Michigan Music Library

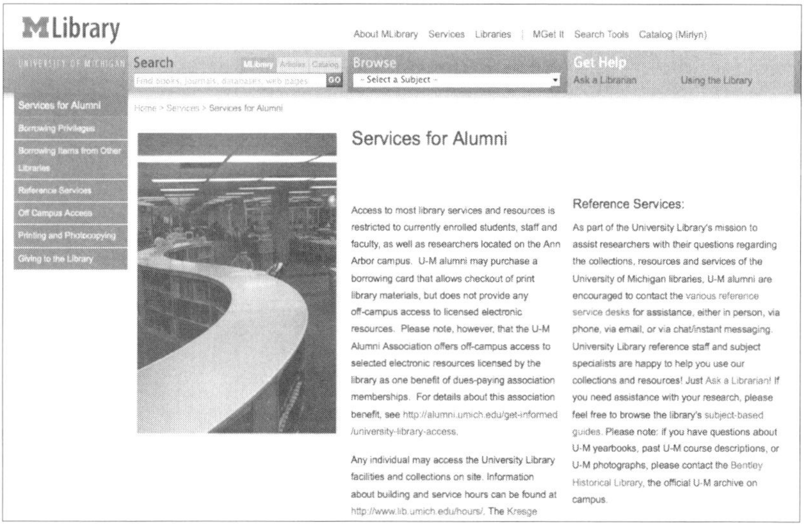

Figure 10.14 University of Michigan Library Services for Alumni

Figure 10.15 McMaster University Library's literature subject guides

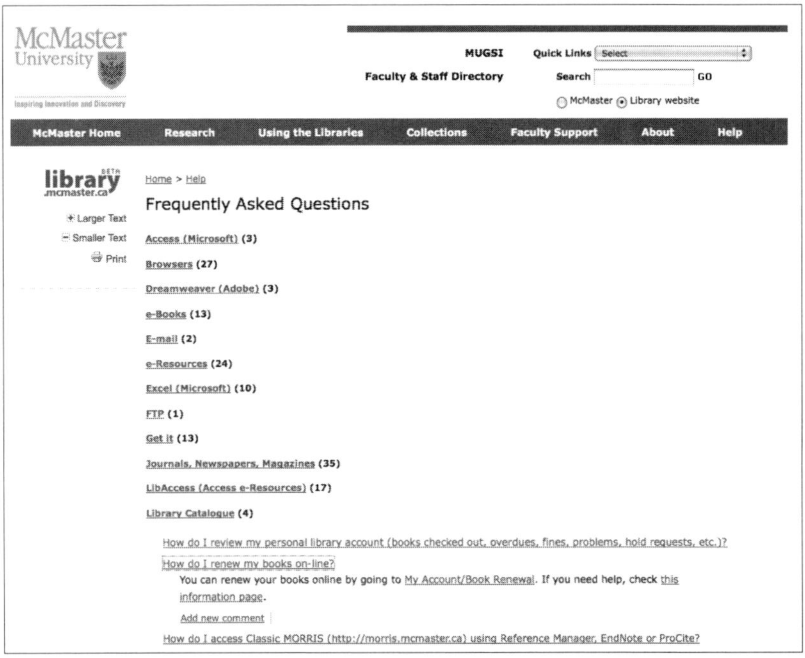

Figure 10.16 FAQs at McMaster University Library website

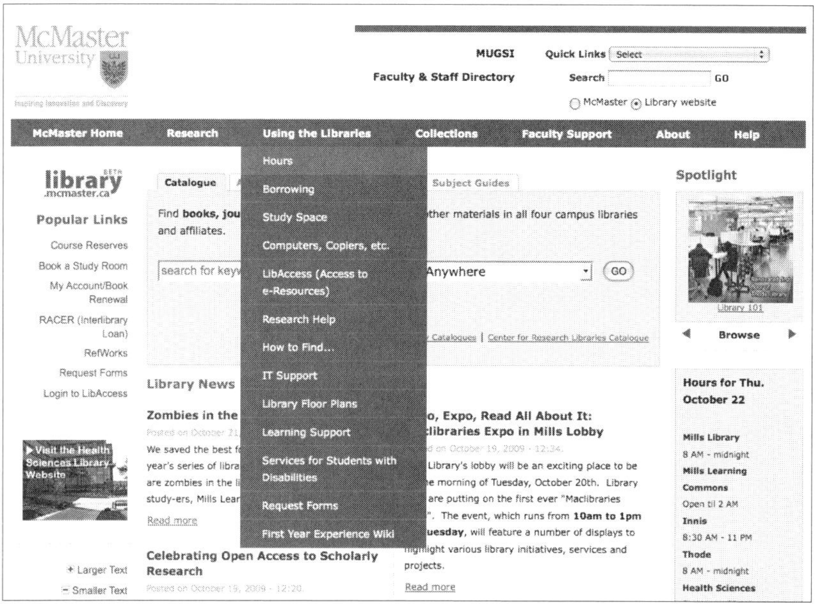

Figure 10.17 Example of Nice Menus

In addition to using Drupal for its website, the McMaster University Library decided also to use Drupal as the primary access point for its digital collections and as the tool for organizing and cataloging these digital collections. McMaster has accomplished this using several Drupal modules, some custom code, and lots of know-how. The collections are primarily built using CCK, which allows for the creation of new custom fields and content types. Using CCK, McMaster was able to use an extended Dublin Core metadata schema to capture the relevant information about the items in each collection. The Views module and Drupal themes enabled the library to create customized display screens. In addition, it has implemented a variety of tools to improve the user interface. These include some fantastic modules for images including: ImageAPI, ImageCache, ImageField, ImageAPI Reflect, Thickbox, and Lightbox2. These modules, which can all be found at the Drupal Modules directory (drupal.org/project/Modules), allow the McMaster University Library to highlight images in a shadowbox and add a timeline feature that enhances the user interface by providing a chronological look at objects (Figure 10.19). The Facet Search module enables the library to expose CCK metadata in facets, which allow users to navigate easily between related objects (Figure 10.20).

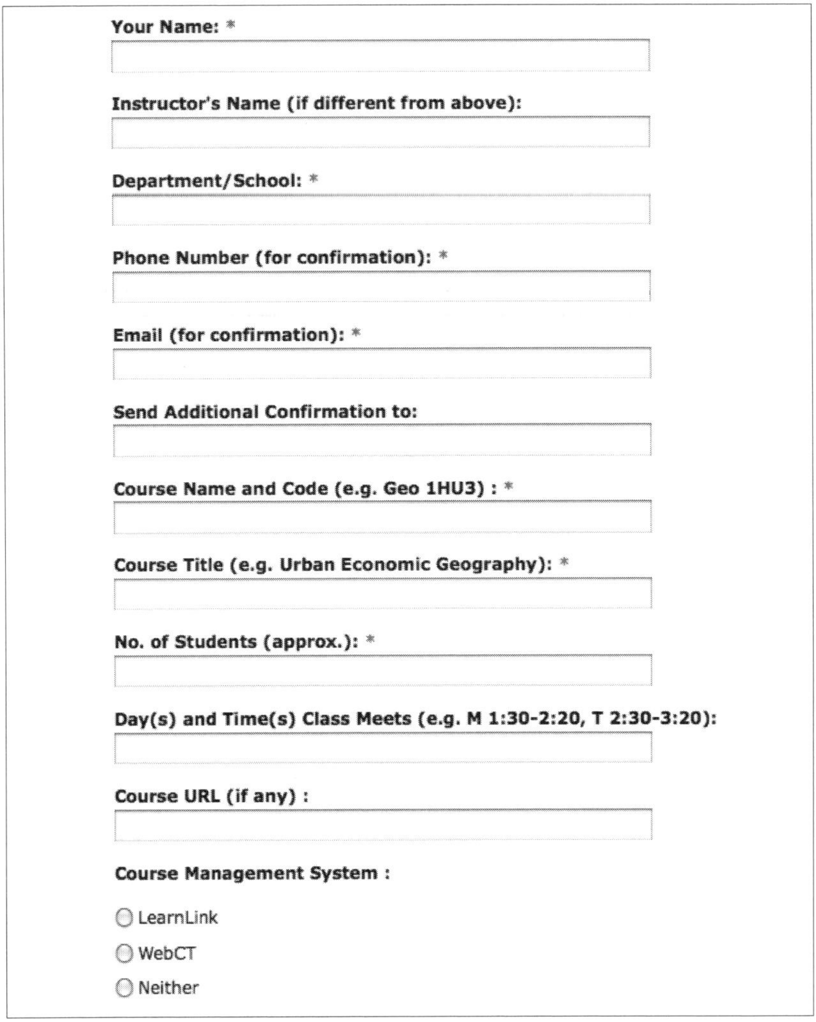
Your Name: *

Instructor's Name (if different from above):

Department/School: *

Phone Number (for confirmation): *

Email (for confirmation): *

Send Additional Confirmation to:

Course Name and Code (e.g. Geo 1HU3) : *

Course Title (e.g. Urban Economic Geography): *

No. of Students (approx.): *

Day(s) and Time(s) Class Meets (e.g. M 1:30-2:20, T 2:30-3:20):

Course URL (if any) :

Course Management System :

LearnLink

WebCT

Neither

Figure 10.18 Instruction request web form

In addition, the digital collections incorporate Web 2.0 functionality, such as tagging, reviews, and ratings. The result is a unique digital collections interface that offers users a rich experience, similar to digital photo sharing sites or other web-based media galleries. Another incredible feature of the McMaster site is the integration of encyclopedic content with its individual objects. This combination is especially effective in the Peace and War in the 20th Century collection, which is both easily searchable and browseable via an exhibit-like interface.

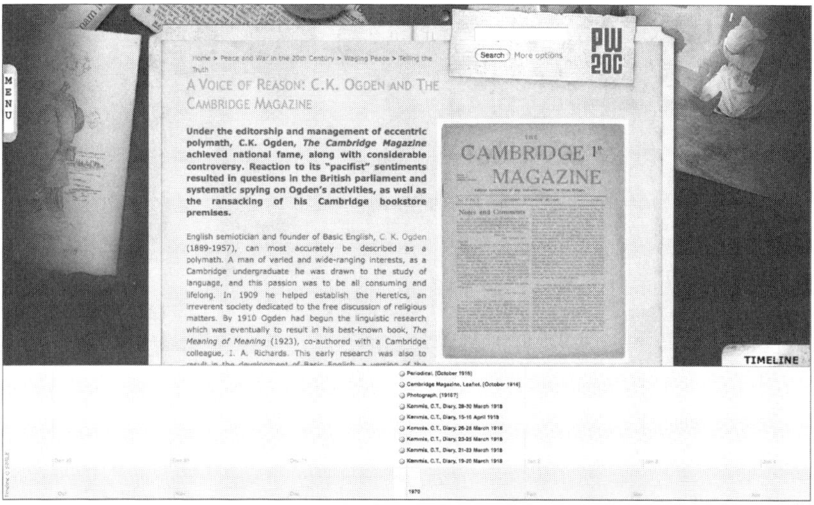

Figure 10.19 Timeline module

Figure 10.20 Faceted search module

Part IV

Reference and Instruction Tools

CHAPTER 11

Reference and Instruction Tools

Many academic and public libraries have expanded their reference and instruction services to include reference support via chat, email, and text messaging services, and they are also providing an increasing amount of online library instruction and tutorials. As these services expand, so does the need for software to support these services, such as software that tracks reference statistics and software to create online quizzes. Open source reference and instruction tools are plentiful; with a bit of creativity, many programs designed for other uses can also be repurposed into these types of tools. This chapter will highlight a few different open source projects that are useful for reference and instruction, including Assignment Calculator, Libstats, LimeSurvey, and refbase.

Assignment Calculator

The Assignment Calculator (www.lib.umn.edu/help/calculator) is a joint creation of the University of Minnesota Libraries, its Center for Writing, and its Center for Teaching and Learning. This tool was created in 2001 to help students complete research papers by providing a timeline of the steps involved in writing a paper. The program creators have divided the process of writing a research paper into twelve steps, and each step includes links to online guides and contact information for help. The goal of the Assignment Calculator is to make it easier for students to begin their research projects and to seek out help. The current version of Assignment Calculator was released in September 2006 and is available with or without the capability to send students email reminders as deadlines approach.

Installing Assignment Calculator

Assignment Calculator requires a web server with PHP installed. To run the version with email reminders, you will also need to create a MySQL database and enter the database information into the instructions.php file. Instructions for creating the database are on the Assignment Calculator blog (blog.lib.umn.edu/jveldof/calculator/003883.html).

Once installed, Assignment Calculator allows students to select the start and due date of their projects (Figure 11.1). The results page lists a breakdown of the basic steps involved in writing a research paper, along with suggested due dates (Figure 11.2).

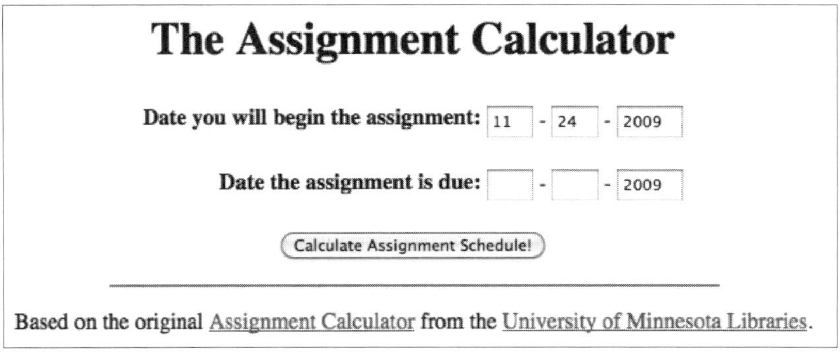

Figure 11.1 Assignment Calculator main panel

Customizing Assignment Calculator

Out of the box, Assignment Calculator comes prepopulated with links to tutorials and guides on writing a research paper. To change these links to point to guides and resources of your own, you will need to edit the instructions.php file (Figure. 11.3).

To change the look and feel of Assignment Calculator, you will need to edit the index.php, date.php, ac_header.php, and ac_footer.php files. For example, the University Libraries at the University of Arkansas have customized Assignment Calculator by adding its library template, a description of the tool, and a link to get help from a librarian (Figure 11.4).

At the time of this writing, there is a new version of Assignment Calculator in development. The Assignment Calculator beta includes additional assignment types, such as speeches and video assignments, and also adds the ability to create and save customized guides for individual assignments. In the examples shown in Figure 11.5 and

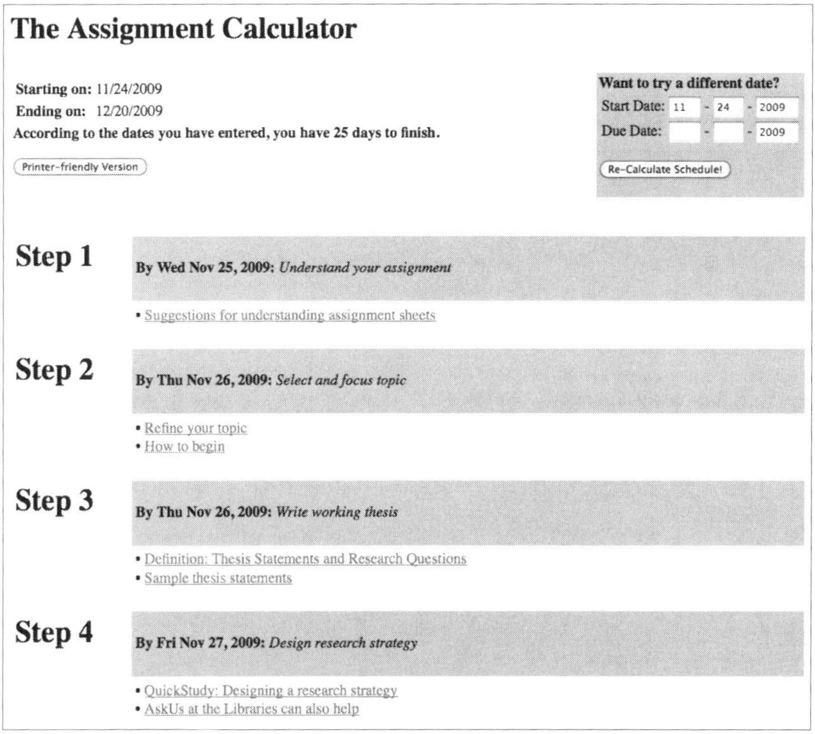

Figure 11.2 Assignment Calculator results page

```
//main array.  Each element has three parts.  A decimal that
//represents fraction of total time, a description, and an
//array of tips

$instructions = Array(

//Step 1
Array(.03,
  "Understand your assignment",
   Array("<a href='http://www.unc.edu/depts/wcweb/handouts/readassign.html'>Suggestions for understanding assignment sheets</a>")
),

//Step 2
Array(.04,
  "Select and focus topic",
  Array("<a href='http://owl.english.purdue.edu/workshops/hypertext/researchW/topic.html'>Refine your topic</a>",
  "<a href='http://www.owc.umn.edu/Handouts/HowtoBegin.cfm'>How to begin</a>")
),

//Step 3
Array(.01,
  "Write working thesis",
  Array("<a href='http://owl.english.purdue.edu/workshops/hypertext/ResearchW/thesis.html'>Definition: Thesis Statements and Research Questions</a>",
  "<a href='http://www.gmu.edu/departments/writingcenter/handouts/g_b_thes.html'>Sample thesis statements</a>")
),

//Step 4
Array(.03,
  "Design research strategy",
    Array("<a href='http://tutorial.lib.umn.edu/infomachine.asp?moduleID=13'>QuickStudy: Designing a research strategy</a>",
    "<a href='http://infopoint.lib.umn.edu/'>AskUs at the Libraries can also help</a>")
),

//Step 5
Array(.10,
  "Find, review, and evaluate books",
  Array("Keep careful notes, with source clearly indicated",
  "<a href='http://www.lib.umn.edu/books/'>Search the library's catalog</a>",
  "<a href='http://tutorial.lib.umn.edu/infomachine.asp?moduleID=5'>QuickStudy: Finding Books</a>")
),

//Step 6
Array(.25,
  "Find, review, and evaluate journal/magazine/newspaper articles",
  Array("Keep careful notes, with source clearly indicated",
  "<a href='http://tutorial.lib.umn.edu/infomachine.asp?moduleID=6'>QuickStudy: Finding Articles</a>",
  "<a href='http://research.lib.umn.edu/'>Research QuickStart</a>")
),
```

Figure 11.3 Assignment Calculator configuration

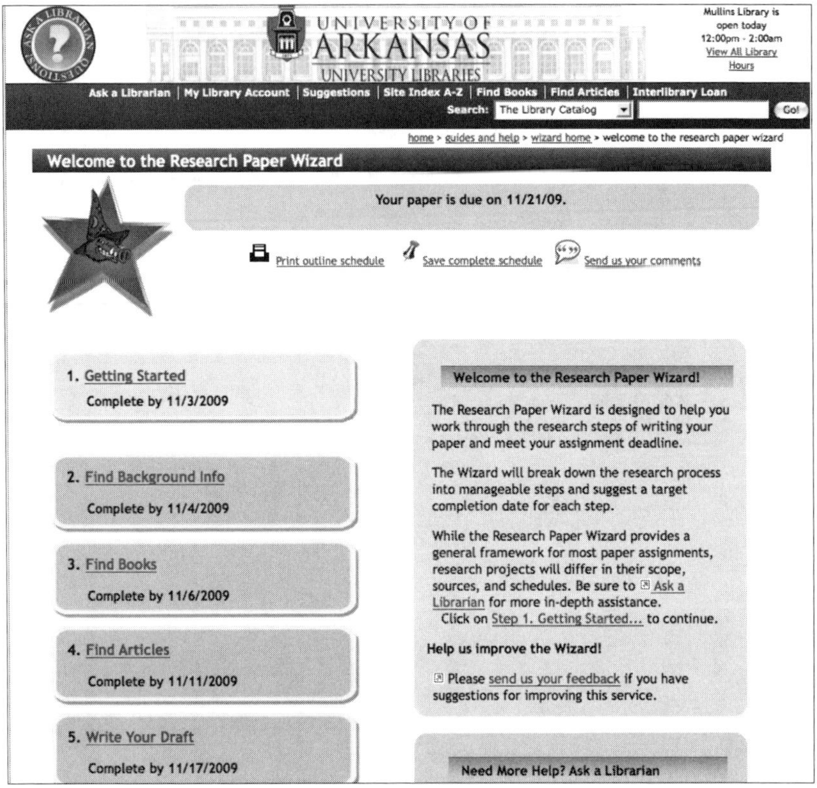
ASK A LIBRARIAN QUESTIONS
UNIVERSITY OF
ARKANSAS
UNIVERSITY LIBRARIES
Mullins Library is open today 12:00pm - 2:00am
View All Library Hours
Ask a Librarian | My Library Account | Suggestions | Site Index A-Z | Find Books | Find Articles | Interlibrary Loan
Search: The Library Catalog
Go!
home > guides and help > wizard home > welcome to the research paper wizard
Welcome to the Research Paper Wizard
Your paper is due on 11/21/09.
Print outline schedule
Save complete schedule
Send us your comments
1. Getting Started
Complete by 11/3/2009
2. Find Background Info
Complete by 11/4/2009
3. Find Books
Complete by 11/6/2009
4. Find Articles
Complete by 11/11/2009
5. Write Your Draft
Complete by 11/17/2009
Welcome to the Research Paper Wizard!
The Research Paper Wizard is designed to help you work through the research steps of writing your paper and meet your assignment deadline.
The Wizard will break down the research process into manageable steps and suggest a target completion date for each step.
While the Research Paper Wizard provides a general framework for most paper assignments, research projects will differ in their scope, sources, and schedules. Be sure to Ask a Librarian for more in-depth assistance.
Click on Step 1. Getting Started... to continue.
Help us improve the Wizard!
Please send us your feedback if you have suggestions for improving this service.
Need More Help? Ask a Librarian

Figure 11.4 Assignment Calculator custom CSS

Figure 11.6, the beta version was used to create a guide to writing lab reports and a guide to creating a poster.

Research Project Calculator

A modified version of Assignment Calculator called the Research Project Calculator (RPC; rpc.elm4you.org) has been available since April 2009. The RPC is a joint project of Minitex (the Library Information Network) and the Minnesota Library Information Network (MnLINK) for use in Minnesota secondary schools. The RPC includes the ability to select videos and presentations as well as research papers. Installation is simple; follow the instructions at https://wiki.minitex.umn.edu/ResearchProjectCalculator. Once installed, the RPC loads with a simple interface (Figure 11.7).

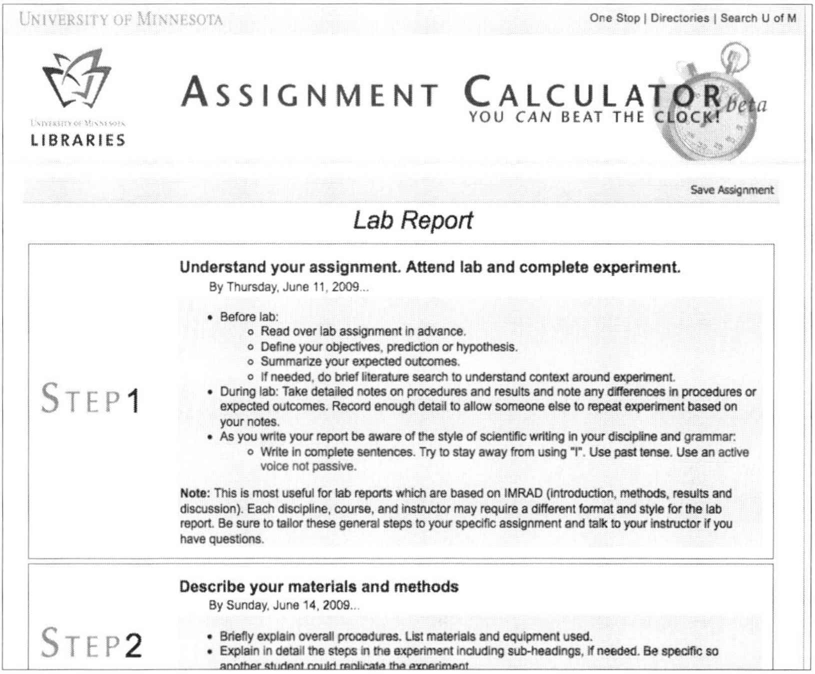
UNIVERSITY OF MINNESOTA
One Stop | Directories | Search U of M
UNIVERSITY OF MINNESOTA LIBRARIES
ASSIGNMENT CALCULATOR beta
YOU CAN BEAT THE CLOCK!
Save Assignment
Lab Report
STEP 1
Understand your assignment. Attend lab and complete experiment.
By Thursday, June 11, 2009...
Before lab:
Read over lab assignment in advance.
Define your objectives, prediction or hypothesis.
Summarize your expected outcomes.
If needed, do brief literature search to understand context around experiment.
During lab: Take detailed notes on procedures and results and note any differences in procedures or expected outcomes. Record enough detail to allow someone else to repeat experiment based on your notes.
As you write your report be aware of the style of scientific writing in your discipline and grammar:
Write in complete sentences. Try to stay away from using "I". Use past tense. Use an active voice not passive.
Note: This is most useful for lab reports which are based on IMRAD (introduction, methods, results and discussion). Each discipline, course, and instructor may require a different format and style for the lab report. Be sure to tailor these general steps to your specific assignment and talk to your instructor if you have questions.
STEP 2
Describe your materials and methods
By Sunday, June 14, 2009...
Briefly explain overall procedures. List materials and equipment used.
Explain in detail the steps in the experiment including sub-headings, if needed. Be specific so

Figure 11.5 Assignment Calculator beta lab report guide

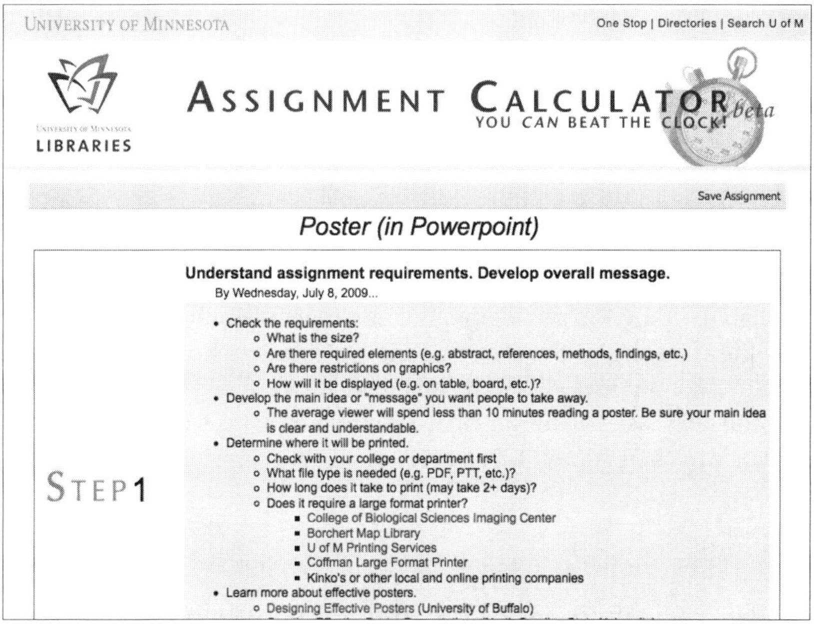
UNIVERSITY OF MINNESOTA
One Stop | Directories | Search U of M
UNIVERSITY OF MINNESOTA LIBRARIES
ASSIGNMENT CALCULATOR beta
YOU CAN BEAT THE CLOCK!
Save Assignment
Poster (in Powerpoint)
STEP 1
Understand assignment requirements. Develop overall message.
By Wednesday, July 8, 2009...
Check the requirements:
What is the size?
Are there required elements (e.g. abstract, references, methods, findings, etc.)
Are there restrictions on graphics?
How will it be displayed (e.g. on table, board, etc.)?
Develop the main idea or "message" you want people to take away.
The average viewer will spend less than 10 minutes reading a poster. Be sure your main idea is clear and understandable.
Determine where it will be printed.
Check with your college or department first
What file type is needed (e.g. PDF, PTT, etc.)?
How long does it take to print (may take 2+ days)?
Does it require a large format printer?
College of Biological Sciences Imaging Center
Borchert Map Library
U of M Printing Services
Coffman Large Format Printer
Kinko's or other local and online printing companies
Learn more about effective posters.
Designing Effective Posters (University of Buffalo)

Figure 11.6 Assignment Calculator beta poster guide

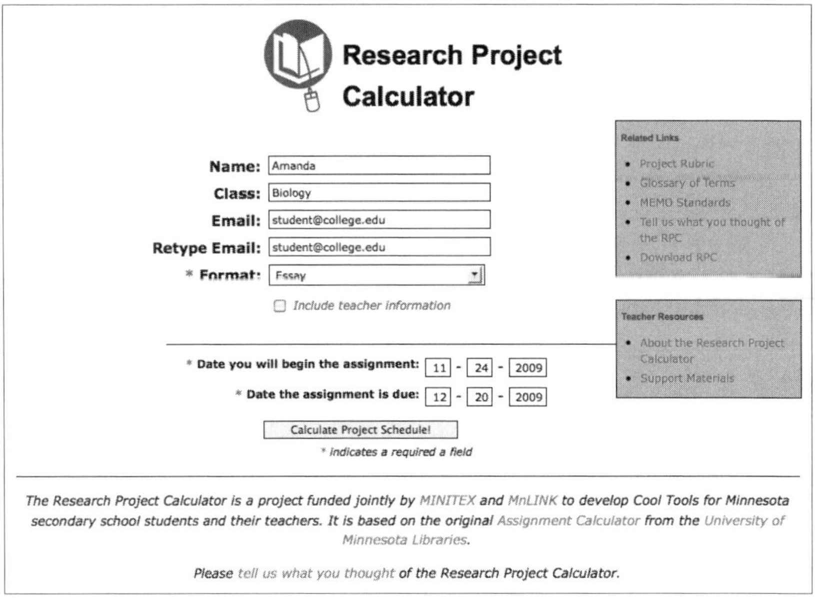

Figure 11.7 Research Project Calculator main panel

The RPC expands upon Assignment Calculator by adding teacher resources and a teacher view of the project outline (Figure 11.8). The teacher view not only allows the teacher to see what help is being provided to the student but also provides guidelines and tutorials for teachers on creating the assignment, working with students during the project, and working with a librarian. The RPC includes copies of the tutorials and guides, which makes keeping usage statistics possible for these resources.

Both the Assignment Calculator and the Research Project Calculator are useful tools. A quick demonstration of one of these tools in a library instruction session will alert students that help is available online for writing papers. A survey of some of the blogs of the libraries using the Assignment Calculator showed that these libraries are reporting not only an increase in reference questions but also an increase in the number of students who seek help well in advance of their project's due date.

Libstats

Libstats (code.google.com/p/libstats) was created by Nate Vack and Eric Larson at Wendt Library at the University of Wisconsin–Madison.

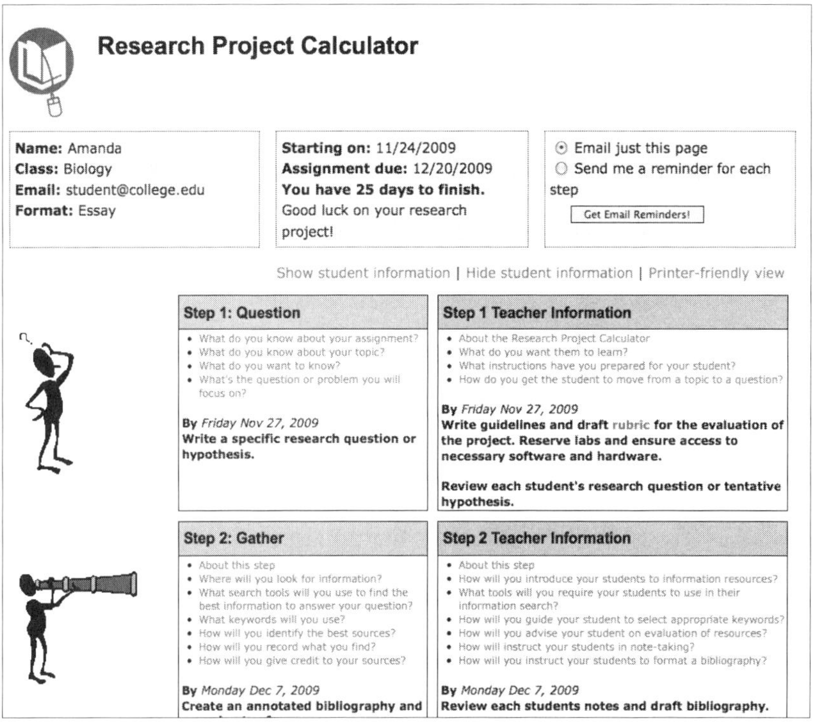
Research Project Calculator
Name: Amanda
Class: Biology
Email: student@college.edu
Format: Essay
Starting on: 11/24/2009
Assignment due: 12/20/2009
You have 25 days to finish.
Good luck on your research project!
Email just this page
Send me a reminder for each step
Get Email Reminders!
Show student information | Hide student information | Printer-friendly view
Step 1: Question
What do you know about your assignment?
What do you know about your topic?
What do you want to know?
What's the question or problem you will focus on?
By Friday Nov 27, 2009
Write a specific research question or hypothesis.
Step 1 Teacher Information
About the Research Project Calculator
What do you want them to learn?
What instructions have you prepared for your student?
How do you get the student to move from a topic to a question?
By Friday Nov 27, 2009
Write guidelines and draft rubric for the evaluation of the project. Reserve labs and ensure access to necessary software and hardware.
Review each student's research question or tentative hypothesis.
Step 2: Gather
About this step
Where will you look for information?
What search tools will you use to find the best information to answer your question?
What keywords will you use?
How will you identify the best sources?
How will you record what you find?
How will you give credit to your sources?
By Monday Dec 7, 2009
Create an annotated bibliography and
Step 2 Teacher Information
About this step
How will you introduce your students to information resources?
What tools will you require your students to use in their information search?
How will you guide your student to select appropriate keywords?
How will you advise your student on evaluation of resources?
How will instruct your students in note-taking?
How will you instruct your students to format a bibliography?
By Monday Dec 7, 2009
Review each students notes and draft bibliography.

Figure 11.8 Research Project Calculator results page

The first public version was 0.9, released in May 2005. The Libstats slogan, "more fun than hash marks," is a reference to the fact that Libstats was designed to replace the practice of keeping reference statistics by making hash marks on a sheet of paper. Libstats is much more than a simple stat counter for reference questions, though; it also replaces the spiral-bound notebook of frequently asked questions found at many reference desks. Lastly, as a web-based application, it gives libraries the ability to track questions across multiple branches and service points.

Installing and Using Libstats

Libstats can be downloaded from code.google.com/p/libstats. The current version is 1.0.6, released in May 2006. Libstats requires PHP 5.x, MySQL 5.x, Pear::DB, and Apache with mod_rewrite. Libstats can be run on a web server or, if you will only be using it at one service point, on a desktop with WAMP installed. Once you have created the

Libstats database and have updated init.php with the database user information, Libstats is ready to run. When you log into Libstats, the top section of the page allows question entry, while the bottom part of the page contains a listing of all the entered questions (Figure 11.9).

Before you begin to use Libstats, you will want to customize the Libstats settings to fit your library. To do this, click on the Admin link on the upper top right of the Libstats main panel. From here, you can customize your library locations (service points), your patron types, the question formats, the question types, and the time spent on breakdowns (Figure 11.10). If you are using Libstats for a number of libraries, these settings can be customized for each library that you have entered (Figure 11.11).

While any library-specific setting marked as Visible will show on the Add Question page, adding multiple library branches or locations will allow you to create branch-specific reports. The last part of the installation and setup of Libstats is to add users (Figure 11.12).

Librarians and staff will add questions on the Add a Question page. A minimal entry consists of selecting the question parameters, such as place and format, and hitting enter. This will add a blank question to the Libstats records (Figure 11.13).

However, the options for entering questions provided by Libstats can also turn Libstats into a knowledge database. If library staff members enter their initials, the questions they receive, and the answers

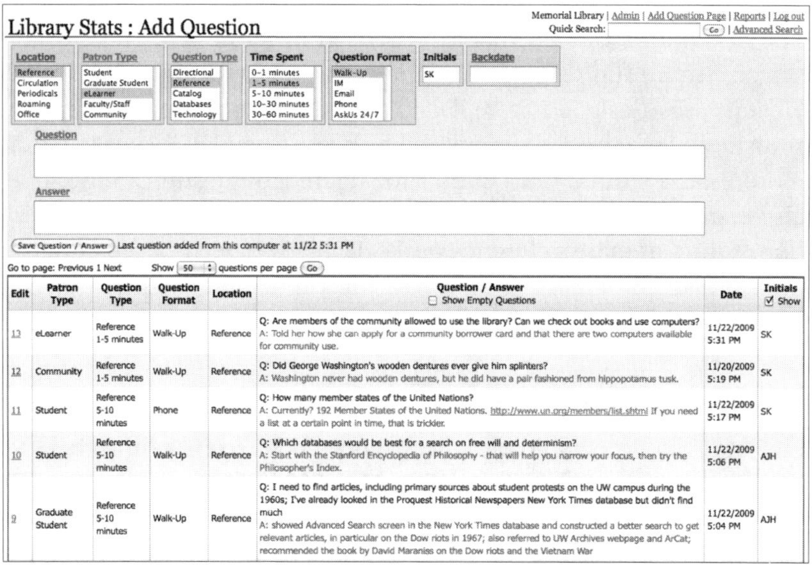

Library Stats : Add Question
Memorial Library | Admin | Add Question Page | Reports | Log out
Quick Search: Go | Advanced Search
Location
Reference
Circulation
Periodicals
Roaming
Office
Patron Type
Student
Graduate Student
eLearner
Faculty/Staff
Community
Question Type
Directional
Reference
Catalog
Databases
Technology
Time Spent
0-1 minutes
1-5 minutes
5-10 minutes
10-30 minutes
30-60 minutes
Question Format
Walk-Up
IM
Email
Phone
AskUs 24/7
Initials
SK
Backdate
Question
Answer
Save Question / Answer
Last question added from this computer at 11/22 5:31 PM
Go to page: Previous 1 Next
Show 50 questions per page Go
Edit
Patron Type
Question Type
Question Format
Location
Question / Answer
Show Empty Questions
Date
Initials
Show
13
eLearner
Reference 1-5 minutes
Walk-Up
Reference
Q: Are members of the community allowed to use the library? Can we check out books and use computers?
A: Told her how she can apply for a community borrower card and that there are two computers available for community use.
11/22/2009 5:31 PM
SK
12
Community
Reference 1-5 minutes
Walk-Up
Reference
Q: Did George Washington's wooden dentures ever give him splinters?
A: Washington never had wooden dentures, but he did have a pair fashioned from hippopotamus tusk.
11/20/2009 5:19 PM
SK
11
Student
Reference 5-10 minutes
Phone
Reference
Q: How many member states of the United Nations?
A: Currently? 192 Member States of the United Nations. http://www.un.org/members/list.shtml If you need a list at a certain point in time, that is trickier.
11/22/2009 5:17 PM
SK
10
Student
Reference 5-10 minutes
Walk-Up
Reference
Q: Which databases would be best for a search on free will and determinism?
A: Start with the Stanford Encyclopedia of Philosophy - that will help you narrow your focus, then try the Philosopher's Index.
11/22/2009 5:06 PM
AJH
9
Graduate Student
Reference 5-10 minutes
Walk-Up
Reference
Q: I need to find articles, including primary sources about student protests on the UW campus during the 1960s; I've already looked in the Proquest Historical Newspapers New York Times database but didn't find much
A: showed Advanced Search screen in the New York Times database and constructed a better search to get relevant articles, in particular on the Dow riots in 1967; also referred to UW Archives webpage and ArCat; recommended the book by David Maraniss on the Dow riots and the Vietnam War
11/22/2009 5:04 PM
AJH

Figure 11.9 Libstats main panel

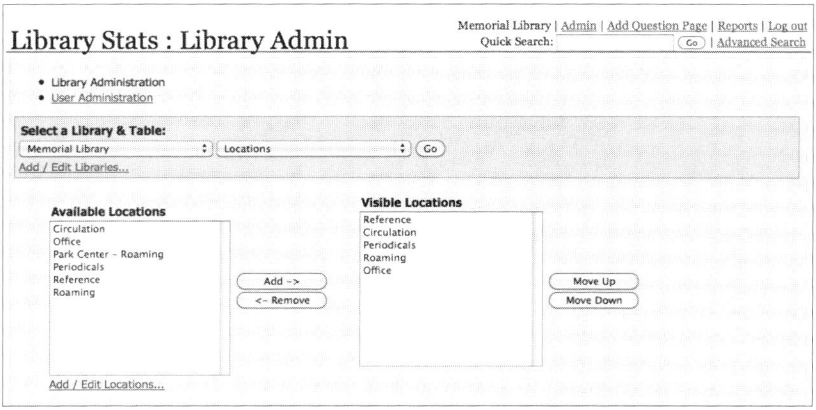

Figure 11.10 Libstats Admin panel

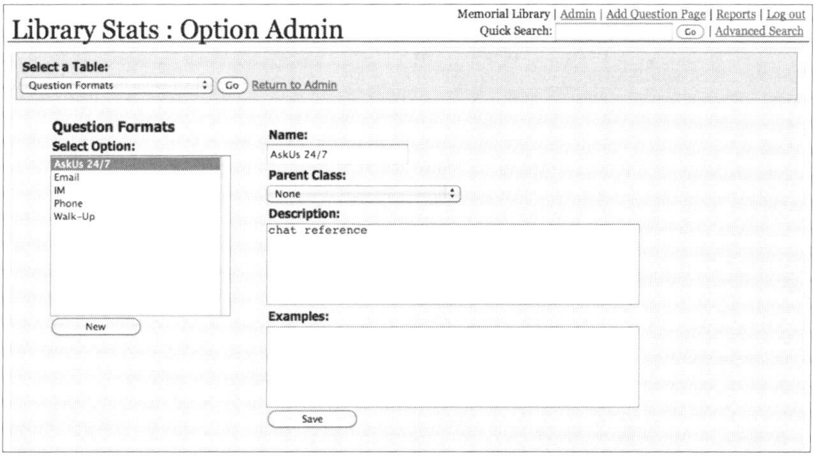

Figure 11.11 Libstats configuration

that they supply, Libstats becomes a searchable knowledgebase. Using the advanced search, you can search for questions and answers by location, date, and user. This can save your staff time subsequently when answering similar questions (Figure 11.14).

Reports

One of the great strengths of Libstats is the reports that it can produce. Libstats greatly simplifies keeping track of questions; statistics from multiple service points are tracked in a single database, eliminating

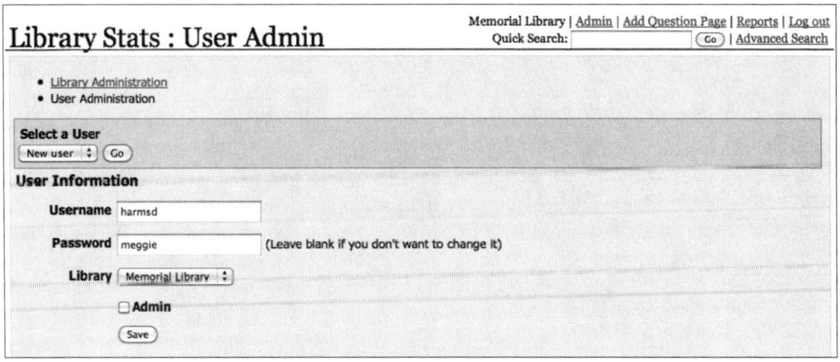

Figure 11.12 Adding a user to Libstats

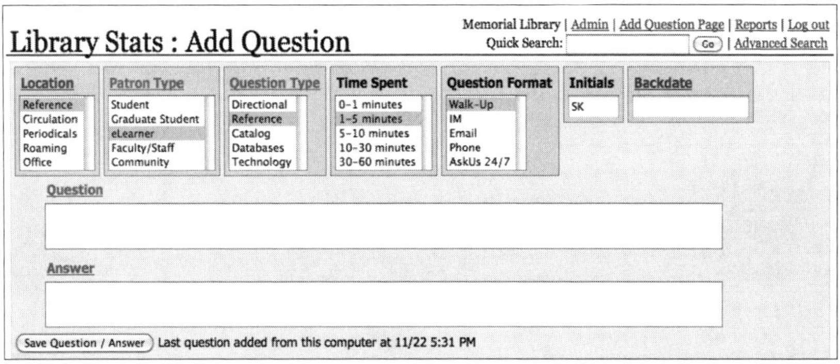

Figure 11.13 Adding a question to Libstats

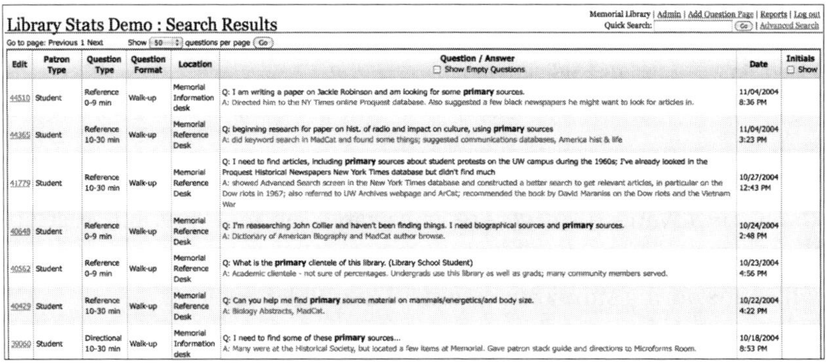

Figure 11.14 Libstats advanced search results

the need to manually input hash marks into a spreadsheet. Libstats also improves upon paper statistics by tracking the data as each question is received. Libstats provides reports on:

- Questions by initials: Track the number of questions answered by each librarian.
- Questions by patron type: Useful for assessing the needs of your user base.
- Questions by time of day: When do you get the most questions?
- Questions by weekday: What days of the week do you receive the most questions?
- Questions by date: The total number of questions received, sorted by day.
- Questions by question format: In what formats do your users prefer to ask questions?

These kinds of statistics are invaluable for assessing your reference services. The ability to export or "dump" all data into a csv spreadsheet format provides an opportunity for further data analysis (Figure 11.15).

Support

Support for Libstats can be found on the Libstats Google group (groups.google.com/group/libstats). This is an active community so questions are usually answered the same day. Mark Mace currently maintains the Libstats project; however, one of the project's creators, Nate Vack, still frequents the group. Technology support for Libstats is also available; if your library cannot host Libstats, the creators of

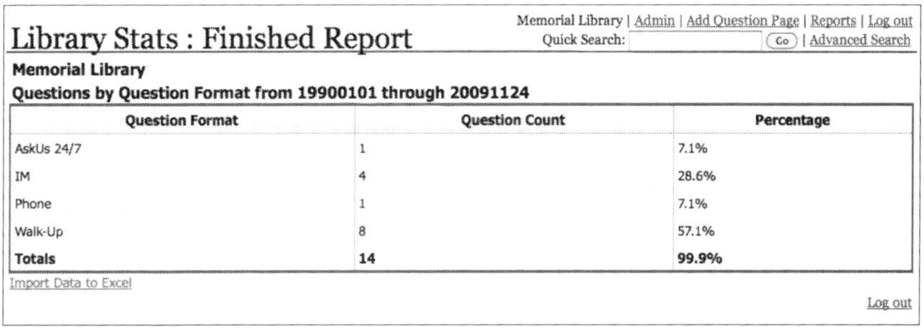

Library Stats : Finished Report

Memorial Library | Admin | Add Question Page | Reports | Log out
Quick Search: Go | Advanced Search

Memorial Library
Questions by Question Format from 19900101 through 20091124

Question Format	Question Count	Percentage
AskUs 24/7	1	7.1%
IM	4	28.6%
Phone	1	7.1%
Walk-Up	8	57.1%
Totals	**14**	**99.9%**

Import Data to Excel

Log out

Figure 11.15 Example of Libstats statistics

Libstats have started Gimlet (gimlet.us), a company that provides hosting and support for Libstats. Gimlet runs $10 a month for each site and adds the ability to tag questions and an improved reports display.

LimeSurvey

LimeSurvey (www.limesurvey.org), formerly PHPSurveyor, is an open source survey application. Initially released in 2003, LimeSurvey has amassed a large user base due to its capabilities and ease of use. The feature set of LimeSurvey makes it comparable to commercial survey software. It includes support for more than 50 languages; an unlimited number of surveys, users, and survey participants; 20 types of questions; a variety of export formats; and the ability to create templates.

Installing and Using LimeSurvey

LimeSurvey requires a server running PHP 5+ and either a MySQL, MS SQL, or a PostgreSQL database. Download LimeSurvey from sourceforge.net/projects/limesurvey/files and unpack it to your web directory. Create a database in your database application and update config.php with your database settings. To complete the install, point your browser to http://yourdomain/limesurvey/admin/install and run the setup. Once logged into LimeSurvey, you will become aware of one of the primary complaints about LimeSurvey: that the Administrator panel is icon-based and not very intuitive (Figure 11.16).

The Administrator panel contains such functions as creating and managing users, managing surveys, and exporting the LimeSurvey database. One function that can be confusing at first is the Label Sets function. Label sets establish consistent choices across all of your

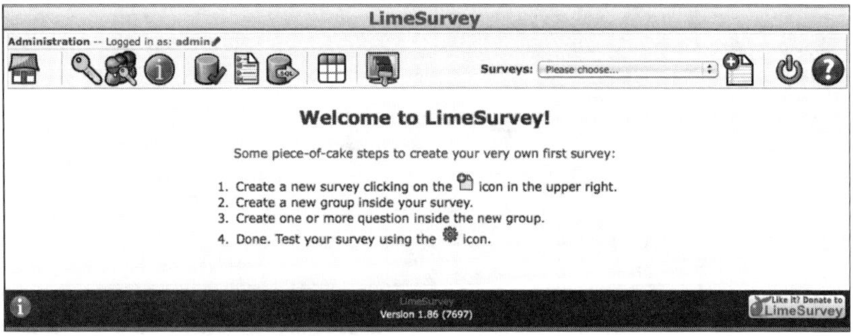
LimeSurvey
Administration -- Logged in as: admin
Surveys: Please choose...
Welcome to LimeSurvey!
Some piece-of-cake steps to create your very own first survey:
1. Create a new survey clicking on the icon in the upper right.
2. Create a new group inside your survey.
3. Create one or more question inside the new group.
4. Done. Test your survey using the icon.
Version 1.86 (7697)
Like it? Donate to LimeSurvey

Figure 11.16 LimeSurvey Admin panel

Figure 11.17 Creating a label set in LimeSurvey

surveys for questions that are answered via a dropdown list of choices or a Likert scale (Figure 11.17).

When you create a label set, you have the option of adding an assessment value. Adding an assessment value to a label set or to a question provides survey participants with ongoing feedback on their progress. For example, if you created a quiz to test a student's knowledge of library skills, as the student progressed through the quiz he would see his score and be able to review your instruction materials.

Survey creation in LimeSurvey is straightforward. LimeSurvey also lets you import surveys that you or other LimeSurvey users have previously created. Each survey has three basic elements: a survey name, at least one question group, and at least one question. Once a survey is created, the first step is to create a question group. Question groups are used to group together questions into topics, survey sections, or pages. Question groups can be quite useful, as the description field of the group can be used to give information about a set of questions. Also, when organizing your survey, you can move an entire group of questions (Figure 11.18).

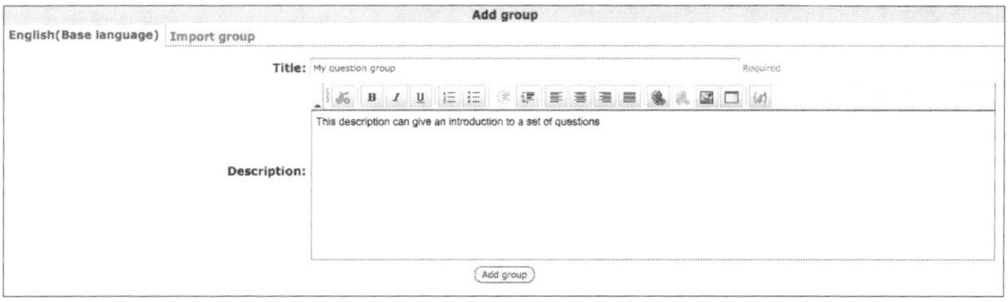

Figure 11.18 Creating a question group in LimeSurvey

Questions are added to the survey by clicking the Add New Question to Group icon. You will need to enter a code for each question. Think of the code as a keyword that will help you identify the question in a data export. Compared to other survey software, LimeSurvey can be somewhat confusing at first, especially when it comes to creating questions. In many survey programs, the question entry form changes when you select a question type. For example, if you are creating a multiple-choice question in SurveyMonkey, it prompts you to enter the answers as you are creating the question (Figure 11.19 and Figure 11.20).

In LimeSurvey, however, the question entry form remains the same regardless of the question format chosen. When you create a multiple-choice question, you are not prompted to enter the multiple choice answers (Figure 11.21) until after the question is saved. At that point LimeSurvey will warn you that you need to add answers to the question (Figure 11.22).

When you have finished adding questions to your survey, there are some survey settings that you may want to consider. Under Survey Settings > Publication and Access Control, you may wish to specify a date range when the survey will be active. We also recommend that you use cookies to prevent repeated participation and turn on CAPTCHA to prevent survey spam (Figure 11.23).

To deploy a survey, click on the small green Activate This Survey arrow. You can test the survey by clicking the Execute This Survey icon.

Survey Results

To access the results of a survey, click on the Browse Responses for This Survey icon. While you have the options to view individual responses and export the data, you will most likely want to click on the icon labeled Get Statistics from These Responses (Figure 11.24).

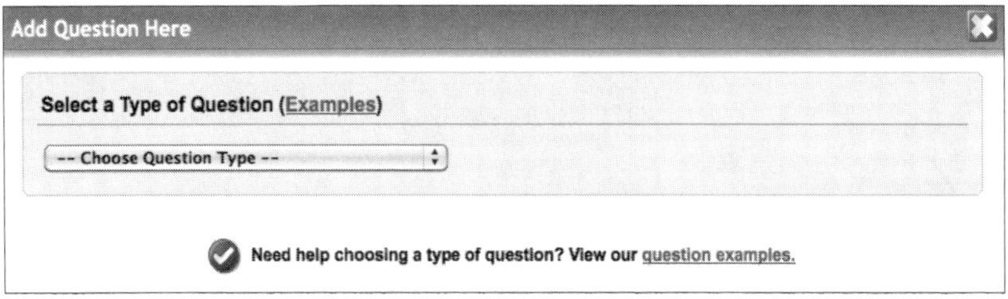

Figure 11.19 Creating a question in SurveyMonkey, step 1

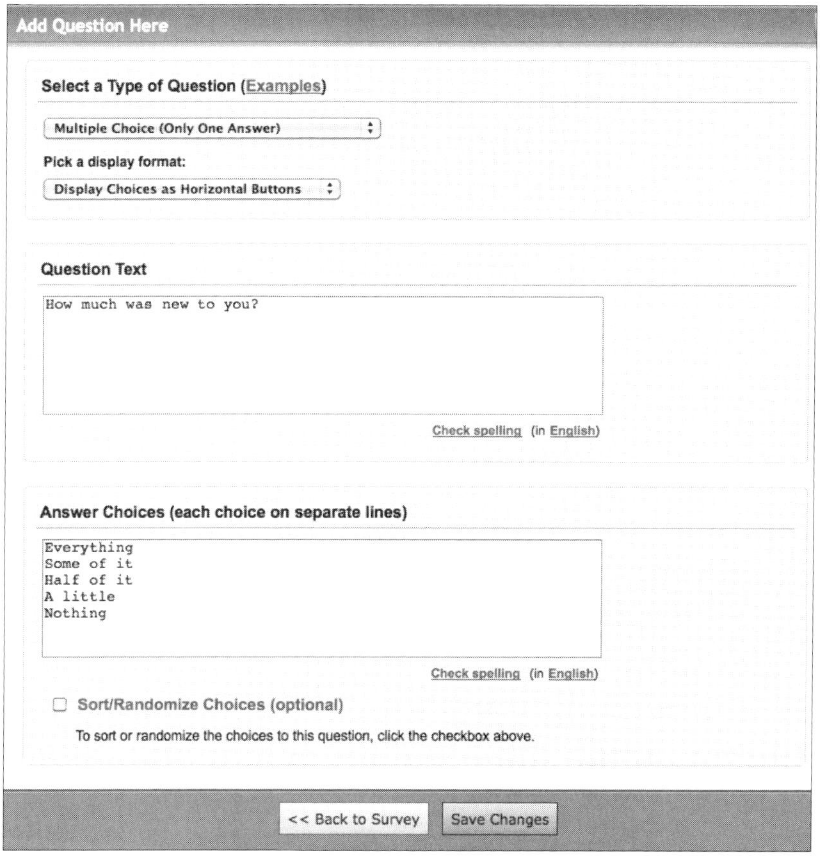

Figure 11.20 Creating a question in SurveyMonkey, step 2

On the survey filter settings page, you can select the questions for which you wish to view data, and choose to view the data for each question with or without a graph (Figure 11.25).

Survey data can be exported in Microsoft Excel format or as an SPSS file. You have the option to export the complete data set or, if you are browsing a filtered data set, to export data only from selected questions.

LimeSurvey 2.0

The next release of LimeSurvey, version 2.0, is currently available as a beta. Version 2.0 is a complete rewrite of the code and will ease template creation, increase the number of data export formats, and improve the user interface with AJAX (Figure 11.26).

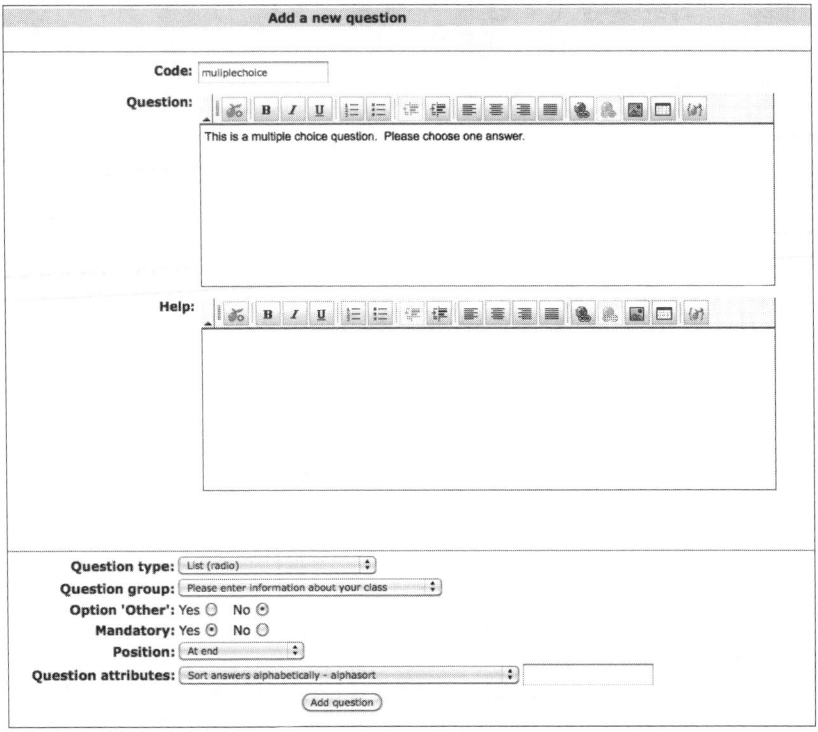

Figure 11.21 Creating a question in LimeSurvey, step 1

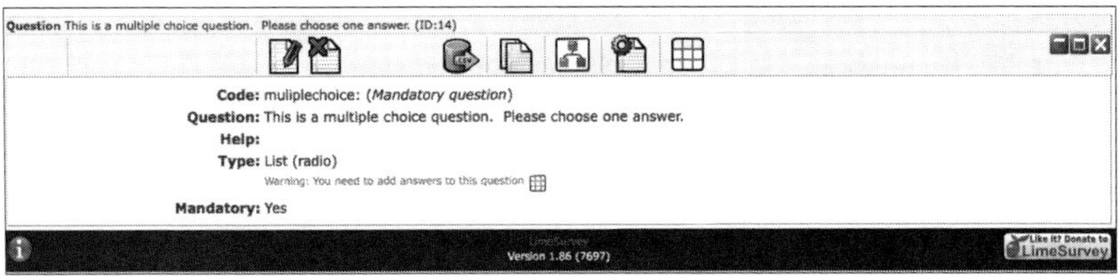

Figure 11.22 Creating a question in LimeSurvey, step 2

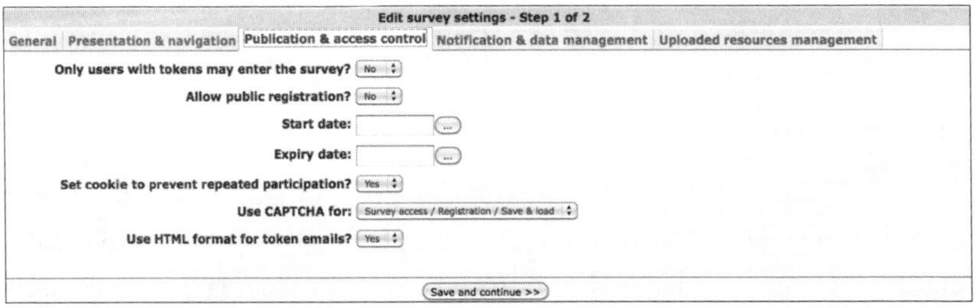

Figure 11.23 Survey settings in LimeSurvey

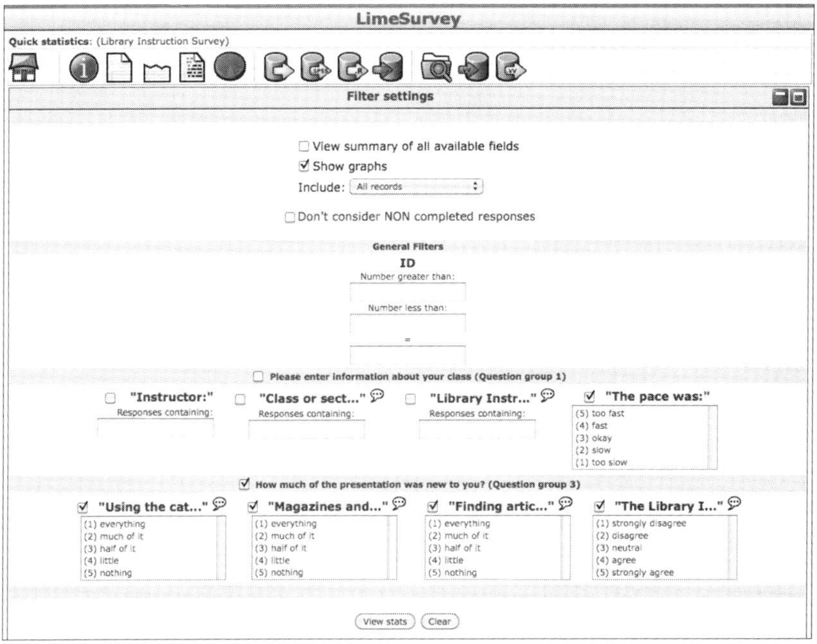

Figure 11.24 Filtering survey results in LimeSurvey

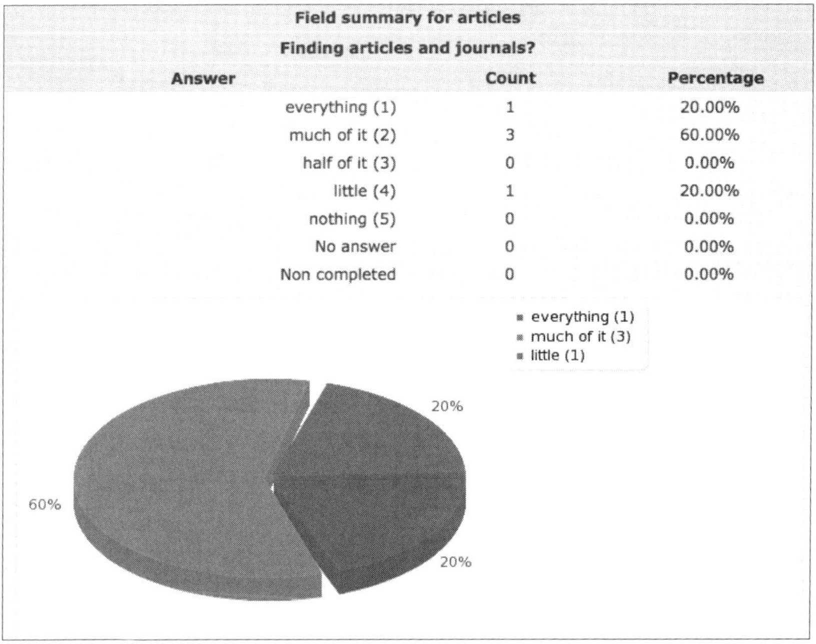

Figure 11.25 LimeSurvey survey results

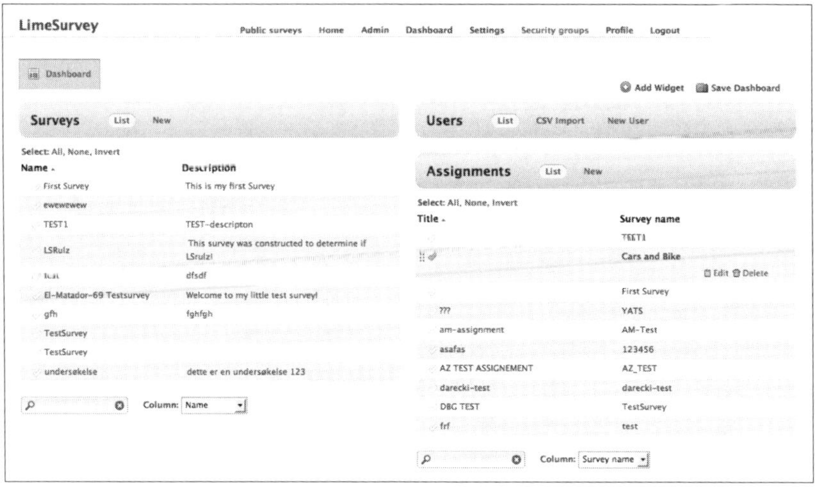

Figure 11.26 LimeSurvey 2.0 Admin panel

Even at the beta stage LimeSurvey 2.0 shows great promise. The dashboard features interactive widgets and a much improved user interface. Procedures for creating and editing surveys have been simplified, and the process of adding questions to a survey has been greatly improved. Questions can now be added via a drag-and-drop interface (Figure 11.27).

Support

LimeSurvey is a well-documented, active open source project. Documentation for LimeSurvey can be found at docs.limesurvey.org/tiki-index.php. Help for LimeSurvey can be found on the forums at www.limesurvey.org/en/support/forums. LimeSurvey encourages active community participation in LimeSurvey development on its Ideas page at ideas.limesurvey.org. Finally, regular updates about LimeSurvey are posted to limesurvey.org and to Twitter at twitter.com/limesurvey.

refbase

refbase (www.refbase.net) is an open-source, web-based citation database intended as a citation repository for a department or for an institution. For example, Washington State University is using refbase to provide access to its collection of the *Pullman Herald* newspaper

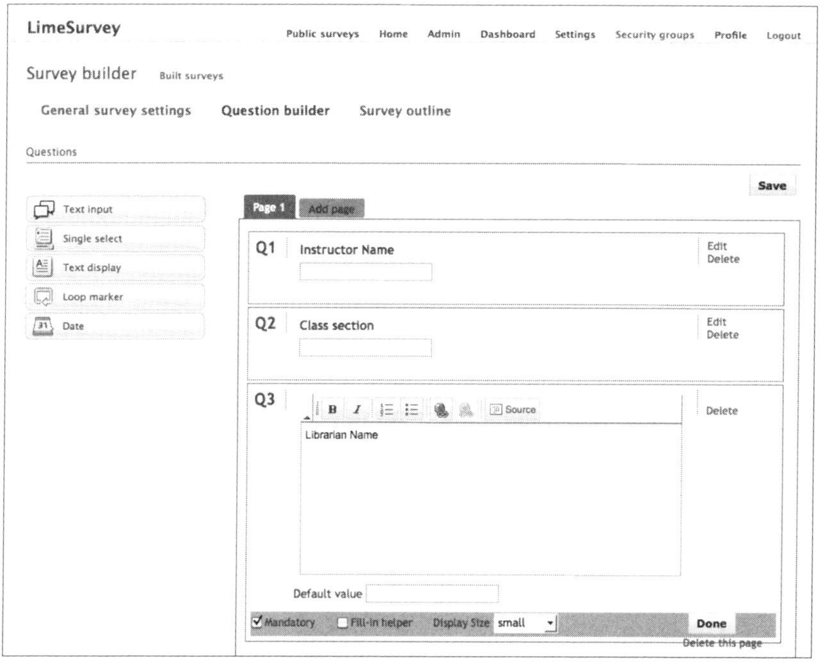

Figure 11.27 Adding a question in LimeSurvey 2.0

(Figure 11.28). refbase lets multiple users create or upload citations and search the database for citations.

Installing and Using refbase

As of this writing, the most recent version of refbase is version 0.9.5. refbase requires a server with PHP and MySQL. To install refbase, unpack the downloaded refbase file onto your web server, create an MySQL database and user, and then update the db.inc.php file with your database settings. You should also edit the ini.inc.php file; this file contains some of the basic refbase settings, such as language, user account access, user permissions, and the default citation style. Additionally, to increase the import and export capability of refbase, you should install Bibutils (www.scripps.edu/~cdputnam/software/bibutils).

Once refbase is installed and configured, your users can start importing citations. Citation records can be imported in two ways: by clicking the Add Record link and entering the citation by hand, or by clicking the Import link (Figure 11.29).

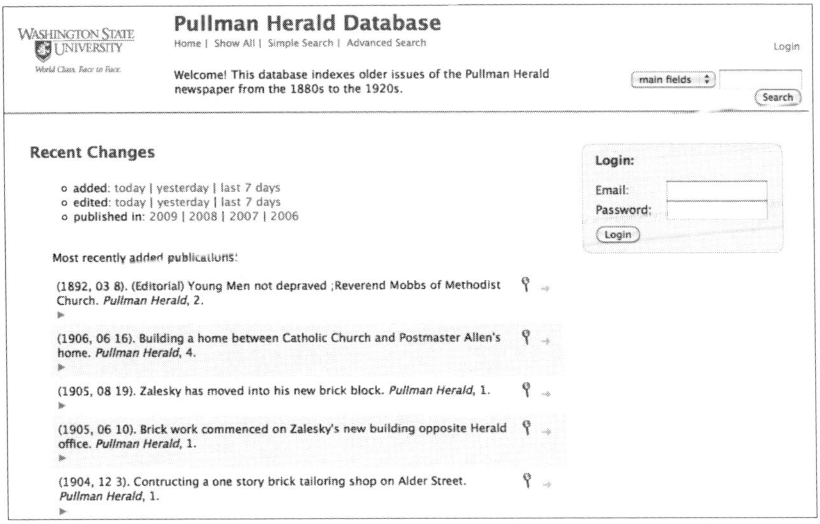

Figure 11.28 refbase at Washington State University

The Import Record screen allows you to paste in a record exported from a database, upload a saved file of citations, or use the accession ID from one of the supported databases. If refbase is configured to use Bibutils, it will import records from Endnote, RefWorks, Reference Manager, BibTeX, and MODS XML. Once a record is imported, the user has a chance to edit the new record, with options for adding "user keys" and "user notes" and adding the record to a "user group." User groups can be topics or assignments that you wish to add records to; adding records to a group can make exporting records easier (Figure 11.30).

refbase provides multiple options for exporting citations to a bibliography. You can select the citations you wish to export and choose to save the citations as HTML, a PDF file, an RTF file, or a LaTeX format. refbase also gives you the option to export records in the formats of other citation managers (Figure 11.31).

refbase has a fairly active user community. Support is available on the refbase forums at sourceforge.net/projects/refbase/support. Future development plans include improving integration with desktop citation managers such as Zotero, adding more citation formats, and providing an API.

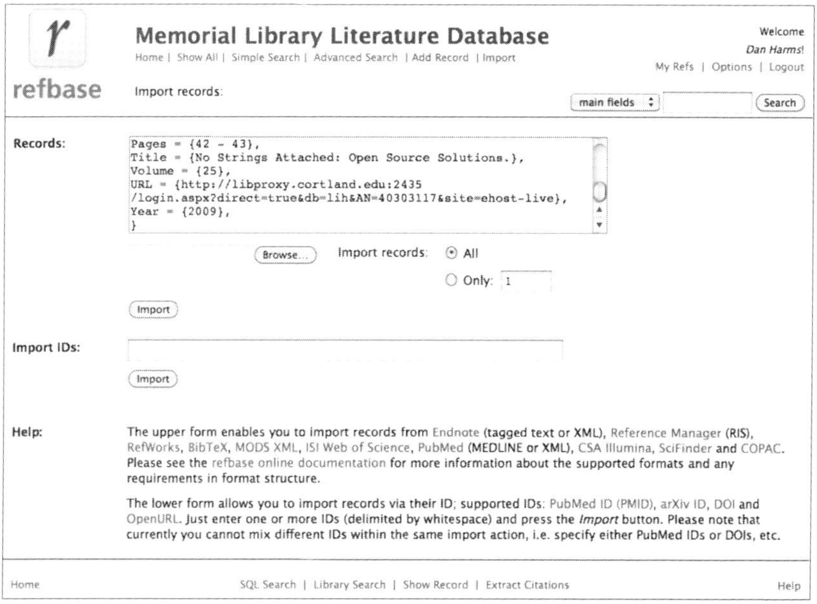

Figure 11.29 Importing a record into refbase

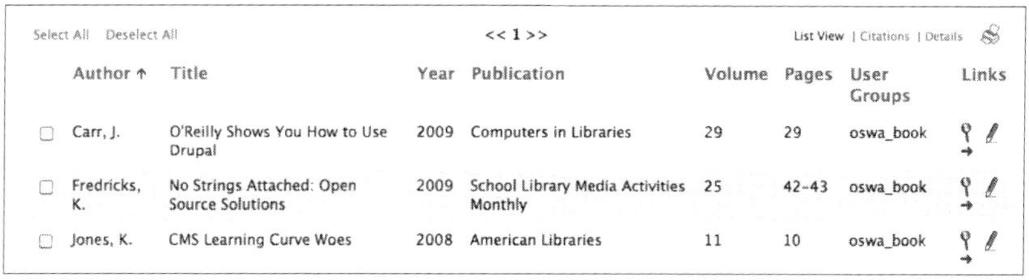

Figure 11.30 refbase user groups

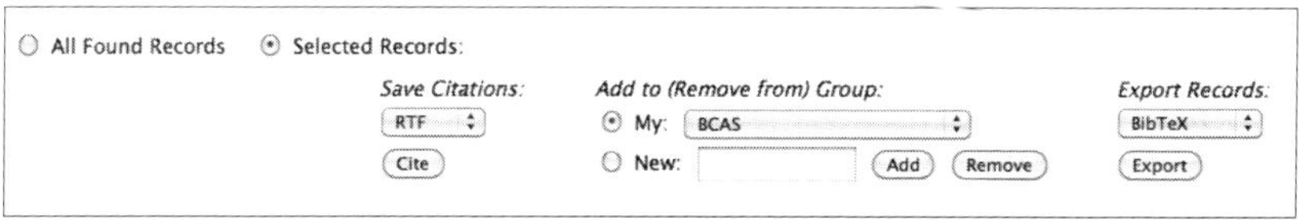

Figure 11.31 Exporting records out of refbase

## CHAPTER 12

Subject Guide Tools

Subject-oriented research guides have been a popular mainstay in libraries for decades. Once delegated to racks of curled-corner paper handouts, subject guides migrated to library websites in the 1990s. Initially, online subject guides were static HTML pages of helpful tips on using the library's online catalog and the journal indexes. While a few adventurous librarians also included links to external resources on the internet, these guides for the most part did not require frequent updating. The nature of subject guides changed with the appearance of online subscription databases and other electronic resources. The prospect of having to update multiple subject guides whenever the URL for an online resource changed led to the creation of database-driven subject guides. This chapter will cover one widely used open source subject guide tool, and the next chapter will cover a second.

Pirate Source

Pirate Source was developed at Eastern Carolina University in response to the need for database-driven subject guides. It launched in December 2001 with 1,300 records in 55 subjects. By April 2003, Pirate Source had 2,150 records in 71 subjects.[1] While Pirate Source is still in use at Eastern Carolina University, it is unfortunately no longer updated or available to download.

SubjectsPlus

Developed by Andrew Darby at Ithaca College in 2004, SubjectsPlus is a spin-off of Pirate Source. Darby had been looking at using Pirate Source as a subject guide tool but found that since it was written in PHP v.4 the code would need considerable updating. He also wished to add more polish to both the public and administration interfaces.

As word of his work to update Pirate Source spread, Darby began receiving requests to use his updated version. He asked Eastern Carolina University if he could redistribute his work on Pirate Source with a GNU GPL license. The university agreed, and in early 2007, SubjectsPlus was born.

As of this writing, there are two versions of SubjectsPlus available: version 0.8 and version 0.9. Both versions can be used to create subject and course guides, as well as to create an A–Z listing of resources such as databases and staff directories. Version 0.8 was released in January 2009, and there are no future updates planned for this version. Version 0.9 was released in September 2009. As of this writing, SubjectsPlus is used by 25 library websites.

SubjectsPlus derives its name from the fact that it does more than create subject and course guides: It can drive your website's list of databases by title as well as your staff directories. SubjectsPlus also has the ability to create database-driven suggestions and frequently asked questions, or FAQs. For example, Holland College has integrated SubjectsPlus into its site, as seen by the screenshot of their FAQ page (Figure 12.1).

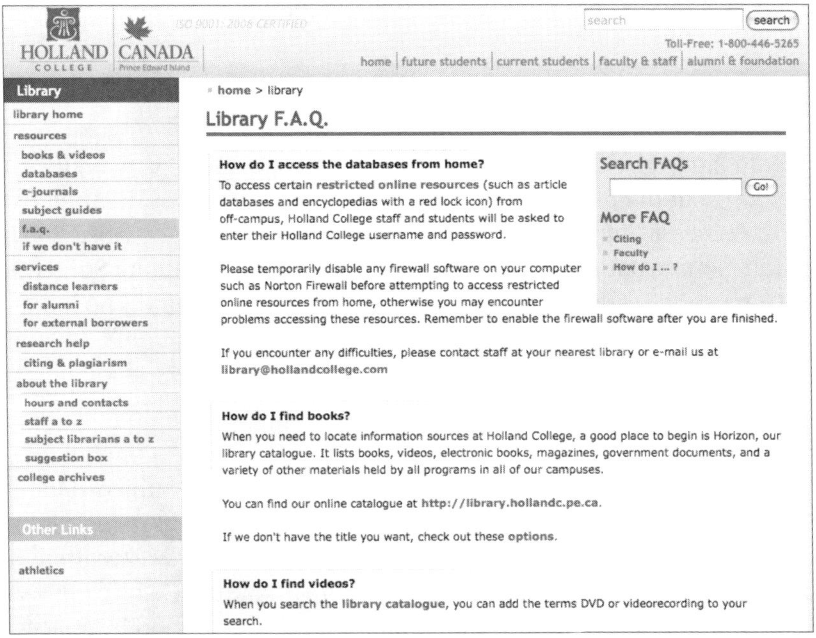
HOLLAND COLLEGE
CANADA
search
Toll-Free: 1-800-446-5265
home | future students | current students | faculty & staff | alumni & foundation
Library
library home
resources
books & videos
databases
e-journals
subject guides
f.a.q.
if we don't have it
services
distance learners
for alumni
for external borrowers
research help
citing & plagiarism
about the library
hours and contacts
staff a to z
subject librarians a to z
suggestion box
college archives
Other Links
athletics
home > library
Library F.A.Q.
How do I access the databases from home?
To access certain restricted online resources (such as article databases and encyclopedias with a red lock icon) from off-campus, Holland College staff and students will be asked to enter their Holland College username and password.
Please temporarily disable any firewall software on your computer such as Norton Firewall before attempting to access restricted online resources from home, otherwise you may encounter problems accessing these resources. Remember to enable the firewall software after you are finished.
If you encounter any difficulties, please contact staff at your nearest library or e-mail us at library@hollandcollege.com
Search FAQs
Go!
More FAQ
Citing
Faculty
How do I ... ?
How do I find books?
When you need to locate information sources at Holland College, a good place to begin is Horizon, our library catalogue. It lists books, videos, electronic books, magazines, government documents, and a variety of other materials held by all programs in all of our campuses.
You can find our online catalogue at http://library.hollandc.pe.ca.
If we don't have the title you want, check out these options.
How do I find videos?
When you search the library catalogue, you can add the terms DVD or videorecording to your search.

Figure 12.1 Holland College FAQ

Installing SubjectsPlus

Installation of SubjectsPlus is fairly simple. While there is no step-by-step downloadable manual, there is a wiki for SubjectsPlus at www.subjectsplus.com, where you can find videos that will walk you through setting up and using SubjectsPlus.

SubjectsPlus requires a server running Apache, PHP, and MySQL. First, you will need to download and unpack SubjectsPlus to your web folder. For your first install of SubjectsPlus, it is best to leave the unpacked directory name as its default; otherwise, your install may have problems finding the include files on some of the webpages. Once you have unpacked SubjectsPlus, you will need to create a MySQL database and a user with privileges to select, insert, update, and delete, and also import the SubjectsPlus SQL tables. The last step of the install is to edit the configuration settings in config.php. You will need to enter the base URL of your SubjectsPlus install and the MySQL connection information, and then edit the path information for your install. (If you have not changed the default folder name, you probably will not need to edit the path data.) You will also need to enter the proxy string information for your library and change the default salt value (an authentication key). Last, you'll need to edit the catalog form in assets\fixed_pluslets\catalog search.html to match the code for your catalog search tool.

Basic Configuration: Administrator

SubjectsPlus unpacks into four directories: Assets, which has many of the common include files; Control, which has the admin functions; FCKeditor, which is the WYSIWYG editor; and Subjects, which contains the public guides. Once you have finished editing the config.php file, you should be able to log into the control panel of SubjectsPlus (subsplus\control). If your install is configured properly, you should see a login box. If the page looks plain or is full of error messages, you will need to tweak the config.php file or check to see that the header.php include file in the \control\includes directory has the correct include file paths.

After logging into SubjectsPlus, the first thing you will want to do is change the password for the default account. Clicking on the Admin tab will bring up a list of users (Figure 12.2).

To change a user's password, click on the key icon. Before adding other users, you will need to decide if you want to use the staff directory functionality built into SubjectsPlus. If so, you will want to start

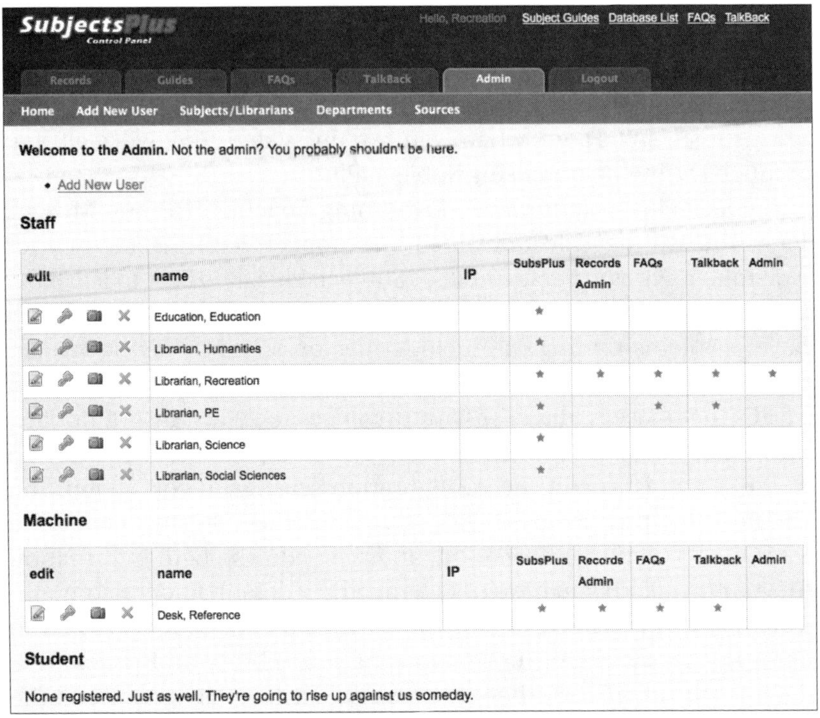

Figure 12.2 SubjectsPlus Administrator panel

by customizing your list of departments by clicking on the Departments tab. After editing the list of departments, click Home to return to the list of users. Under Add New User, you have a choice of user types (Staff, Machine, and Student), and you can set what permissions the new user has. Adding a user as Staff adds that user to the staff listing. The Machine and Student user types allow for the creation of users that will not show up on the staff listing. For each user you have the option of granting access to Subsplus, Records Admin, FAQs, Talkback, and the Admin features. These user groups are described here:

- Subsplus access gives a user the ability to create and edit guides and to add records.
- Records Admin gives the user the Subsplus access, plus the ability to add records to the A–Z list, to add the proxy string, and to delete records.

- FAQ access allows the user to create and edit questions in the FAQ module.
- Talkback gives the user the ability to view and answer feedback submitted from the Talkback page.
- Admin user access gives the user the ability to change and edit all aspects of SubjectsPlus.

You will most likely set up users with a combination of these roles. For example, you may wish to give librarians the ability to create guides and add resources, and give staff at public service desks access to the FAQ and Talkback modules.

Librarians can create guides as soon as they are added as users. However, before any guides are created you will want to enter some data concerning sources, subjects, and resources. Sources describe what type of resource each item is and are used to populate a table of contents on the guides. Some common sources you may wish to add are websites, databases, books, and videos. Resources are links to databases, catalog records, internet sites, and so on. Before adding resources, you will want to edit the sources and add some subject areas, as each resource will be associated with a source and at least one subject area. Ithaca College has added an extensive source list, which makes it possible to use SubjectsPlus to drive their virtual reference desk (Figure 12.3).

Figure 12.3 Ithaca College Virtual Reference Desk

Creating subjects is done on the Subjects/Librarians page. When you create a new subject, you have the option to make it live, or available on your site, and to specify what type of guide the subject is associated with: a subject guide, a course guide, or a topic guide. The library at the University of Southern Maine has created additional subject areas such as Biographies, News Sources, and Primary Sources. These subject areas are then listed under Databases by Type, which gives students another opportunity to stumble upon the resources they need (Figure 12.4).

Once you have finished adding your subject areas, you (or the electronic resources librarian) can start adding resources. To add a resource, click on the records tab and then the Add New Item link (Figure 12.5). Besides the basic title, description, subject, and location fields, you also have the following options:

- Pre: Adds a nonsortable prefix to the title, such as *a* or *the*
- Restricted: Adds the proxy string to the URL

Figure 12.4 University of Southern Maine databases by type

- Open URL, full-text, images, video, and audio: Adds descriptive icons to your database listing
- A–Z list: Adds the title to the database list on databases.php

When you save a new record you immediately have the opportunity to edit the record. This feature allows you to add a record to more than one subject area. If you want the database to have a different description for each subject, choose the Override Description option.

Basic Configuration: Librarian

When a librarian or staff member logs into SubjectsPlus, what they see depends on what rights you have given them. Users who are creating guides will most likely have access just to the SubsPlus user group. This access gives them the ability to create and edit guides and to add and edit resources. They can either create a guide from a subject that was previously entered or choose to create a new subject, course, or topic guide (Figure 12.6).

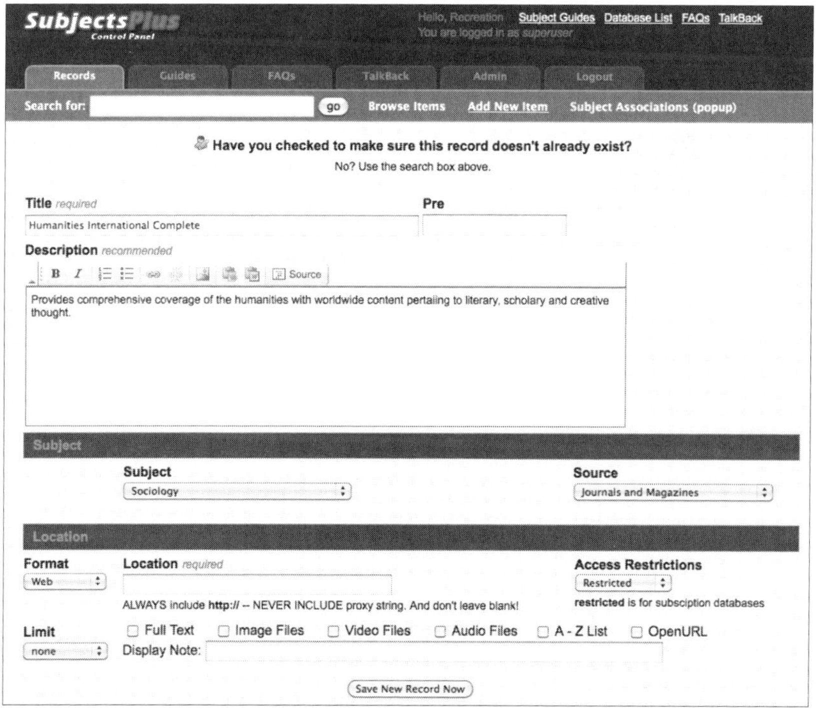

Figure 12.5 Creating new records

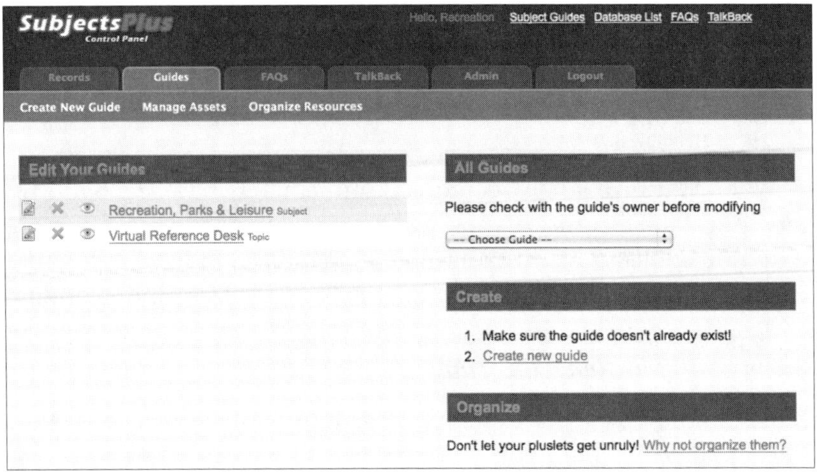

Figure 12.6 Guides tab

If a guide has previously been created for a topic, the librarian has the option to edit the guide properties. A second librarian who is editing the guide properties can also be associated with the guide, and the guide can be marked as a "child" of another guide. Marking a guide as a child guide adds the option of having a link to the guide appear on guides of similar topics. If the librarian chooses instead to create a new guide, he or she can clone an existing guide.

Version 9 of SubjectsPlus has completely changed how guides are created. In version 8, guides were created when a subject or course topic was added, as the resources were automatically pulled into the guide. Version 8 of SubjectsPlus had limited customization capabilities; the guide owners could only customize the sidebar. Version 9 gives you a blank slate and the ability to drag and drop content blocks, called "pluslets," where you want them. When you first enter the guide editing panel, your guide is a blank slate. Clicking on the New Pluslet menu brings down a menu of pluslets, or content blocks, that can be added to the guide. There are 11 types of pluslets:

- Base pluslet: Adds a WYSIWYG editor for adding blocks of text. There are also icons to quickly add a link to a database item, catalog record, or search; to upload an item; or to insert an FAQ.
- Heading: Creates a header bar.

- RSS Feed: Pulls in a chosen number of posts from an external RSS feed.
- Delicious Links: Pulls in links associated with a tag or tags from a Delicious account.
- Twitter Feed: Pulls in Twitter posts.
- Flickr Images: Pulls in the RSS from a Flickr set.
- All Items by Source: Pulls in all the resources associated with a particular subject.
- Legend: Creates a legend for the icons in the source listing.
- Subject Specialist: Provides user contact information for the guide creators.
- Related Guides: Pulls in links to "parent" guides.
- Books: Using the library catalog, provides a search toolbar for your library.

Creating a new guide is as simple as dragging and dropping the pluslets that you wish to appear in the guide. The content will not appear in each pluslet until the guide has been saved and refreshed. You may wish to start by creating a minimal guide for each subject consisting simply of the Legend pluslet, the Subject Specialist pluslet, and the All Items by Source pluslet (Figure 12.7).

Any of the pluslets that have a pencil icon are editable. For example, once content is loaded into the All Items by Source pluslet, editing the pluslet gives you the ability to drag and drop resources. This functionality allows you to arrange the resources in order of preference, rather than alpha order. Any changes that you make to the pluslets that are editable or that require user input, such as a Twitter pluslet, will be saved; the edited pluslet will then be available for use in other guides.

Two other features are available to guide creators: Organize Resources and Manage Assets. Organize Resources is the drag-and-drop function just mentioned: the ability to rearrange the order in which resources appear in the All Items by Source pluslet. Manage Assets gives you an overview of all the files you have uploaded and of all the unused pluslets you have created. From here, you can choose to delete your unused pluslets and files (Figure 12.8).

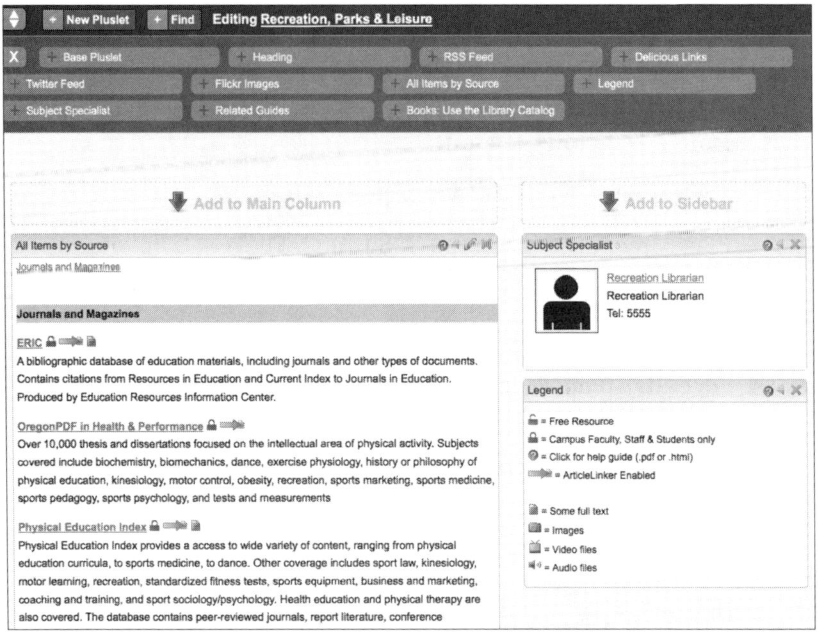

Figure 12.7 Basic subject guide

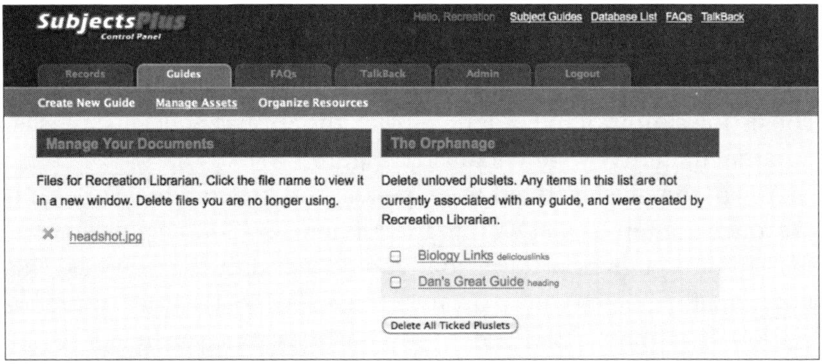

Figure 12.8 Manage Assets screen

Many library websites feature a page of FAQs and a form for submitting questions or suggestions to the library. Quite often the FAQs are static HTML pages that are rarely updated, and the emailed suggestions disappear into a single library email account. The FAQ and Talkback modules of SubjectsPlus make FAQs and patron questions database-driven and accessible to everyone who has access to these modules. Questions and answers are entered one-by-one into

SubjectsPlus and then added to any of the subject areas or to an FAQ collection. For example, the Cardinal Cushing Library at Emmanuel College has created collections of FAQs on both finding books and finding articles (Figure 12.9).

The Talkback module contains the questions and suggestions from your library's website users. These user suggestions are held in moderation until a librarian with access to the Talkback module answers the question. The Talkback module provides the option to delete submitted questions or to answer them and mark them as "active." Active questions and answers will appear on the database-driven talkback.php page (Figure 12.10).

Customizing SubjectsPlus

Once you have a few guides created, SubjectsPlus is almost ready for public view. The public webpages for SubjectsPlus have a simple, attractive design (Figure 12.11).

All that is required before going live with SubjectsPlus is to edit the header include file in subjects/includes by adding a link to your

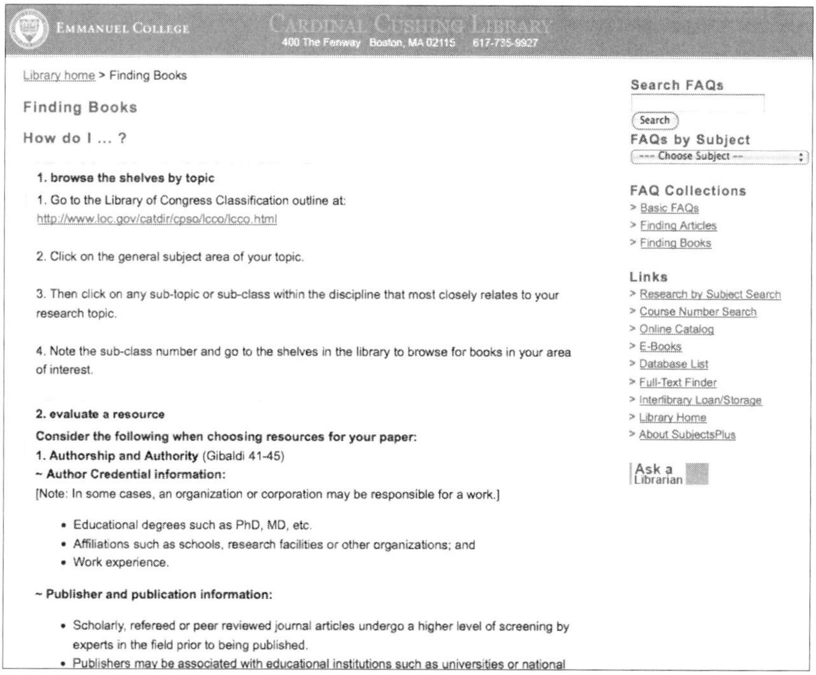
EMMANUEL COLLEGE
CARDINAL CUSHING LIBRARY
400 The Fenway Boston, MA 02115 617-735-9927
Library home > Finding Books
Finding Books
How do I ... ?
1. browse the shelves by topic
1. Go to the Library of Congress Classification outline at:
http://www.loc.gov/catdir/cpso/lcco/lcco.html
2. Click on the general subject area of your topic.
3. Then click on any sub-topic or sub-class within the discipline that most closely relates to your research topic.
4. Note the sub-class number and go to the shelves in the library to browse for books in your area of interest.
2. evaluate a resource
Consider the following when choosing resources for your paper:
1. Authorship and Authority (Gibaldi 41-45)
~ Author Credential information:
[Note: In some cases, an organization or corporation may be responsible for a work.]
• Educational degrees such as PhD, MD, etc.
• Affiliations such as schools, research facilities or other organizations; and
• Work experience.
~ Publisher and publication information:
• Scholarly, refereed or peer reviewed journal articles undergo a higher level of screening by experts in the field prior to being published.
Search FAQs
Search
FAQs by Subject
--- Choose Subject ---
FAQ Collections
> Basic FAQs
> Finding Articles
> Finding Books
Links
> Research by Subject Search
> Course Number Search
> Online Catalog
> E-Books
> Database List
> Full-Text Finder
> Interlibrary Loan/Storage
> Library Home
> About SubjectsPlus
Ask a Librarian

Figure 12.9 Emmanuel College FAQ

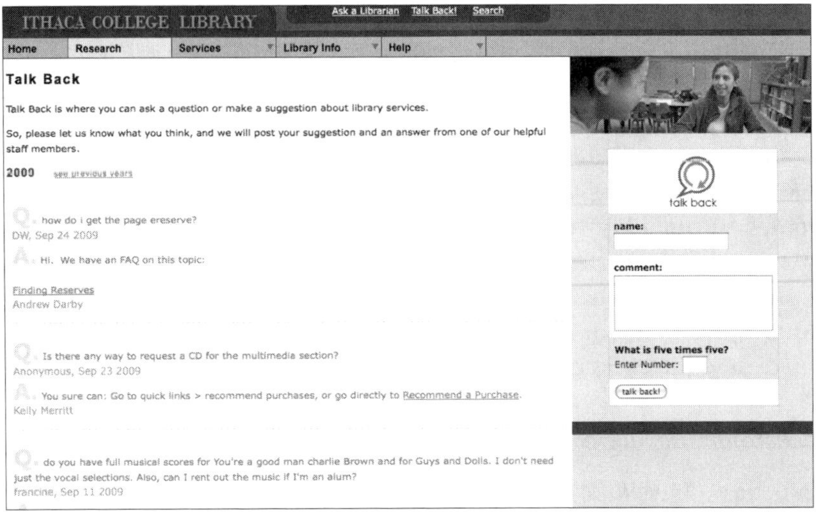
ITHACA COLLEGE LIBRARY
Ask a Librarian
Talk Back!
Search
Home
Research
Services
Library Info
Help
Talk Back
Talk Back is where you can ask a question or make a suggestion about library services.
So, please let us know what you think, and we will post your suggestion and an answer from one of our helpful staff members.
2009
see previous years
how do i get the page ereserve?
DW, Sep 24 2009
Hi. We have an FAQ on this topic:
Finding Reserves
Andrew Darby
Is there any way to request a CD for the multimedia section?
Anonymous, Sep 23 2009
You sure can: Go to quick links > recommend purchases, or go directly to Recommend a Purchase.
Kelly Merritt
do you have full musical scores for You're a good man charlie Brown and for Guys and Dolls. I don't need just the vocal selections. Also, can I rent out the music if I'm an alum?
francine, Sep 11 2009
talk back
name:
comment:
What is five times five?
Enter Number:
talk back!

Figure 12.10 Ithaca College Talk Back page

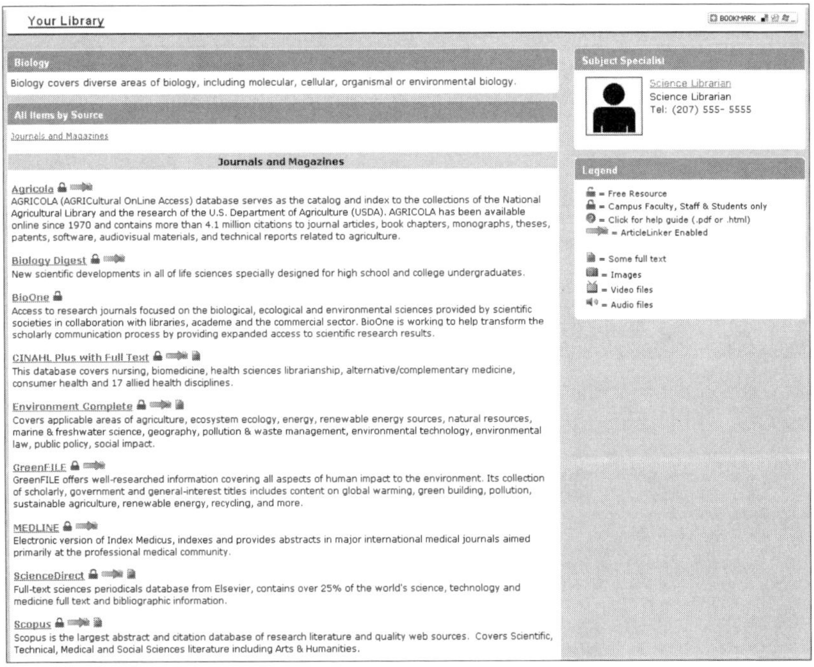
Your Library
BOOKMARK
Biology
Biology covers diverse areas of biology, including molecular, cellular, organismal or environmental biology.
All Items by Source
Journals and Magazines
Journals and Magazines
Agricola
AGRICOLA (AGRICultural OnLine Access) database serves as the catalog and index to the collections of the National Agricultural Library and the research of the U.S. Department of Agriculture (USDA). AGRICOLA has been available online since 1970 and contains more than 4.1 million citations to journal articles, book chapters, monographs, theses, patents, software, audiovisual materials, and technical reports related to agriculture.
Biology Digest
New scientific developments in all of life sciences specially designed for high school and college undergraduates.
BioOne
Access to research journals focused on the biological, ecological and environmental sciences provided by scientific societies in collaboration with libraries, academe and the commercial sector. BioOne is working to help transform the scholarly communication process by providing expanded access to scientific research results.
CINAHL Plus with Full Text
This database covers nursing, biomedicine, health sciences librarianship, alternative/complementary medicine, consumer health and 17 allied health disciplines.
Environment Complete
Covers applicable areas of agriculture, ecosystem ecology, energy, renewable energy sources, natural resources, marine & freshwater science, geography, pollution & waste management, environmental technology, environmental law, public policy, social impact.
GreenFILE
GreenFILE offers well-researched information covering all aspects of human impact to the environment. Its collection of scholarly, government and general-interest titles includes content on global warming, green building, pollution, sustainable agriculture, renewable energy, recycling, and more.
MEDLINE
Electronic version of Index Medicus, indexes and provides abstracts in major international medical journals aimed primarily at the professional medical community.
ScienceDirect
Full-text sciences periodicals database from Elsevier, contains over 25% of the world's science, technology and medicine full text and bibliographic information.
Scopus
Scopus is the largest abstract and citation database of research literature and quality web sources. Covers Scientific, Technical, Medical and Social Sciences literature including Arts & Humanities.
Subject Specialist
Science Librarian
Science Librarian
Tel: (207) 555- 5555
Legend
= Free Resource
= Campus Faculty, Staff & Students only
= Click for help guide (.pdf or .html)
= ArticleLinker Enabled
= Some full text
= Images
= Video files
= Audio files

Figure 12.11 Example subject guide

library homepage. Further customizations can be done to integrate SubjectsPlus into your library site. The CSS for the public side of SubjectsPlus is found in assets\css\default.css. Content from SubjectsPlus is pulled onto webpages into two div tags: the "content" div, which holds the main guide section, the database A–Z listing, and the staff directory: and the "sidebar" div, which holds the legend, subject liaison information, and so on. It is fairly easy to add the color scheme and basic layout from your library site to the SubjectsPlus pages by adding the css include files and div tags from your design to the header and footer include files from SubjectsPlus (Figure 12.12).

The addition of the pluslets to version 0.9 provides the potential for using SubjectsPlus as a content management system (CMS). Out of the box, SubjectsPlus has the ability to create most of the database-driven webpages on most library sites. Each page on an existing website can be created as a new guide. Content from static HTML pages can entered into a Base pluslet, and each page can have links to contact information, recent FAQs, and related pages. Navigation modules that could be shared between pages can be created by entering links to other guides into a base pluslet. A library news page could be

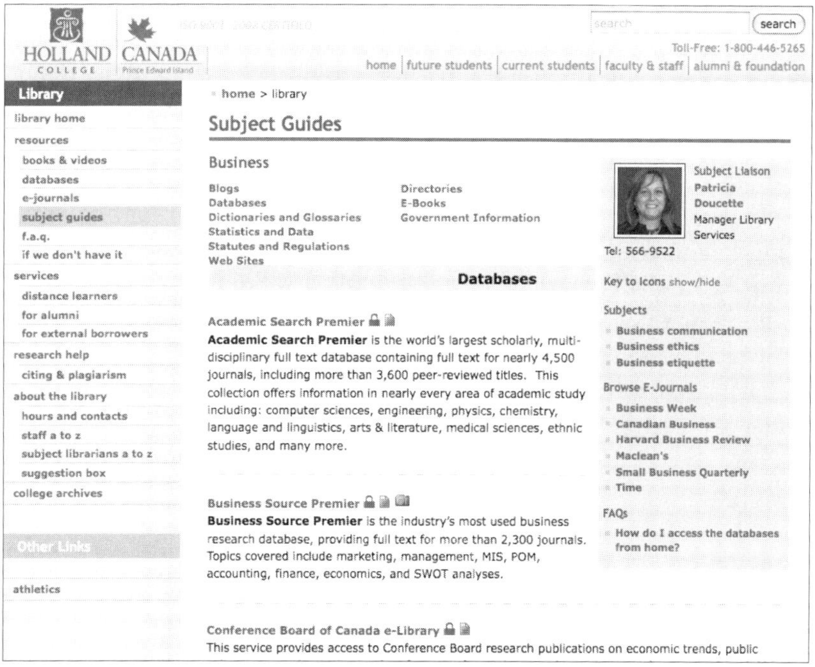

Figure 12.12 Holland College subject guide

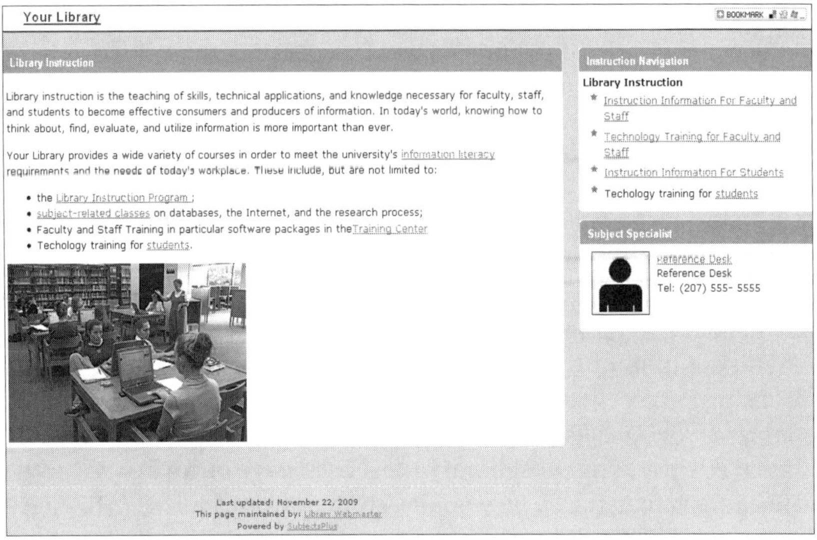
Your Library
BOOKMARK
Library Instruction
Library instruction is the teaching of skills, technical applications, and knowledge necessary for faculty, staff, and students to become effective consumers and producers of information. In today's world, knowing how to think about, find, evaluate, and utilize information is more important than ever.
Your Library provides a wide variety of courses in order to meet the university's information literacy requirements and the needs of today's workplace. These include, but are not limited to:
the Library Instruction Program ;
subject-related classes on databases, the Internet, and the research process;
Faculty and Staff Training in particular software packages in the Training Center
Techology training for students.
Instruction Navigation
Library Instruction
Instruction Information For Faculty and Staff
Technology Training for Faculty and Staff
Instruction Information For Students
Techology training for students
Subject Specialist
Reference Desk
Reference Desk
Tel: (207) 555- 5555
Last updated: November 22, 2009
This page maintained by: Library Webmaster
Powered by SubjectsPlus

Figure 12.13 SubjectsPlus as a CMS

created by using the RSS pluslets to pull in posts from external blog and Twitter accounts (Figure 12.13).

One final customization you may wish to do is more troubleshooting than customizing. If you plan to use mod_rewrite with SubjectsPlus, you may need to tweak the htaccess file. If you have changed the file names of either guide.php or staff_details.php you will need to change the file names in the htaccess file accordingly. Also, the staff directories included with SubjectsPlus provide links to the staff_details.php page for more information about each staff member. SubjectsPlus uses the email address of each staff member to create the link to the staff details page, as this provides a unique identifier for each staff member. If your email addresses are in the form name.name@college.edu however, Apache mod_rewrite will fail to display the staff details page due to the period in the user portion of the email address. You will need to replace "`RewriteRule ^staff/([^/\.]+)/?$ staff_details.php?name=$1 [L]`" with "`RewriteRule ^staff/([^/]+)/?$ staff_details.php?name=$1 [L]`".

Support

Support for SubjectsPlus is available on the SubjectsPlus wiki (www.subjectsplus.com), through the SubjectsPlus Google Group (groups.google.com/group/subjectsplus), and from the developer and maintainer, Andrew Darby. There is also an online manual for SubjectsPlus on the wiki. While this may not be as convenient as a manual that you can download and print, the wiki has links to videos that are very helpful for learning the basics of SubjectsPlus quickly. The SubjectsPlus Google Group is an active group, and questions are answered quickly by group members or by Andrew Darby.

SubjectsPlus is an easy-to-use subject guide tool. Out of the box, SubjectsPlus is attractive enough to use with minor modification and is easy to integrate into an existing library website. SubjectsPlus earns the plus in its name by being far more than a tool for creating subject guides; it can run most, if not all, of the database driven sections of a library website, including the database A–Z list, the staff directories, and the FAQs. With a little creativity, SubjectsPlus can be used to drive an entire library website.

Endnotes

1. Clark Nall and Janice Steed Lewis, "Integrating Print and Electronic Resources: Joyner Library's 'Pirate Source'," *Acquisitions Librarian* 17, no. 33/34 (2005), 107–120.

CHAPTER 13

LibData

LibData was released at the University of Minnesota in the fall of 2003 and was developed as a tool to make creating subject guides (Research QuickStart), course guides (CourseLib), and other web pages (PageScribe) easy.

Installing LibData

LibData (sourceforge.net/projects/libdata) requires Apache, PHP, and MySQL, and is an easy install due to the developer's step-by-step instructions. There is a Perl script included in the LibData installation folder to aid with the installation. However, if you do not have Perl installed you will need to create three MySQL databases called libdata, libstats, and libsessions. Each database has a corresponding MySQL dump to import. To finish the MySQL setup, you will need to create two user accounts, "libdata" and "libsessions," and give these accounts permissions to the LibData databases.

Basic Configuration: Administrator

The first thing you will want to do after installing LibData is to remove the libdata installation directory from your web server directory. This will prevent anyone from running the install script and overwriting your install. Next, log into libdata_admin to access the authoring console (Figure 13.1).

The LibData Administrator panel consists of Authoring Console, Manager Functions, and DBA Tools. The Authoring Console is used to create guides and add resources; the Manager Functions panel is used to create staff accounts and to create and manage the subject and information types associated with each resource; and the DBA Tools give the ability to troubleshoot errors that may come up. Each of these will be discussed further in the following sections.

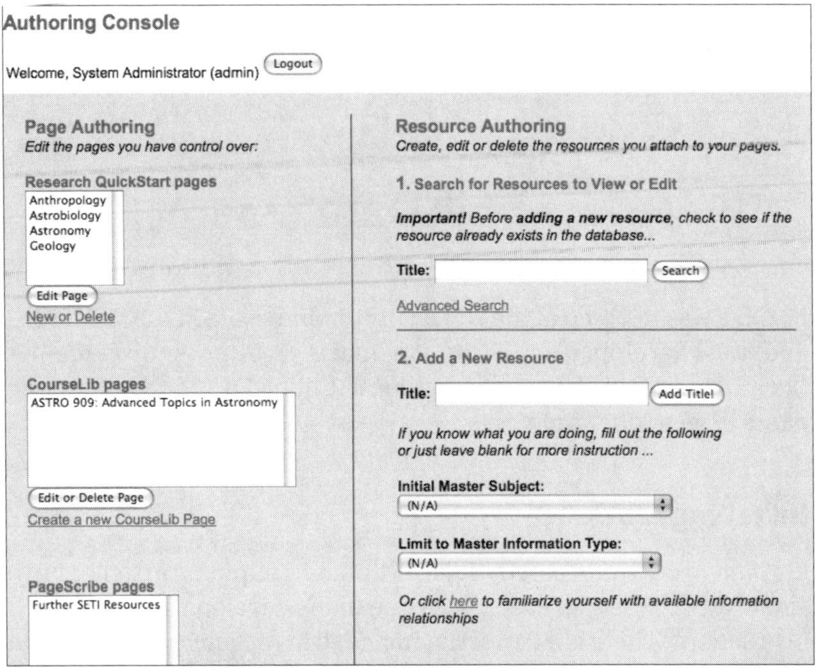

Figure 13.1 Authoring Console

LibData has three types of user accounts: authors, managers, and DBAs. Authors have the ability to create and edit any resource, to create new guides, and to edit guides that have been assigned to them. Authors have access only to the authoring console. Managers can create or edit any resource and may edit any guides that they created or are assigned to. A manager can also be marked as the head of a library unit, which gives him or her the ability to edit any of the guides created by that unit. Managers also have access to the Manager Functions panel, where they can configure the information associated with a resource or guide and can add or edit staff members. DBA accounts have full rights to LibData; they can create or edit any resource or guide and have access to all three administrator panels.

Users are added to LibData in the manager functions panel. Select Manage Staff at the bottom of the panel, and you will be taken to a screen that lists all of the staff, their access levels, and the time of their last login. To add a new user, select Add New and add the basic user information (Figure 13.2).

Once you have saved the basic user information, you will have the opportunity to give the account a password and to assign subject areas.

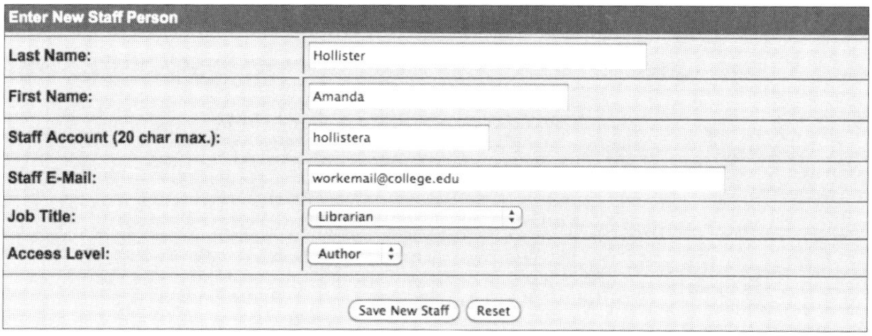

Figure 13.2 Adding a new user

After creating your LibData user accounts, you will want to customize LibData for your library's needs. The first step is to edit or delete the sample data that came with LibData. The sample data helps to demonstrate how resources are associated with at least a master subject or a master information type. The information types provide a hierarchal structure of your resources on your guides. For example, a newspaper index may be listed under the master information type Article Databases, then the information type Newspapers (Figure 13.3).

Resources are the links to the content that you wish to provide in your guides. Editing or deleting resources is done using the General Subject drilldown menu found at the bottom of the Authoring Console (Figure 13.4).

Select a master subject area, and you will see a screen that lists the subjects that fall under that master subject and the resources associated with them. To delete a resource, click on the radio button of that resource and then click Edit. At the bottom of the resource-editing screen, you have the option to delete the resource.

Once you have removed the resources that come installed with LibData, you can begin to customize the master subjects and master information types. The information types are tailored to the University of Minnesota Libraries and may not suit your needs (Figure 13.5).

Click the Lookup button on the master information type to see a list. As you are editing the master information types, you may wish to see what information types are associated with it. This information is available on the Authoring Console, either by selecting "Or click here to familiarize yourself with available information relationships" or by using the drilldown menus at the bottom of the page. You may also

Information Structure Summary

Master Subject	Master -> Base Information Type
(All)	Article Databases -> Article Databases, Broad Topic Article Databases -> Article Databases, Subject Specific Article Databases -> Best Sources for this Subject Article Databases -> Newspapers Internet Resources -> Electronic Texts Internet Resources -> Gateways & Megasites Internet Resources -> Internet Directory Internet Resources -> Library Web Sites Internet Resources -> Official Agency and Organization Web Sites Internet Resources -> Search Engines Internet Resources -> Web Sites Primary Source Materials -> Archival Materials Primary Source Materials -> Correspondence Primary Source Materials -> Government Documents Primary Source Materials -> Historical Documents Primary Source Materials -> Reports Primary Source Materials -> Speeches Reference Reources -> Almanacs Reference Reources -> Atlases & Maps Reference Reources -> Bibliographies Reference Reources -> Biographical Sources Reference Reources -> Dictionaries Reference Reources -> Directories Reference Reources -> Dissertations and Theses Reference Reources -> Encyclopedias Reference Reources -> Forms, Tests, Inventories Reference Reources -> General Reference Works Reference Reources -> Guides Reference Reources -> Handbooks and Manuals Reference Reources -> Societies, Agencies, and Organizations Reference Reources -> Standards Reference Reources -> Statistics and Data Reference Reources -> Style Guides
(N/A)	(N/A) -> (N/A)
Arts and Sciences	Primary Source Materials -> Diaries
Education	Reference Reources -> Lesson Plans

Figure 13.3 Information types

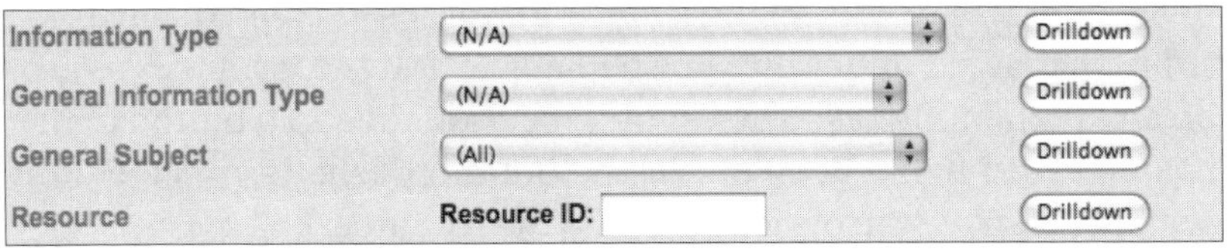

Figure 13.4 Authoring Console drilldown menu

want to customize the master subjects, which can be changed to reflect the schools on your campus or kept as broad subject areas. The master subjects can become a research starting point for your patrons, as shown by the example in Figure 13.6 by the University of Minnesota Libraries.

Before adding resources, there are a few more things to customize. In the Manager Functions panel, you can edit the Location, Feature, Service, Service Type, and Vendor. Locations give the

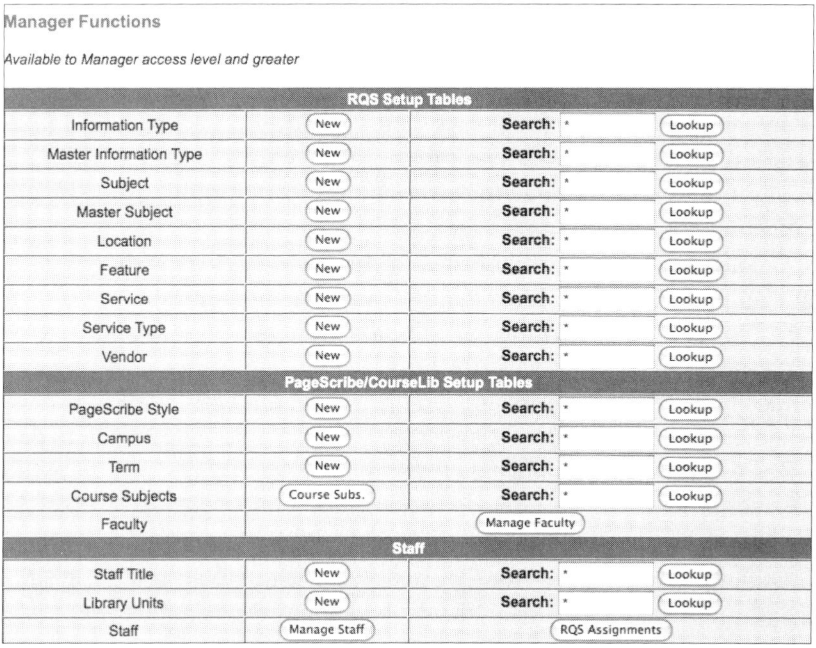

Figure 13.5 Manager Functions

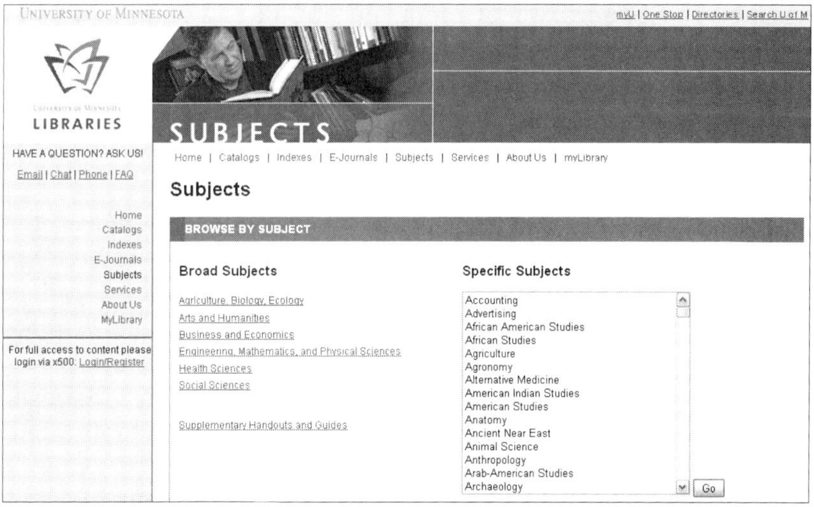

Figure 13.6 University of Minnesota Libraries master subjects

contact information for your library and library branches. While locations can be associated with particular resources and subjects, this information is only displayed on the subject guide. If your library does not have any branches, you could add librarian contact information as a location. Associating a librarian with a guide as a location will populate the guide with the contact information for that subject librarian.

Features can be the attributes of the item, such as Web, Book, or Campus ID Required. Each feature can have an icon associated with it (upload the desired images to libdata\images). Service and Service Type are fields used to describe library services such as reference and interlibrary loan. Vendors are usually associated with paid resources, such as subscription databases. The Vendor feature allows you to flag all resources from a particular vendor if the vendor is experiencing down time.

Once you have customized the master subjects, information types, and features to fit your library's needs, it is time to start adding subjects and resources for your library. LibData was designed to separate the procedures for creating and managing resources from the procedures for creating guides. The developers felt that it would be much easier for library staff to assemble research and course guides if most of the resources they needed could be added with a single click. To facilitate this, you will want to populate LibData with a list of subjects and resources before any guides are created.

Subjects can be added via the Authoring Console or the Manager Functions panel. From the Authoring Console, click New or Delete under the subject listings and then New on the next page. After you have entered your subject name and clicked Save New Subject, you will have new options available, such as assigning the subject to a master subject, to a location, or to a librarian. Once a subject has been created, editing the subject to change the name, the location, the description, or the librarians associated with it can only be done in the Manager Functions panel.

The PageScribe/CourseLib setup section of the Manager Functions panel contains the style settings for PageScribe and CourseLib webpages, which are discussed in greater detail later in this chapter. The PageScribe style function gives the ability to offer multiple layout options for the guides. Campus, term, course subjects, and faculty are used on the CourseLib pages. Staff titles are used in conjunction with guides to provide contact information for the creators and the faculty associated with each page. Library units are

RQS Subject	Created	Updated	Public?	Assigned Staff
Africana Studies	2009-10-14 (hollistera)	2009-10-14 (hollistera)	Y	Librarian, SocialSci (soclib)
Anthropology	2008-07-29 (admin)	2009-10-14 (admin)	Y	Administrator, System (admin)
Art and Art History	2009-10-14 (hollistera)	2009-10-14 (hollistera)	Y	Librarian, SocialSci (soclib)
Asian Studies	2009-10-14 (hollistera)	0	N	Librarian, SocialSci (soclib)
Biology	2009-10-14 (hollistera)	2009-11-22 (admin)	Y	Librarian, Science (scilib)
Business	2009-10-14 (admin)	0	N	Librarian, Arts (artlib)
Chemistry	2009-10-14 (hollistera)	0	N	Librarian, Science (scilib)
Cinema and Photography	2009-10-14 (admin)	2009-10-15 (admin)	Y	Librarian, Arts (artlib)
Communication Disorders and Sciences	2009-10-14 (admin)	0	N	Librarian, Science (scilib)
Geology	2008-08-20 (admin)	2009-10-14 (admin)	Y	Administrator, System (admin)
Health	2009-10-15 (admin)	2009-10-15 (admin)	Y	Librarian, Science (scilib)
Research Quick Start	2009-10-14 (admin)	2009-11-22 (admin)	Y	Desk, Reference (refdesk)
		Total Rows: 12		

Figure 13.7 Research QuickStart assignments

most useful when used as a broad topic subject area. Designating a staff member as a Unit Lead, allows that staff member to edit any of the guides created by the members of that unit. Lastly, the Research QuickStart Assignments function gives an overview of the subject guides that have been created, including information on when the guide was last updated, whether the guide is public, and who is assigned to the guide (Figure 13.7).

Basic Configuration: Guide Authors

Resources are added using the Resource Adding interface of the Authoring Console. Enter a new title, choose a master subject type and/or a master information type, and click Add Title. On the Enter New Resource page, there are many configuration options for each resource. For example, for a subscription database, you will want to fill out the coverage details, the URL for the resource (including the proxy string if needed), the base information type, the vendor, and the description. Once you have saved this information, additional options appear: the ability to assign a location, features such as Full Text or Campus Access Only, and a master subject. Make sure to specify a master information type for each resource, otherwise the resource will "float" to the top of the guide and be listed under N/A. You can also edit resources from the Authoring Console. One thing to note: When you update the information type for a resource, that field is not updated system-wide, so each guide using that resource will need to update that resource (Figure 13.8).

After the subjects and resources have been added, creating guides is simple. Choose one of the subjects listed on the page authoring

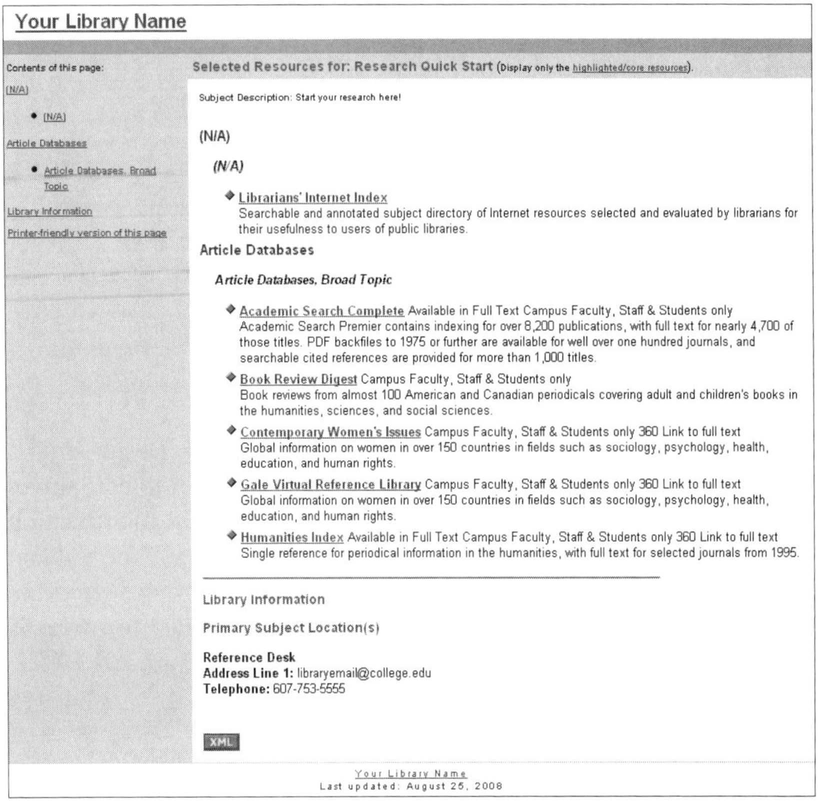
Your Library Name
Contents of this page:
[N/A]
[N/A]
Article Databases
Article Databases, Broad Topic
Library Information
Printer-friendly version of this page
Selected Resources for: Research Quick Start (Display only the highlighted/core resources).
Subject Description: Start your research here!
(N/A)
(N/A)
Librarians' Internet Index
Searchable and annotated subject directory of Internet resources selected and evaluated by librarians for their usefulness to users of public libraries.
Article Databases
Article Databases, Broad Topic
Academic Search Complete Available in Full Text Campus Faculty, Staff & Students only
Academic Search Premier contains indexing for over 8,200 publications, with full text for nearly 4,700 of those titles. PDF backfiles to 1975 or further are available for well over one hundred journals, and searchable cited references are provided for more than 1,000 titles.
Book Review Digest Campus Faculty, Staff & Students only
Book reviews from almost 100 American and Canadian periodicals covering adult and children's books in the humanities, sciences, and social sciences.
Contemporary Women's Issues Campus Faculty, Staff & Students only 360 Link to full text
Global information on women in over 150 countries in fields such as sociology, psychology, health, education, and human rights.
Gale Virtual Reference Library Campus Faculty, Staff & Students only 360 Link to full text
Global information on women in over 150 countries in fields such as sociology, psychology, health, education, and human rights.
Humanities Index Available in Full Text Campus Faculty, Staff & Students only 360 Link to full text
Single reference for periodical information in the humanities, with full text for selected journals from 1995.
Library Information
Primary Subject Location(s)
Reference Desk
Address Line 1: libraryemail@college.edu
Telephone: 607-753-5555
XML
Your Library Name
Last updated: August 25, 2008

Figure 13.8 Orphaned resource on a Research QuickStart guide

side of the Authoring Console and click Edit Page. The subject_builder.phtml page provides the following options: page status, adding resources, and adding related guides. The page status shows you when the guide was last updated and whether the guide is published. A guide will not be available on the public side of LibData until the guide is published. To add a resource to the guide, you can locate the resource using the A–Z list, search for it by title, or limit to a master information type or feature (Figure 13.9).

Resources can be identified as "core" resources, which enables the guide creator to prioritize resources. As resources are added to the guide, a preview of the guide appears at the bottom of the page. In the guide preview, you have the options to Edit the Base Resource, Edit This Instance of the resource, or to Remove the Resource from the guide. Editing the base resource changes the resource system-wide; however, these changes will only appear when the resource is newly

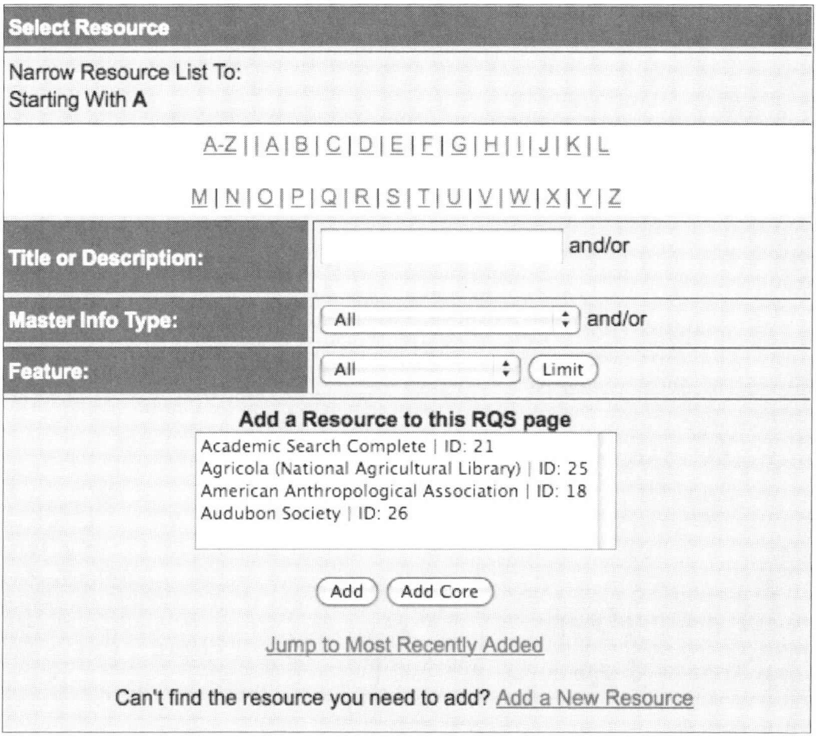

Figure 13.9 Adding resources to a Research QuickStart guide

added to a guide. The change will not appear in guides already using the resource until the guide owner updates the resource on the guide. The Edit This Instance function gives you the ability to add or remove the “core resource” flag and to override system-wide settings such as the information type and resource description. Finally, while creating or editing a guide, you have the ability to add links to related guides. The finished guide includes a table of contents of the resources, a link to show only the “core” resources, the library contact information, and links to related guides (Figure 13.10).

CourseLib and PageScribe Pages

The ability to create CourseLib and PageScribe pages is particularly useful if you are not using a content management system (CMS) for your library site, as you can create webpages easily with this function. The process for creating CourseLib and PageScribe pages is

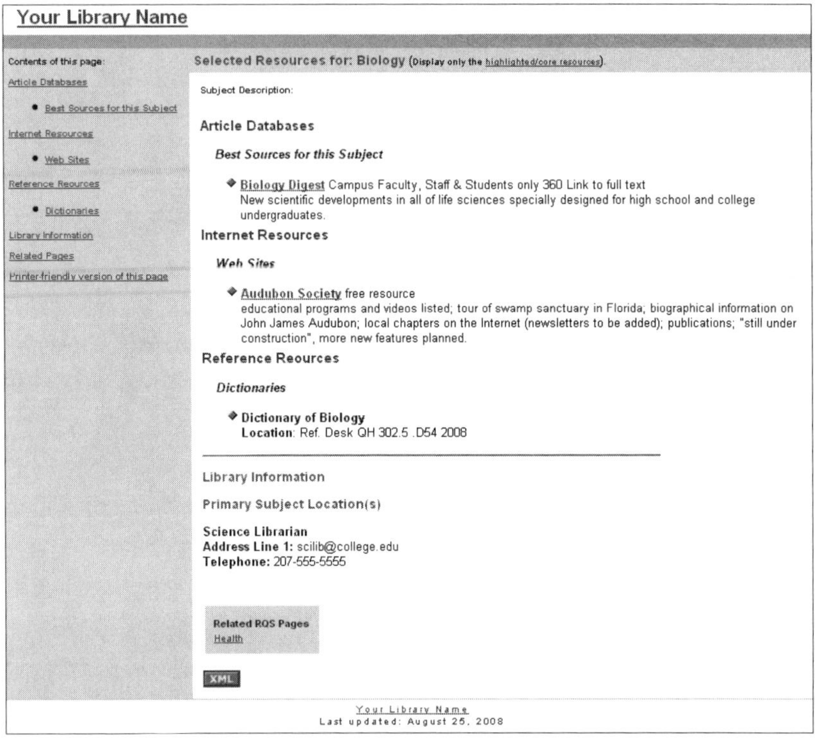

Figure 13.10 Example Research QuickStart guide

very similar, so these will be covered together in a quick overview. Pages can be created on the Authoring Console by selecting Create a New CourseLib or PageScribe Page. The scribe_start.phtml page gives the option to create a new page, edit a page you have previously created, or "clone" or copy an existing page to use as a base for a new page. The section at the top of the scribe.phtml page contains information about the page, such as its last modified date, published state, and basic functions for the page. You can choose to hide or display the table of contents, choose what staff can edit the page, and choose a page style. The Activate Up Anchors function is useful if the page is long; it automatically inserts a link to the top of the page after every element added to the page. Last, a handy style key shows you how each header will look on the page.

Content is added to a page by adding elements. An element can be a free-text box, a resource, a link to another guide or page, or links to library staff or services. Creating CourseLib and PageScribe pages differs only in terms of creating the introductory section of the page.

PageScribe pages have an element called Page Header, which is essentially a free-text box. The entire page could in fact be built using the Page Header element, as this element will render text and HTML. CourseLib pages include additional elements such as course title, section and term, course faculty, and introductory text (Figure 13.11).

The main body of each page is created by a flexible layout of elements. At the bottom of scribe.phtml is a small, green icon. Click on that icon to add an element to your page. After you have added an element such as text or a resource, that element appears both on the page and in the table of contents. Each element added to the page will have several small icons next to it: a yellow box to edit the element, a red box to delete the element, links to increase the element's text size, and an arrow to move the element up or down on the page (Figure 13.12). The published CourseLib or PageScribe guide will include the contact information for the page maintainer and an RSS feed for that page (Figure 13.13).

LibData Statistics

One definite strength of LibData is its ability to keep statistics on guide usage, page usage, and resource usage. You will find a link to LibData statistics at the bottom of the page authoring side of the Authoring Console. The stats_libdata.phtml page shows you links to the subject guides and to the CourseLib and PageScribe pages that you maintain. At the bottom of the page, you can also drill down to see statistics for any of the guides, pages, and resources in LibData.

LibData not only tracks how many users are accessing the pages directly but also how many users are using the RSS feeds. LibData keeps track of every time a user clicks on a resource link on a page, giving you usage statistics for each resource and the exit points from which your users left your site. LibData lets you export page statistics as an Excel spreadsheet (Figure 13.14).

Customizing LibData

Customizing the appearance of LibData can be as simple as editing the page header and footer include files, found in the \LibData folder, or as complex as completely changing the layout of LibData. At a minimum you should add the banner from your library website to the header, and your library contact information to the footer. Adding

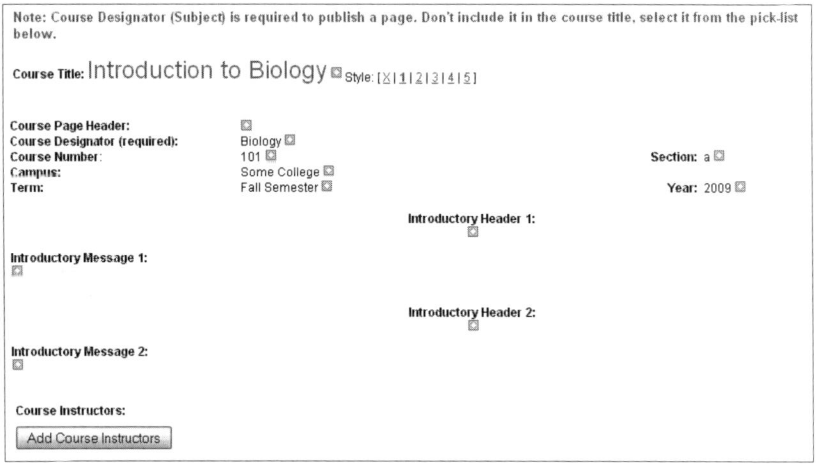

Figure 13.11 CourseLib page builder

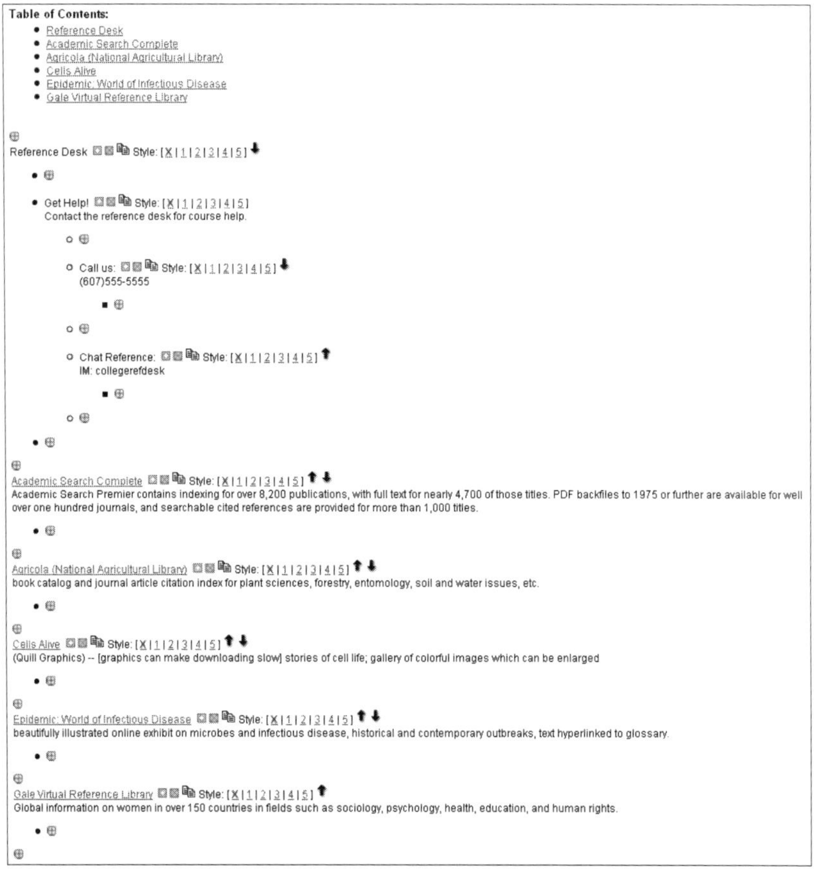

Figure 13.12 PageScribe page elements

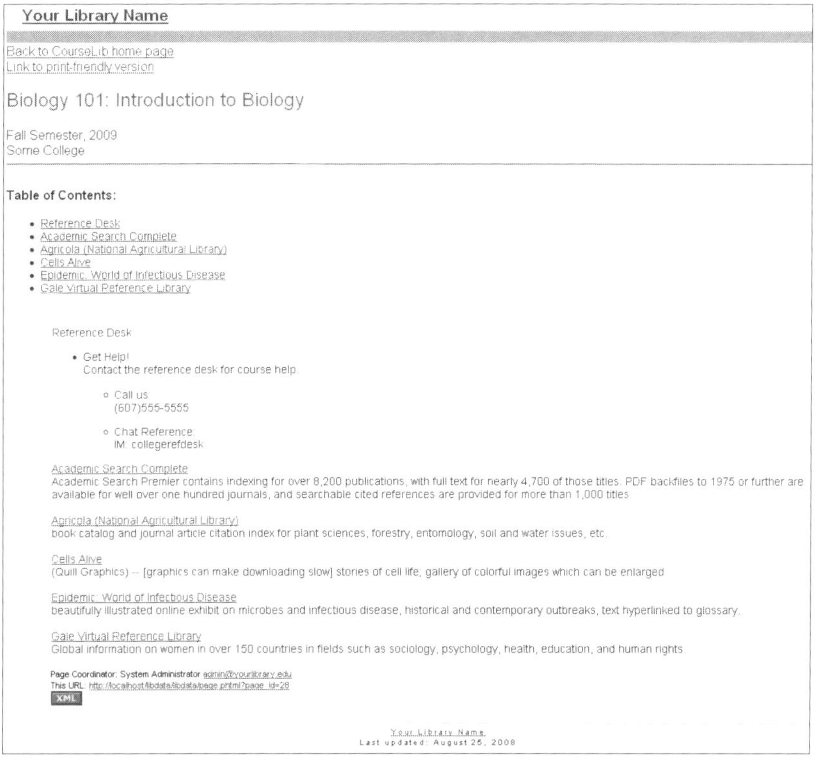
Your Library Name
Back to CourseLib home page
Link to print-friendly version
Biology 101: Introduction to Biology
Fall Semester, 2009
Some College
Table of Contents:
Reference Desk
Academic Search Complete
Agricola (National Agricultural Library)
Cells Alive
Epidemic: World of Infectious Disease
Gale Virtual Reference Library
Reference Desk
Get Help!
Contact the reference desk for course help.
Call us
(607)555-5555
Chat Reference:
IM: collegerefdesk
Academic Search Complete
Academic Search Premier contains indexing for over 8,200 publications, with full text for nearly 4,700 of those titles. PDF backfiles to 1975 or further are available for well over one hundred journals, and searchable cited references are provided for more than 1,000 titles.
Agricola (National Agricultural Library)
book catalog and journal article citation index for plant sciences, forestry, entomology, soil and water issues, etc.
Cells Alive
(Quill Graphics) -- [graphics can make downloading slow] stories of cell life; gallery of colorful images which can be enlarged
Epidemic: World of Infectious Disease
beautifully illustrated online exhibit on microbes and infectious disease, historical and contemporary outbreaks, text hyperlinked to glossary.
Gale Virtual Reference Library
Global information on women in over 150 countries in fields such as sociology, psychology, health, education, and human rights.
Page Coordinator: System Administrator admin@yourlibrary.edu
XML
Your Library Name
Last updated: August 25, 2008

Figure 13.13 Example CourseLib guide

a print style sheet to the header include file will allow you to remove the “link to print-friendly version” link from each page.

The current version of LibData makes use of a table layout. It is relatively easy to replace the table layout on the public pages with a CSS-driven layout by changing the courses.phtml, page.phtml, rqs.phtml, and subjects.phtml files. A simple layout would include a content div for the resources and a sidebar div for the table of contents, links to related guides, and the librarian or library location (Figure 13.15).

Libraries Using LibData

Academic libraries running LibData include:

- University of Minnesota Libraries (www.lib.umn.edu)
- St. Cloud State University Library (research.stcloudstate.edu)

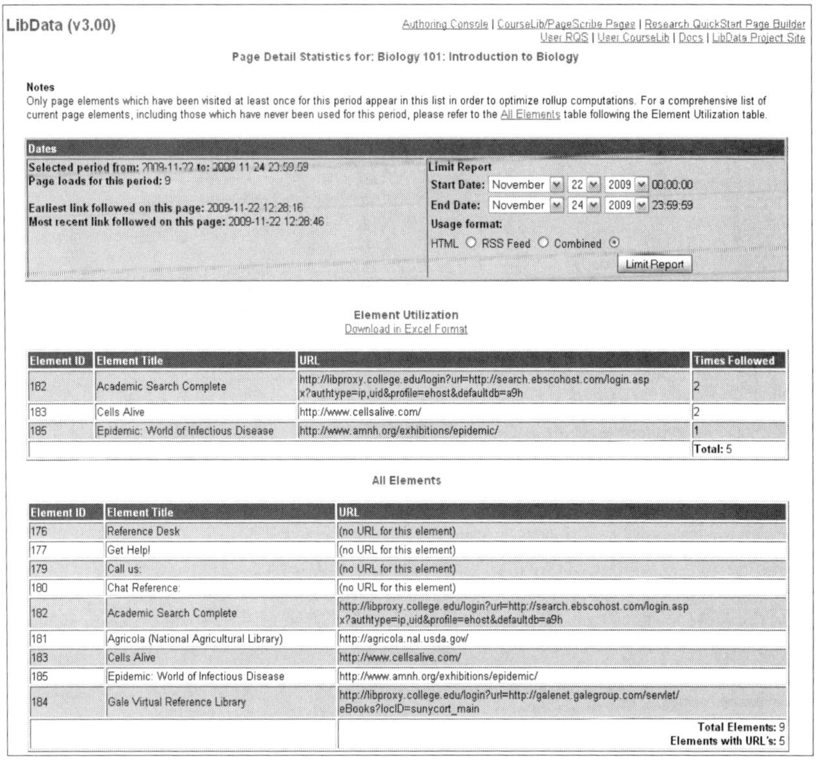

Figure 13.14 LibData statistics

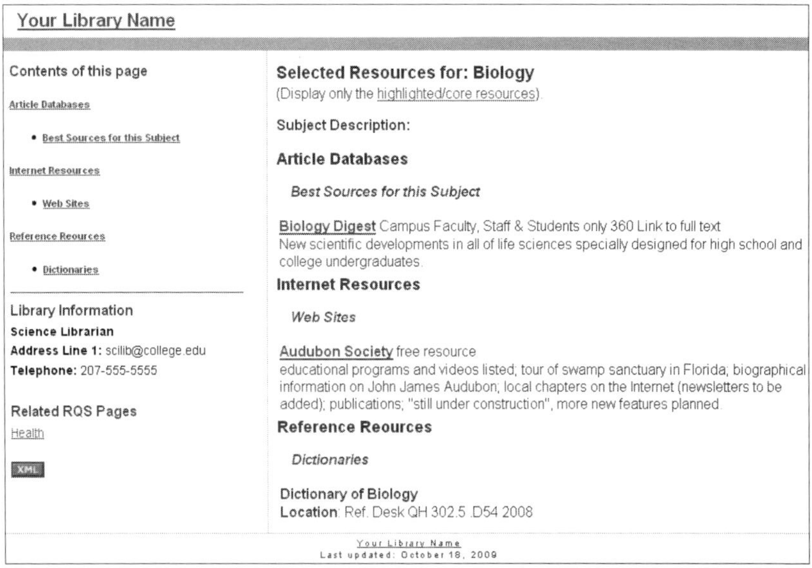

Figure 13.15 Customized layout

- Macalester College DeWitt Wallace Library (libdata.macalester.edu/disciplineguides.php)
- Middle Tennessee State University James E. Walker Library (library.mtsu.edu)
- Georgetown University Library (resources.library.georgetown.edu/libdata)
- University of Wisconsin–La Crosse Murphy Library (www.uwlax.edu/murphylibrary)

Conclusion

LibData is a subject and course guide tool that is also capable of functioning as a simple CMS. The ability to build custom styles or templates for each page adds to the flexibility of the system. One of the greatest strengths of LibData is the built-in resource tracking system, which tracks not only the number of clicks a resource is getting but also from which page on your library site users are accessing that resource.

Open source subject guide tools are a viable alternative to commercial products such as LibGuides. The two current open source subject guide tools covered here, LibData and SubjectsPlus, offer a degree of flexibility and customization that may not be possible in a commercial product. In addition, the open source options give you the ability to easily integrate the content, guides, and other features into your library website.

Out of the box, LibData offers the abilty to create subject guides and course guides and to serve as a mini CMS. The main strength of LibData lies in the functionality behind the system. Built into LibData is a system that tracks how often your links to resources are used. While this feature is not built into LibData, with a little SQL editing, you could create a report that shows you the top resources used on your library site. This same SQL query could then be used on your library homepage to show a dynamic listing of popular resources. The developers of LibData are working to increase the functionality behind LibData and have announced that the next version of LibData will include "REST/XML calls to nearly all of the public interfaces … [including] the Drupal CMS, the University enterprise portal, and probably course management tools which can then simply parse the XML with XSLT."

SubjectsPlus offers the ability to create subject, course, and topic guides. With a little creativity, SubjectsPlus can also be used as a CMS. The main strengths of SubjectsPlus are in its astounding flexibility in creating guides and in the extras, such as the database-driven staff listings, FAQs, and database listings. The latest version of SubjectsPlus, released at the end of September 2009, features content modules called pluslets, which can be moved around by the guide creators via Ajax. These pluslets can provide the capability of pulling in Delicious links, images from Flickr, and Twitter and blog posts.

All of the pages included with LibData have a table-driven layout, so when compared to SubjectsPlus, LibData looks out of date. However, changing the table layout of LibData to a CSS layout can allow you to take full advantage of the database-driven templates that you can create in LibData. When you combine the template system with the ability to use LibData as a CMS, you have the ability to create webpages that have differing layouts and color schemes.

Overall, both these subject guide tools are extremely capable. Your choice comes down to whether your needs are better served by the data tracking and CMS built into LibData or the very flexible, Web 2.0 friendly guides created by SubjectsPlus.

Part V

Resource Discovery Tools

CHAPTER 14

Federated Search Tools

Federated search tools are designed to bring together content from disperse silos of data. Each individual silo of data sends information back to the federated search tool, which ranks, de-duplicates, and organizes the results into a single result list. The goal of these tools is to simplify searching for users by allowing them to search several key resources simultaneously. Typically, federated search tools need some way to programmatically interact with the silo of data, and for library databases, this has typically been the Z39.50 search protocol. However, since not all resources can be searched via this protocol, some federated search tools use screen scraping to obtain data from particular resources. One limitation of federated search technologies is that the speed at which they can return a complete result set is decreased as the number of sources of data is increased.

Open source federated search tools have several advantages over proprietary federated search tools. The software is free of cost, the interfaces are highly customizable, and libraries have the ability to participate in the development process. In addition, some open source federated search tools have built-in application programming interfaces (APIs) and return search results relatively quickly as compared to their commercial competitors. However, these tools also require an investment of staff time and effort in order to customize and configure them successfully.

The tools outlined here and in the next chapter are more complex to set up and configure than the tools discussed earlier in this book. In order to properly test and configure federated search tools, it is necessary to configure search targets that are specific to each individual library. Similarly, the resource discovery tools discussed in Chapter 15 require library-specific configuration in order to harvest records from a local library catalog. Because of the level of complexity and the specific configurations required, we are not providing installation instructions for these tools. Consult each project's website for the specific installation and configuration instructions you will need to implement the tools in your institution.

dbWiz

dbWiz (dbwiz.lib.sfu.ca/dbwiz) is a federated search tool developed by the Simon Fraser University (SFU) Library in Canada and requires a variety of technologies, including Apache, Perl, and MySQL. The project was originally funded by the following nine partner universities and colleges:

- Concordia University College
- Malaspina University College [now Vancouver Island University]
- Royal Roads University
- Simon Fraser University
- University College of the Fraser Valley
- University of Northern British Columbia
- University of Regina
- University of Victoria
- University of Winnipeg

dbWiz is part of a larger suite of tools called reSearcher (researcher.sfu.ca), which SFU provides for managing electronic resources. It works with SFU's GODOT OpenURL resolver (researcher.sfu.ca/godot) and can be run either separately or in conjunction with the other components of the reSearcher suite.

In the spring of 2010, Simon Frasier discontinued development of dbWiz. However, the source code is still available for download, and another institution or the community could choose to continue development of the application.

In order to connect and search the widest possible number of databases, dbWiz uses search plugins, which are small Perl modules that connect to databases. Since the inception of the project, more than 200 search plugins have been written for the project, and these are distributed as part of the standard dbWiz download. Because of the changing nature of many proprietary resources, the code for searching a particular resource often breaks. In this scenario, using a modular approach for search plugins has two advantages. First, changes to a single resource don't break the entire search tool. Second, because the plugins are compartmentalized, it makes them easier to debug and fix.

In order to allow searching across multiple resources, only a limited number of indexes are searchable. Currently, dbWiz can be searched by keyword, author, title, and subject. Resources within dbWiz can be searched via predefined, typically subject-oriented categories of resources, such as Anthropology. Users can also select individual resources to search, creating their own custom suite of resources to be queried. The dbWiz search box can be embedded in a webpage (Figure 14.1), which allows the library to place important library resources where the users are; be that a subject guide on the library website or a course page within a campus learning management system.

A significant difference between dbWiz and the other two federated search tools discussed in this chapter is that dbWiz requires users to be authenticated prior to viewing search results, while both Pazpar2 and LibraryFind show all users the results list and only require authentication for viewing abstracts or full text.

In addition to having the flexibility to build custom sets of resources for library users, libraries using dbWiz can heavily customize the results screen. This includes customizing the number of records returned and their sort order. A result screen can be

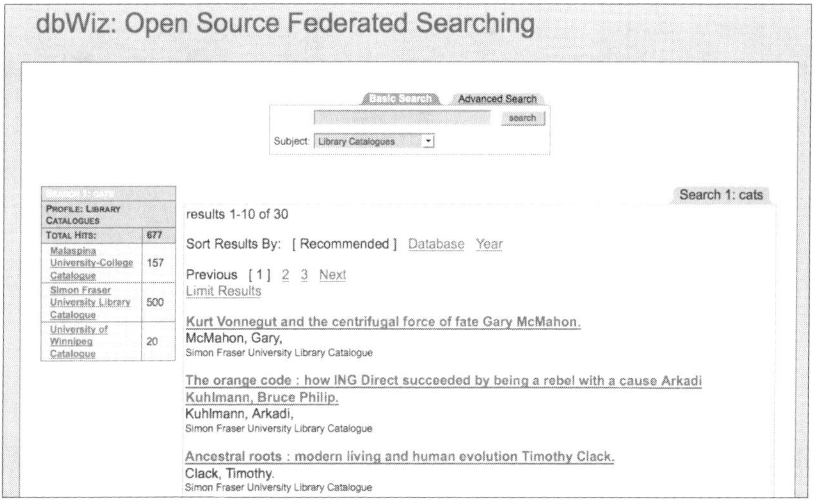

Figure 14.1 dbWiz demo site

extremely simple or highly detailed. However, the results display typically includes item title, author, date, journal title, and a link to the resources if available.

Only two of the original project partners still use dbWiz, but other libraries throughout the world have implemented the software. The software continues to be maintained but active development is limited.

Pazpar2

Pazpar2 (www.indexdata.com/pazpar2) is an open source federated search service developed by Index Data. Unlike dbWiz or LibraryFind, Pazpar2 is primarily a middleware web service and lacks a web-based administrative interface for configuring resources to search. Instead it can be accessed via a REST-like interface. The default installation package comes with an extremely simple search interface that libraries can implement out of the box (Figure 14.2).

This basic JavaScript-based interface can be customized to meet the needs of the library. Colors, fonts, and logos can easily be changed by editing the basic interface's style sheet or main HTML file. Further customization can be made by editing the JavaScript file that drives the interface. For assistance in creating customizations, a library can hire Index Data to develop custom code. OPLIN (Ohio Public Library

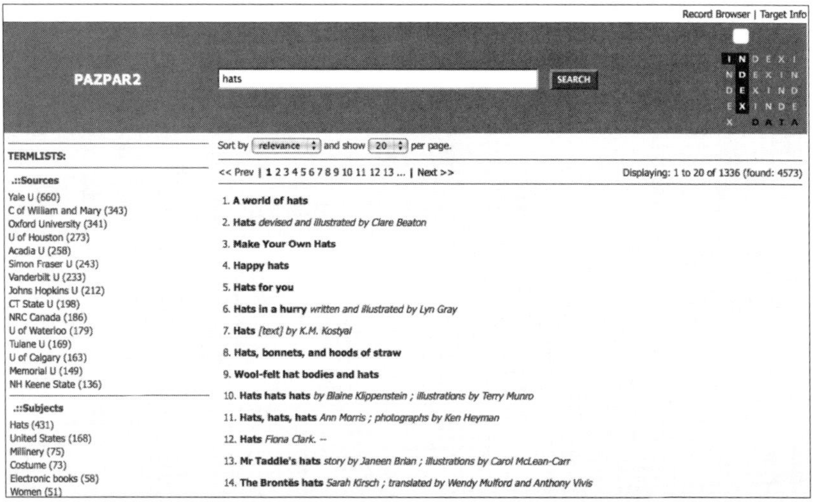

Figure 14.2 Basic Pazpar2 interface

Information Network) in Ohio used a combination of these techniques for its custom implementation of Pazpar2, which supports the Ohio Web Library (www.ohioweblibrary.org). While most of the customizations, including the searching bar, were created by OPLIN staff, Index Data was hired to complete some of the more complex additional features (Figure 14.3).

The success of the Ohio Web Library project depends on the fact that Pazpar2 is at its heart a web service, which can be accessed via any number of programming languages and applications. Because of this structure, OPLIN is able to use the tool in very flexible ways. This includes creating a Facebook application that allows users to access a search box for the Ohio Web Library from within Facebook.

Another option for libraries that don't want to customize the out-of-the-box JavaScript interface is to use Pazpar2 to develop their own interface in the programming language of their choice. This alternative requires significant development time, so, for libraries daunted by this path, Index Data also offers, on a subscription basis, MasterKey (mk2.indexdata.com), a hosted federated search tool, fully

Figure 14.3 Ohio Web Library

customized and configured. (MasterKey is also available from CARE Affiliates or LibLime.) MasterKey is a full-featured, federated search tool, which is built on the basic Pazpar2 software. It includes a web-based interface for configuring search targets, and Index Data is actively working to improve Pazar2 as a tool.

LibraryFind

LibraryFind (libraryfind.org) is a federated search tool based on MySQL and Ruby on Rails, developed by Oregon State University Libraries. The goal of the project was to provide library users with a simple interface for finding and retrieving library resources. To accomplish this goal, the interface is designed to deliver content to users within two clicks. Users search and then are able to immediately click on links to full text if they exist. The LibraryFind project also aimed to improve the speed of federated searching as much as possible and did so using two approaches. First, LibraryFind adds the ability for records to be harvested locally via OAI-PMH. Second, LibraryFind employs a three-tiered caching mechanism, which allows for searches and search results to be cached for future use. The software was initially released in January 2007, and since that time has undergone six revisions, which have improved the software and added new features and functionality.

One of the strengths of LibraryFind is that it can search a source using a variety of protocols, including Z39.50, SRU, Open Archives Initiative (OAI), and OpenSearch. In addition, LibraryFind can be extended to search other resources via a custom search connector. Currently four custom search connectors exist: WorldCat Search API, EBSCOhost XML Gateway, Flickr, and Yahoo!. LibraryFind comes with a built-in OpenURL resolver, which can be configured with your library's holdings information. You can enter the necessary information via the LibraryFind Administrative interface. But in order to save libraries time and avoid the need to manually input holdings information and coverage, LibraryFind also provides a coverage load script (components/coverage_load.rb), which can be used to load holdings data into the LibraryFind OpenURL resolver knowledge base via a spreadsheet. Further information on loading coverage information can be found on the LibraryFind Documentation website (trac.library.oregonstate.edu/projects/libraryfind/wiki/Coverage LoadingIn0.7).

If you have an existing OpenURL resolver with an API, LibraryFind has the capability to query the API and determine whether full text is available. Currently it can query either the SFX or Serials Solutions OpenURL resolvers. Using information from either the built-in OpenURL resolver or a resolver API, LibraryFind then can create a link directly to that full-text object, if one exists. The standard interface for LibraryFind also incorporates book covers and links to Google Book previews (Figure 14.4).

Another strength of LibraryFind is that it allows libraries to create customized Collection Groups of resources for users to search. The University of Houston Libraries uses this functionality extensively to group together resources within a particular subject and provide a simple federated search for that subject area (Figure 14.5).

LibraryFind also includes a mobile style sheet, which enables users on a variety of mobile devices, including iPhones, Android phones, and other smart phones, to access the LibraryFind search tool. The mobile interface greatly simplifies the design of the LibraryFind interface to make it friendly for mobile users (Figure 14.6).

Another advantage of LibraryFind is that, unlike many federated search tools, LibraryFind has a built-in API, which allows developers to create their own interface or use LibraryFind search results in unique ways. The API can be accessed via SOAP or a REST-like JSON

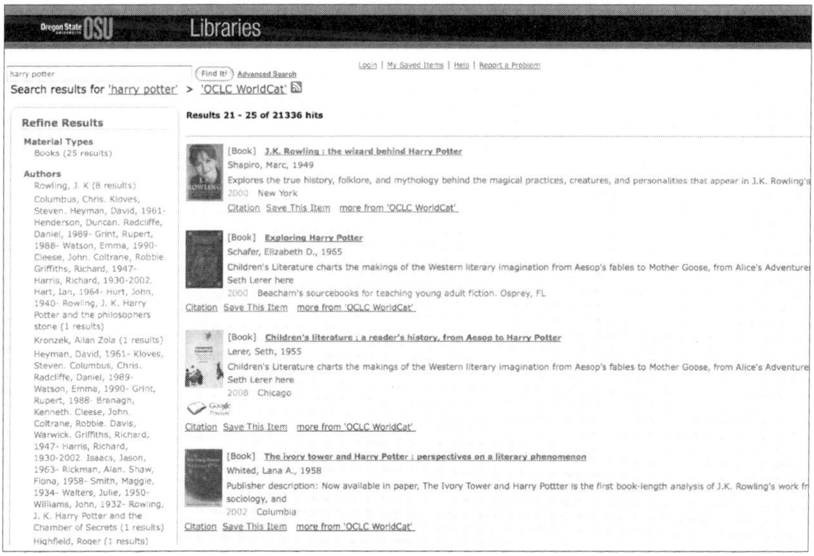

Figure 14.4 LibraryFind search results

Figure 14.5 Subject-oriented collections in LibraryFind

Figure 14.6 LibraryFind mobile interface

interface. Oregon State University Libraries uses the LibraryFind API to incorporate content from LibraryFind into their subject guides created in Library a la Carte.

With nearly all these tools the biggest difficulty is not the installation but rather the configuration of search targets, or "connectors." This means collecting connection information (host, username, and password) from vendors, as well as mapping metadata gathered from each database to fields used by the tool. Getting this information correct can be a time-consuming process and requires a partnership between metadata and technical staff, since both skill sets are necessary. While none of these tools has completely overcome this problem, each has developed solutions for making search target configuration easier. Both dbWiz and LibraryFind provide documentation on how targets for the major database vendors should be configured. Index Data has taken a slightly different route, providing a tutorial on Z39.50, the primary standard used to access library database information. This information is extremely useful when configuring new targets. The developers of LibraryFind are examining still other ways to overcome this challenge. An upcoming release of the LibraryFind software will offer a central repository of target information, which libraries can draw on to create and customize their own targets. This is a huge step forward, and perhaps will remove some of the current barriers to adoption of open source federated search tools.

References

Bisson, C. 2007. Building open source. *Library Technology Reports* 43 (3): 36–39. Library, Information Science & Technology Abstracts, EBSCOhost (accessed November 10, 2009).

Jung, S, J. L. Herlocker, J. Webster, M. Mellinger, and J. Frumkin. 2008. LibraryFind: System design and usability testing of academic metasearch system. *Journal of the American Society for Information Science & Technology* 59 (3): 375–389. Library, Information Science & Technology Abstracts, EBSCOhost (accessed November 10, 2009).

Mah, C., and K. Stranack. 2005. dbWiz: Open source federated searching for academic libraries. *Library Hi Tech* 23 (4): 490–503. Library, Information Science & Technology Abstracts, EBSCOhost (accessed November 10, 2009).

Reese, T. LibraryFind: 2009. The development of a shared library platform at Oregon State University Libraries. *OLA Quarterly* 15 (1): 17–19. Library, Information Science & Technology Abstracts, EBSCOhost (accessed November 10, 2009).

## CHAPTER 15

NextGen Catalogs

Next generation, or "NextGen," catalogs are a set of tools that seek to solve several problems with library user interfaces. The first of these is the siloization of library resources: Library collections exist in separate system silos—the library catalog, article databases, and digital library tools. This structure creates significant problems for library users, who are accustomed to Google-like interfaces that allow them to search across many sets of resources. A second issue is the inability of library systems to support Web 2.0 features and socially created content. Third, data created by library catalogers needs to be leveraged and highlighted in order to facilitate better user access to resources via faceted search. In order to meet these needs, several NextGen catalog tools have been developed.

Scriblio

Scriblio (about.scriblio.net) is a NextGen catalog based on the WordPress blogging platform. The project, originally known as WPopac, was begun at Plymouth State University in 2005 by Casey Bisson. Bisson's basic idea was to create a blog post for every record in the library catalog. The blog posts would be made up of the information in the MARC record, enhanced with additional information—book covers, reviews, and ratings—that would come from external sources such as Amazon, Syndetics, and LibraryThing. The developers chose to use WordPress as the underpinnings for the project because WordPress comes with some key Web 2.0 features built-in: permalinks, comments, and trackbacks. Originally, the software was a customization of WordPress comprised of three major components: a data importer, a plugin, and the WordPress baseline code with some modifications.

These modifications of the base WordPress code made WPopac difficult for others to install and implement. However, in 2007,

WPopac became Scriblio. The software was officially released as open source and the code broken up into a series of WordPress plugins that can be easily installed and configured. Currently Scriblio is comprised of the bSuite plugin (wordpress.org/extend/plugins/bsuite) and the Scriblio plugin (wordpress.org/extend/plugins/scriblio). Libraries can also download a number of plugins that extend Scriblio further (wordpress.org/extend/plugins/search.php?q=scriblio). Many of these plugins are designed to harvest records or to interact with a specific library system. Plugins are currently available that allow records to be harvested from Innovative Interfaces, Horizon, Flickr, and MARC records.

Scriblio has a number of features that make it an improvement over standard library catalog interfaces. The most important of these is the fact that library users can add comments to records. Until recently, this feature was not available in any library catalog. Scriblio also puts all the relevant information about an object onto a single screen, including: title, author, description and reviews, availability, subject, and related objects. Items in Scriblio have tags, faceted browsing, book jackets, and links to other resources (Figure 15.1).

Another distinct advantage of Scriblio is that it contains a built-in RSS feed. This means that a library user can subscribe to the feed and

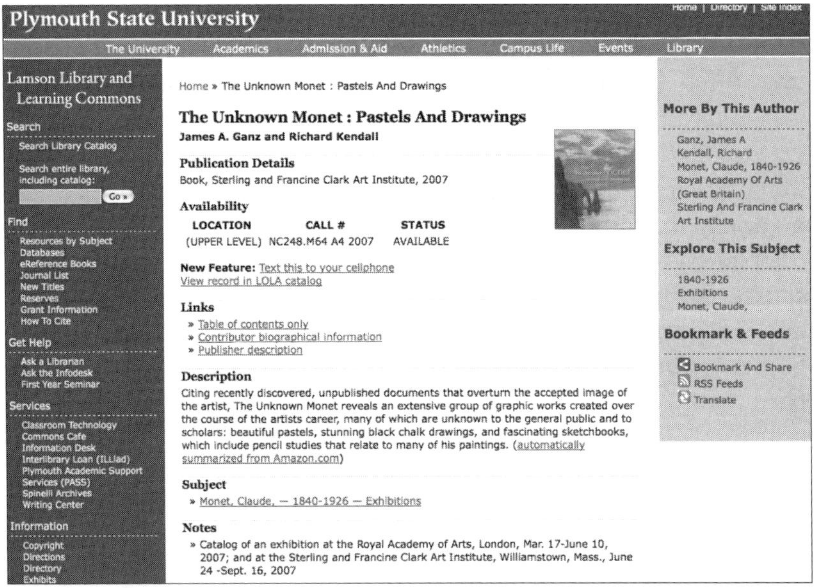

Figure 15.1 Plymouth State University Library Scriblio implementation

see all new items the library has acquired, along with news and other important information. Finally, every item within Scriblio has a persistent URL and can be indexed by web search engines. This makes library resources and collections much more findable.

As a tool, Scriblio has evolved a great deal, from catalog as a blog to a full-featured content management system capable of managing many different kinds of content including physical resources and digital objects such as photos. A terrific example of digital materials organized in Scriblio is Beyond Brown Paper, an archive of photos from the Brown Manufacturing Company in northern New Hampshire (beyondbrownpaper.plymouth.edu). This site contains historical photographs that date from the late-19th century through the mid-1960s. What is fabulous about putting digital collections in a blog-like system is that library users can comment on these collections. In the case of this collection, many users have commented on the photographs and provided important historical details, such as information about the location or people shown in the photo. This project leverages the power of the user-contributed information to enhance metadata about digital objects, a feature most digital library systems do not currently offer (Figure 15.2).

Scriblio has been downloaded more than 1,500 times and is currently used in several public and academic libraries. In addition to powering the Plymouth State University Library website (library.plymouth.edu), Scriblio also powers the Collingswood (NJ) Public Library website (collingswoodlib.org) and the Cook Memorial Library (Tamworth, NH) website (www.tamworthlibrary.org). Like the Plymouth State University Library website, the Cook Memorial Library website features tags and book jackets. Additionally, the library uses Scriblio to provide users with information about new books and new videos in an easily browseable format (Figure 15.3).

Colby-Sawyer College (archives.colby-sawyer.edu) has chosen to catalog and display its digital materials within Scriblio. The site contains photographs, historical diaries, correspondence, yearbooks, and other historical records. The project has leveraged Scriblio in several unique ways. The homepage contains an excellent gallery of exhibit thumbnails (Figure 15.4).

Additionally, each collection has a landing page that allows users to browse by facets such as Subject and Time and Place and also displays thumbnails of images within the collection. Mousing over an image brings up its basic metadata, which allows users to easily scan objects.

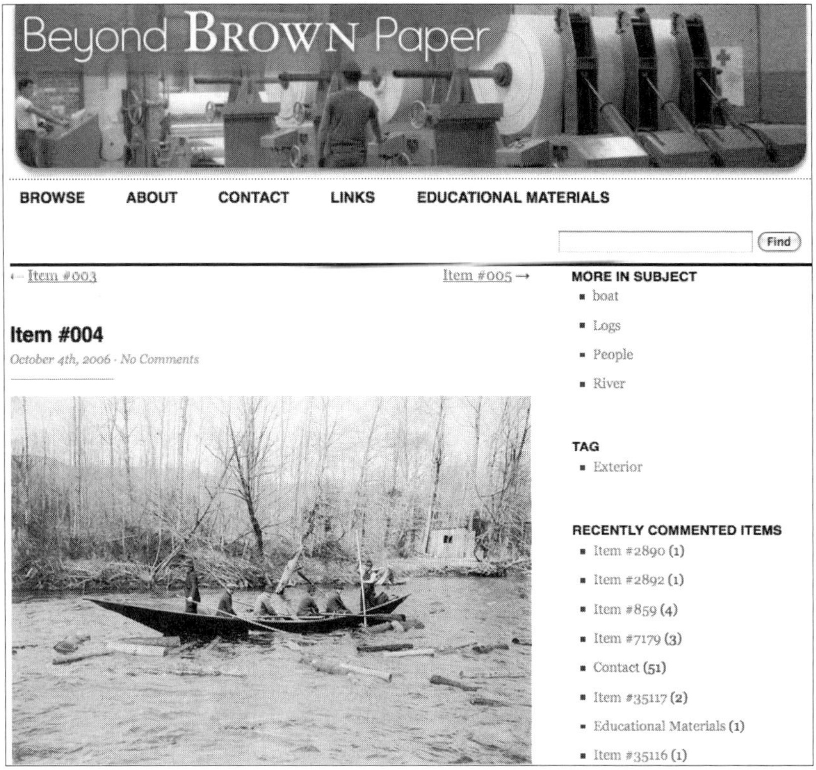
Beyond BROWN Paper
BROWSE
ABOUT
CONTACT
LINKS
EDUCATIONAL MATERIALS
Find
← Item #003
Item #005 →
Item #004
October 4th, 2006 · No Comments
MORE IN SUBJECT
boat
Logs
People
River
TAG
Exterior
RECENTLY COMMENTED ITEMS
Item #2890 (1)
Item #2892 (1)
Item #859 (4)
Item #7179 (3)
Contact (51)
Item #35117 (2)
Educational Materials (1)
Item #35116 (1)

Figure 15.2 Beyond Brown Paper website

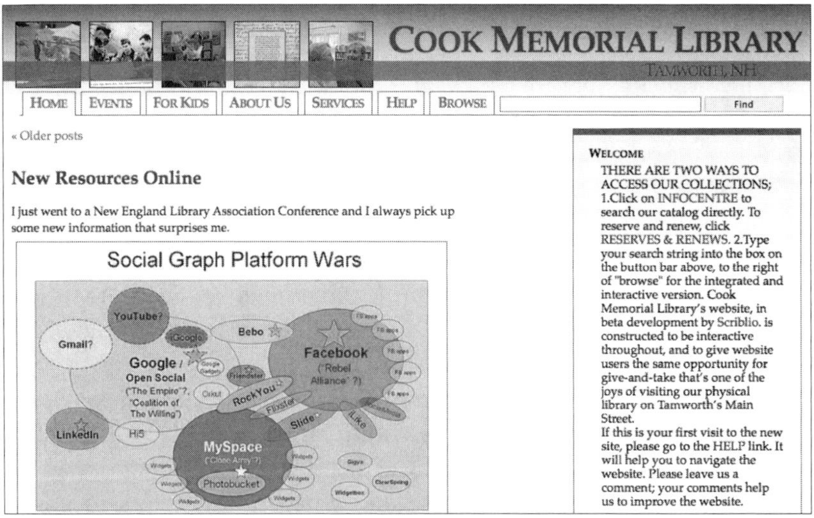
COOK MEMORIAL LIBRARY
TAMWORTH, NH
HOME
EVENTS
FOR KIDS
ABOUT US
SERVICES
HELP
BROWSE
Find
« Older posts
New Resources Online
I just went to a New England Library Association Conference and I always pick up some new information that surprises me.
Social Graph Platform Wars
YouTube?
Gmail?
Google / Open Social
Bebo
Facebook
LinkedIn
Hi5
MySpace
Photobucket
RockYou
Slide
WELCOME
THERE ARE TWO WAYS TO ACCESS OUR COLLECTIONS; 1.Click on INFOCENTRE to search our catalog directly. To reserve and renew, click RESERVES & RENEWS. 2.Type your search string into the box on the button bar above, to the right of "browse" for the integrated and interactive version. Cook Memorial Library's website, in beta development by Scriblio. is constructed to be interactive throughout, and to give website users the same opportunity for give-and-take that's one of the joys of visiting our physical library on Tamworth's Main Street.
If this is your first visit to the new site, please go to the HELP link. It will help you to navigate the website. Please leave us a comment; your comments help us to improve the website.

Figure 15.3 Cook Memorial Library website powered by Scriblio

Home About Browse Exhibits
Haystack
Books, Movies, etc.
Search »
Featured Exhibits
«
»
Explore
Pillsbury Family Papers
James Cleveland Papers
Patience Cleveland Papers
Colby-Sawyer Photo Collection
Letters from Susan B. Anthony and Ralph Waldo Emerson
Explore the 19th and 20th centuries in photographs, diaries, and correspondence
Student Newspapers (exit Haystack to Digital Newspaper Database)
About
Haystack is a portal to digital materials available at Colby-Sawyer College. These materials include photographs, historical diaries, correspondence, yearbooks, and other historical records. The site is part of the Cleveland Colby Colgate Archives and helps to support the Susan C. Cleveland Library/Learning Center in its efforts to stimulate teaching and learning by providing access to research materials relating to the study of New Hampshire and the history of Colby- Sawyer College.
Haystack is funded through a generous donation from the Cleveland family. The Cleveland family has been pivotal in the ongoing work in the Cleveland Colby Colgate Archives and encouraging the college to expand opportunities for use of the collection. The website is a result of our shared desire to increase access to the collection. Funds provided by the Cleveland Archives allowed Colby-Sawyer College to purchase some of the hardware and software needed to create and maintain Haystack. The college would like to express its gratitude for the continued support of the Cleveland family.

Figure 15.4 Colby-Sawyer College Haystack

SOPAC

SOPAC, the social OPAC, was originally created by Ann Arbor (MI) District Library (AADL) in 2007 to improve its users' library experience by integrating catalog content seamlessly with the library website. To accomplish this, John Blyberg created a Drupal module that used cURL to screenscrape data from AADL's Innovative Interfaces catalog and highly customize the data so users were able to tag, rate, and comment on records. However, since this functionality relied on screenscraping it was extremely complex and subject to failure with each Innovative Interfaces upgrade. Another issue AADL encountered was a lack of enough of a critical mass of user-generated metadata to be meaningful. Lastly, although Blyberg released the initial SOPAC code, it was customized to AADL's setup and not meant to work out of the box for other libraries.

These issues prompted Blyberg (now working at Darien [CT] Library) to develop a complete rewrite of SOPAC for version 6.0 of Drupal (SOPAC 2.0). SOPAC 2.0 was written to be a highly configurable, distributable package with the potential to work with any integrated library system (ILS), so it could be implemented and used by any other library. To accomplish this goal, two pieces of SOPAC 2.0, Locum and Insurge, were separated from Drupal and made into stand-alone components that collect and store data, which is manipulated and presented by the Drupal modules to which they are connected.

Locum is responsible for ingesting and indexing bibliographic records for SOPAC, so it requires an ILS-specific connector. Currently, there are three connectors available: one for Innovative Interfaces Millennium 2006, another for SirsiDynix Unicorn, and a third that was recently developed for Koha. Insurge stores user-created tags, ratings, and reviews. Separating these two components from the Drupal module makes it easier for libraries to develop new connectors for different ILSs and to share user-created metadata across libraries. In addition, Locum and Insurge can be used by other applications besides the SOPAC Drupal module.

Another goal of SOPAC 2.0 was to make individual library customization easier. SOPAC does this by taking advantage of the Drupal architecture and using templates. This allows libraries to customize the look and feel of SOPAC for their individual library in a standardized fashion. So, for example, if you wanted to customize the display of the search results screen to change how each result displays, you could simply copy the sopac-results-hitlist.tpl.php file to your Drupal theme directory and make the necessary changes. SOPAC also makes available theme functions, which allow the basic pieces of SOPAC—search form, side blocks, and faceted search browser—to be embedded throughout the Drupal site.

Although the underpinnings of SOPAC 2.0 are different, the seamless integration of the library catalog and website, as well as the NextGen catalog features such as facets, tags, book covers, reviews, and ratings, are still integral (Figure 15.5).

Other important aspects of the SOPAC system include:

- Saved searches
- Integrated renewals, holds placement, and fine payment
- Ability to customize the user experience via the administrative control panel
- Tag clouds

SOPAC 2.0 has also added several new features, such as making user-generated content searchable and enabling libraries to create custom functionality by developing a Drupal submodule. All of these enhancements create a richer experience for library users.

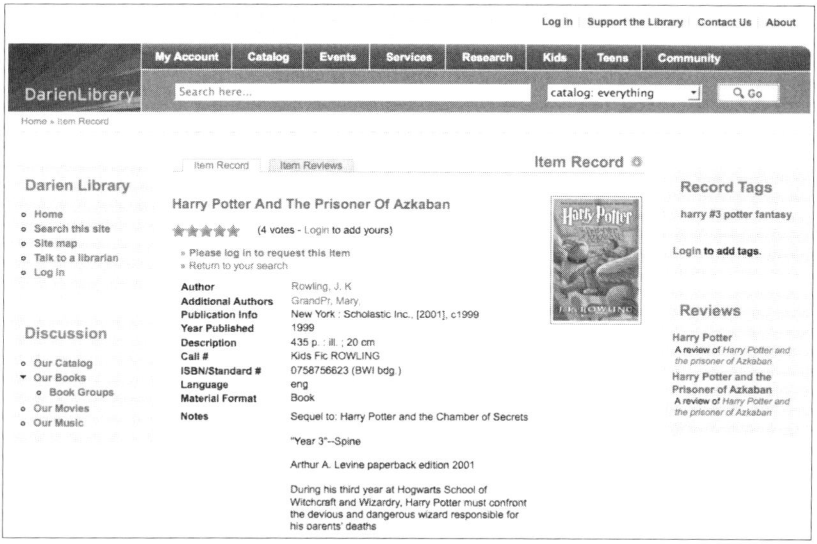

Figure 15.5 Darien Library website

Adoption of and support for SOPAC has grown since version 2.0 was released in September 2008. YourLibrarySite (part of CraftySpace), a company that develops and supports Drupal library websites, assists libraries with implementing SOPAC. In addition to Darien Library, Palos Verdes Library District and the Ann Arbor District Library have already implemented SOPAC (Figure 15.6).

YourLibrarySite is also working with Newport Beach (CA) Public Library (www.newport-beach.ca.us/nbpl) and SAILS (sailsinc.org) to implement SOPAC. SOPAC is also being tested by Allen County Public Library (www.acpl.lib.in.us) in Indiana and BibLibre (www.biblibre.com), a Koha and Drupal development and support vendor. Development on the next version of SOPAC is currently underway, with features and enhancements potentially including: multibranch support, incorporation of third-party data into the discovery index (Syndetics, Amazon, etc.), the ability to limit searches to available items, SMS notifications, and RSS support. Version 2.1 was rolled out in March 2010.

VuFind

The VuFind (vufind.org) project began at Villanova University in 2006 as the result of a desire to create a user interface that would better

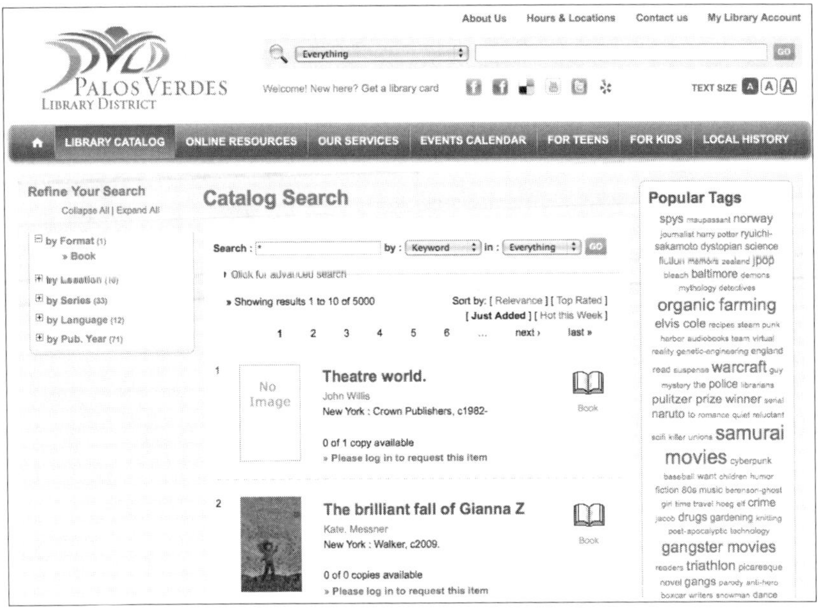

Figure 15.6 Palos Verdes Library District SOPAC

meet users' expectations and would bridge the gaps between the disparate systems of the library catalog, website, and digital repository. Villanova's interest was initially sparked by the deployment of North Carolina State University's Endeca-based catalog project. Upon investigation, however, the Endeca approach proved to be extremely costly. In response, Andrew Nagy, the lead developer at Villanova at the time, suggested an alternative approach: build a NextGen catalog with many features similar to the Endeca-powered catalog using open source technologies. Nagy showed an initial pre-release prototype at the Code4Lib conference in February 2007, which sparked the interest of many library developers. When the project was released as VuFind in July 2007, it received positive reviews, and many libraries began to download the software.

VuFind uses Solr for indexing but has a PHP-driven user interface. Solr, a project of the Apache Foundation, is an open source indexing and searching tool that is written in Java and based on the Lucene search library. Solr's strengths are its powerful full-text search capabilities; the ease of use of its APIs, which facilitate access via XML, JSON, and several other programming languages; its faceted search capabilities; and its scalability. In recent years, Solr has gained a significant following in libraries and is being used for a variety of projects including both Blacklight and VuFind.

Since VuFind relies on local integrated library systems for real-time information such as status, it is necessary to develop what the project called "drivers" for each ILS. Initially, Villanova created a driver for Voyager, its library's ILS. Over time other libraries have begun contributing drivers for various other ILSs. Currently VuFind comes with drivers for Aleph, Evergreen, Horizon (SirsiDynix), Innovative, Koha, Unicorn (SirsiDynix), Virtua (VTLS), and Voyager. Functionality varies across these drivers, and some are more full-featured than others. Some libraries have also customized the driver code locally to add additional functionality; these customizations need to be re-integrated into the main VuFind codebase.

One of the key features of VuFind is that it enhances existing library catalog records with content from other sources, including covers, reviews, and ratings from Amazon, and information from Open Library. Tables of contents and summaries are also provided (Figure 15.7), and users can see similar items. Another key feature is faceted searching, which allows users to limit search results in a browsable way (Figure 15.8).

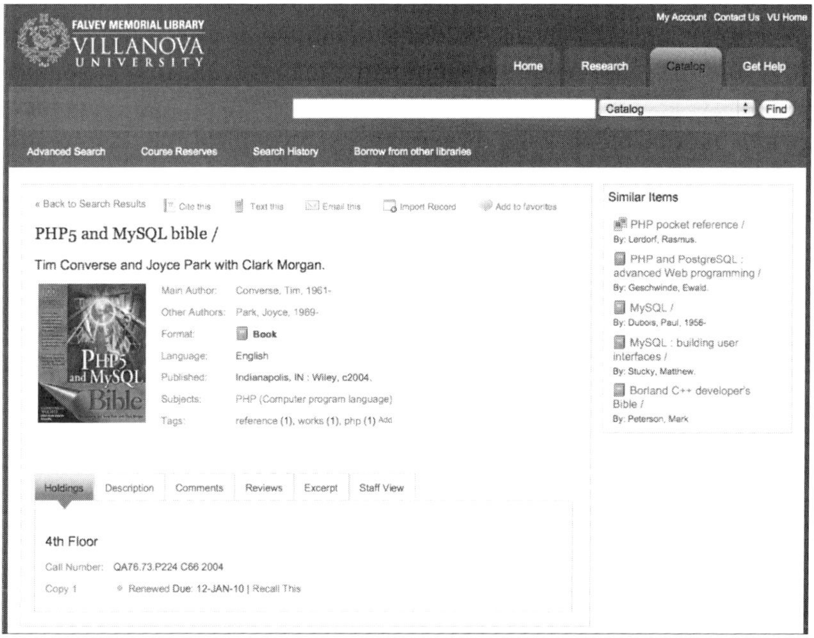

Figure 15.7 VuFind item screen

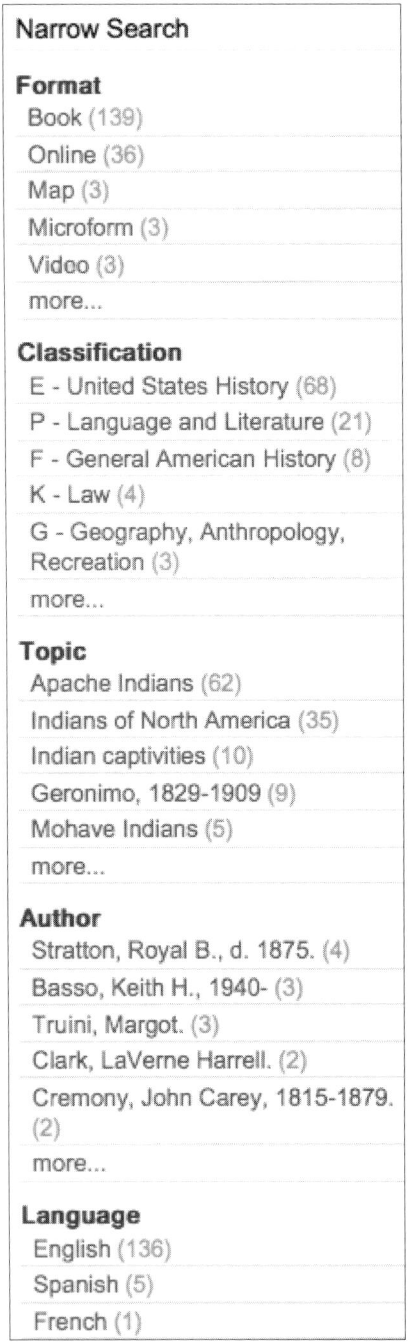

Figure 15.8 VuFind facets

VuFind incorporates Web 2.0 features, allowing users to comment on and tag materials. Users can also text a record to their cell phone, email a record to themselves, see APA or MLA citations format for a particular record, or export a record to a citation tool. Currently VuFind can export records to EndNote, RefWorks, or Zotero (Figure 15.9). In addition, users can email a set of search results to themselves or subscribe to results of a particular search as an RSS feed (Figure 15.10).

Currently VuFind has been implemented at libraries of several colleges and universities, including the Minnesota State Colleges and Universities, Colorado State University, Georgia Tech, University of Southern Queensland, Yale University (beta), University of Michigan, and Wake Forest University. Several other libraries are experimenting with the software. For a complete list of libraries using VuFind, visit the VuFind wiki (www.vufind.org/wiki/installation_status).

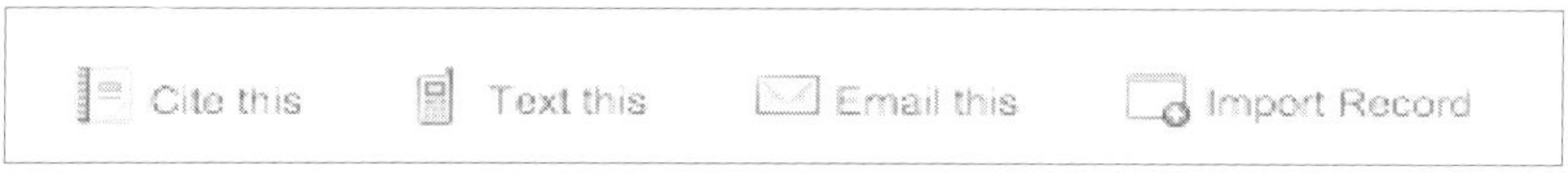

Figure 15.9 VuFind citation export

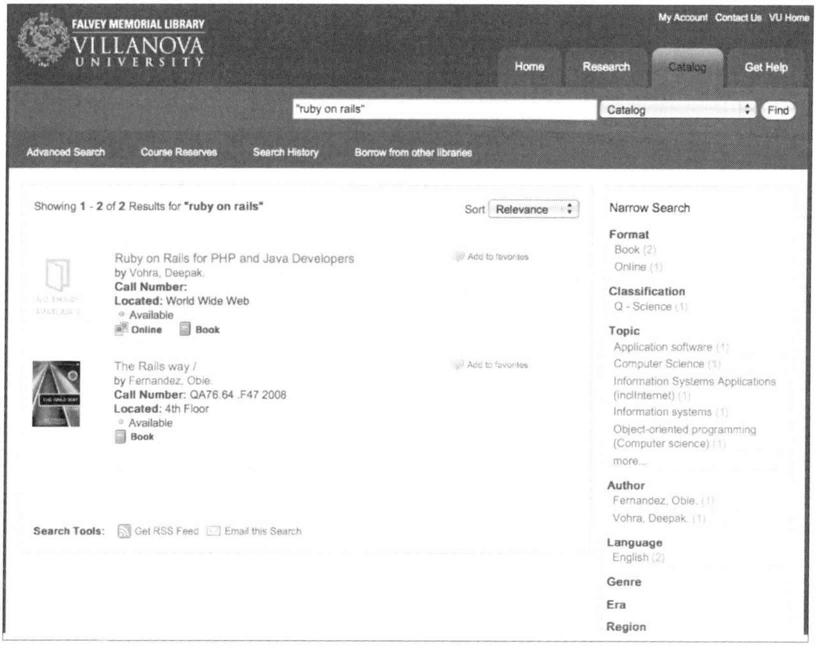

Figure 15.10 VuFind search results with RSS feed

The Minnesota State Colleges and Universities Libraries (libraries.project.mnscu.edu) has a union catalog of materials from 32 member libraries. One of its unique features is an Availability facet, which allows users to see only available materials (Figure 15.11).

Colorado State University Libraries' (lib.colostate.edu) implementation of VuFind features nested facets, which allow users to limit to the Digital Repository or to a specific collection within that repository (Figure 15.12).

Georgia Tech Library's (www.library.gatech.edu) VuFind catalog uses a Call Number facet to group items into broad subject areas based on the Library of Congress call number (Figure 15.13). The individual item display provides links to allow users also to check the local consortium's catalog, WorldCat, or Amazon for an item (Figure 15.14).

University of Southern Queensland Library's (libcat.usq.edu.au) VuFind interface moves the subject facets from the side navigation to

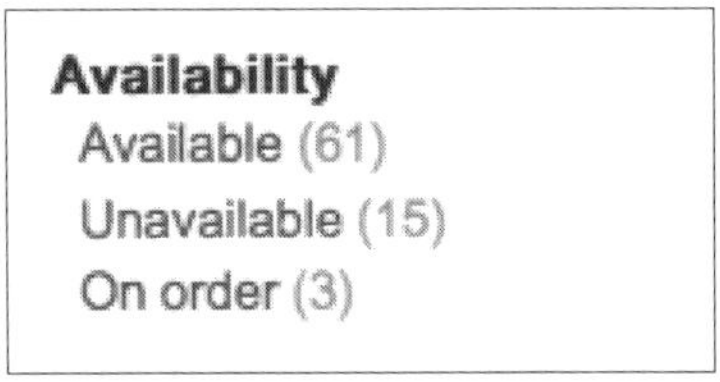

Figure 15.11 Minnesota State Colleges and Universities Libraries' Availability facet

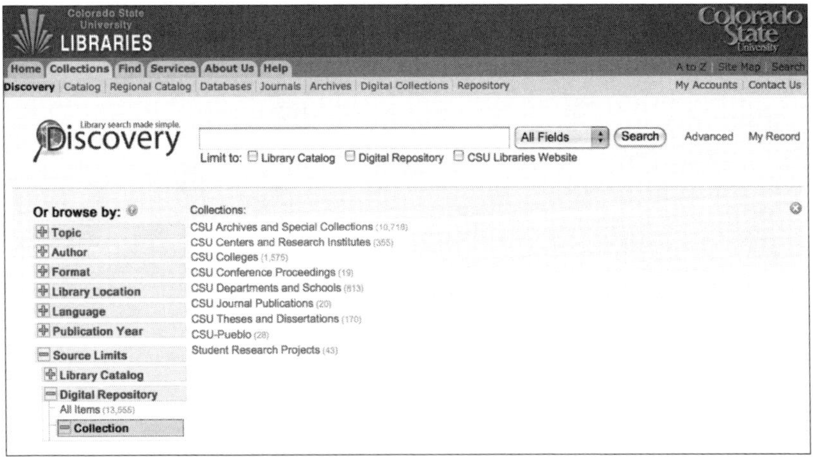

Figure 15.12 Limiting by source/collection on Colorado State University Libraries website

Figure 15.13 Georgia Tech Library's Call Number facet

Figure 15.14 Georgia Tech Library's links to additional information

the top of the results screen and relabels them as Suggested Topics (Figure 15.15). Yale University Library's (www.library.yale.edu) beta implementation of VuFind includes unique author pages, which incorporate information from Wikipedia (Figure 15.16).

These examples illustrate VuFind's flexibility. Each library is able to customize its own interface to incorporate new functionality, features, and additional content. Because of this, the VuFind user community continues to grow.

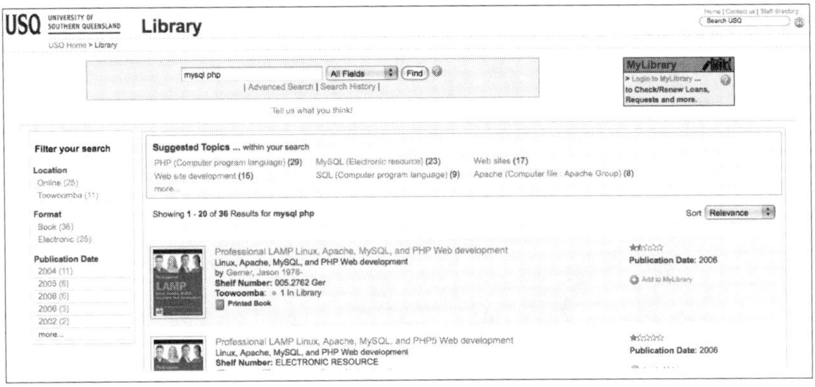

Figure 15.15 University of Southern Queensland Library VuFind implementation

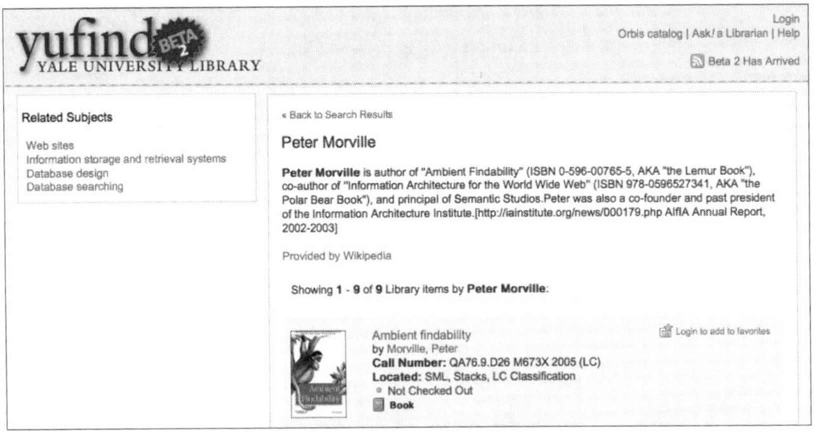

Figure 15.16 Yale University Library Wikipedia information in VuFind

Blacklight

The Blacklight project (projectblacklight.org) began at the University of Virginia (UVA) in 2006. Like many NextGen catalog projects, Blacklight sought to keep pace with the rapid changes in the web environment by decoupling the ILS from its public interface. In addition, the project wanted to bring content in the library catalog and digital objects together in a Fedora repository. Fortunately, another project that tackled some of these issues was already underway at UVA. Collex (www.collex.org), which was built to power the NINES project (www.nines.org), brings together metadata and full text from disparate sources, indexes it, and displays it in a single interface using Solr and Ruby on Rails. In the case of NINES, the content comprises a variety of materials related to the 19th century. Currently, NINES aggregates more than 400,000 digital objects from more than 60 sites (Figure 15.17).

Because Collex was already performing some of the functions that UVA wanted to incorporate, Blacklight developers were able to use that software as a starting point for their project design. Both projects use Solr for indexing and have a user interface developed in Ruby on Rails. However, the developers of Blacklight knew that their tool was going to have to do much more than Collex. One key area they needed to focus on was indexing MARC records in Solr. Here, the developers of Blacklight were able to collaborate with the developers of VuFind to create SolrMarc, a tool for indexing MARC records into Solr. In addition, Blacklight developers needed to index other types of

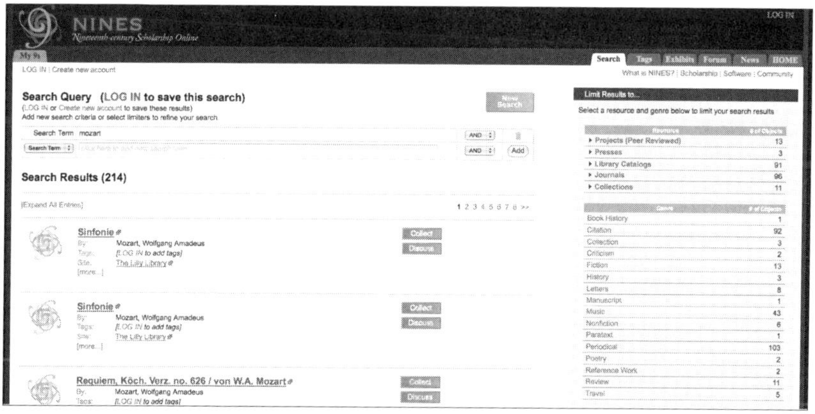

Figure 15.17 NINES Project website search results

content in Solr, including EADs, TEI, Dublin Core, and proprietary and nonstandard metadata formats. In configuring indexing for each of these types of metadata and collections, the Blacklight developers focused on the metadata aspects of each collection that were unique, in order to create custom indexes and facets.

This ability to take advantage of the unique metadata qualities of different collections is one of Blacklight's biggest strengths. The software has the ability to handle different types of objects in different ways: from both an indexing and display perspective (Figure 15.18). In a traditional library catalog, libraries typically have a limited number of indexes at their disposal, which results in a narrow set of general access points for users. While this approach works reasonably well for generalized searching, it hides metadata critical for specialized and discipline specific searching. For example, information about the format of a recording of music is hidden in most catalogs. In the interface of the UVA Music Collection, Blacklight not only exposes this information to users, it highlights it.

The interface also highlights *instrument* as a facet, which is extremely helpful for music students and faculty searching for pieces appropriate for a particular instrument. This kind of search is much more difficult in a traditional library catalog, because this information is located in Library of Congress Subject Headings (LCSH), which are buried within the record. The LCSH terms are also

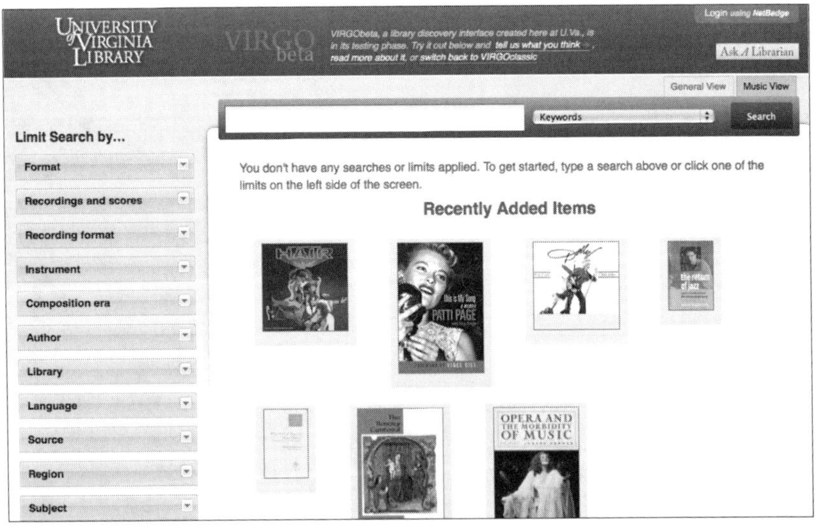

Figure 15.18 Music score record in Blacklight

archaic, particularly when dealing with terms that indicate what voice range a music piece is for. With *instrument* exposed as a facet, users don't need to know the LCSH term. Instead, they can easily browse the possibilities (Figure 15.19).

Specific collections and objects are better showcased via certain types of displays. While books can be appropriately represented by cover art, digital image collections should include a thumbnail of the image. An interesting example of a collection-specific display in action is the display of Greek and Roman coins that are part of UVA's collections (Figure 15.20).

This item screen has a number of unique features. First, it shows users a number of unique metadata fields such as Mint, Denomination, Material, and Regions. Additionally, the display is designed to recognize that coins are three-dimensional objects with a front and back, so the item screen displays images of both the obverse and reverse of the coin. These examples illustrate how Blacklight overcomes many limitations of traditional catalog user interfaces by allowing libraries to highly customize indexes, facets, and displays.

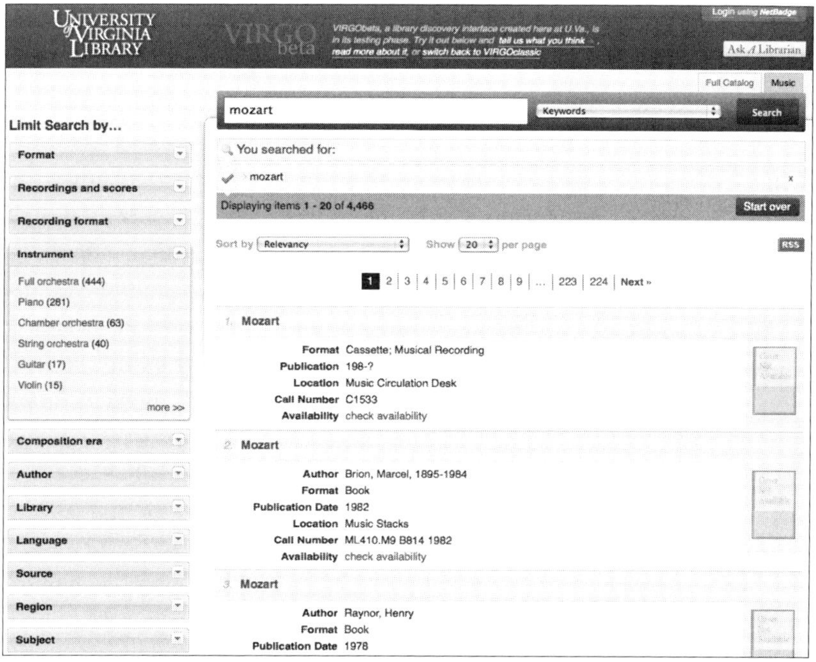

Figure 15.19 Instrument facet in Blacklight

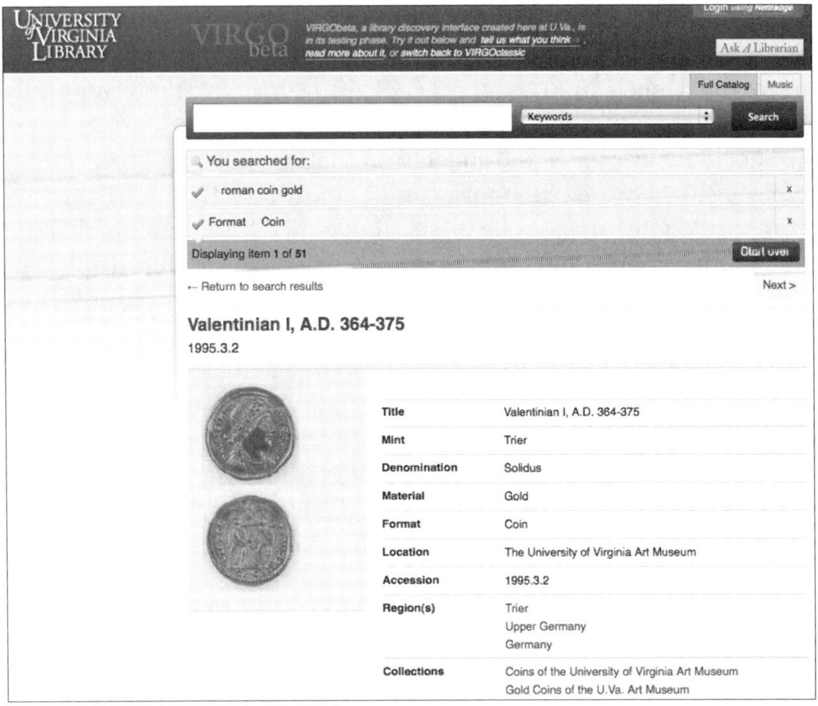

Figure 15.20 Record for ancient coin in Blacklight

Since the software was released in 2008, Blacklight has been undergoing active development. At the time of this writing, its most recent version is the 2.4 release (November 2009), which adds the ability to export citations to Zotero and a basic advanced search user interface, based on Stanford's Blacklight customizations.

The Blacklight project has a mailing list, strong developer documentation, a roadmap for upcoming versions, a good bug-tracking system, and a viewable repository of code. Although the initial adoption rate for Blacklight seems slower than for VuFind, more libraries are becoming aware of the software and are considering it or are in the process of adopting it. Johns Hopkins University Libraries, for instance, is currently in the process of implementing Blacklight. Blacklight has been implemented or is under consideration at a variety of institutions and organizations including:

- Agricultural Network Information Center (www.agnic.org/search)

- Northwest Digital Archives (nwda.projectblacklight.org)
- Stanford University Libraries (searchworks.stanford.edu)
- University of Hull (hydra.hull.ac.uk)
- University of Wisconsin Library System (disco.library.wisc.edu/forward)

Each of these implementations leverages the power of Blacklight in slightly different ways. The Northwest Digital Archives project is primarily a prototype interface for searching digital objects from the Northwest Digital Archives and the Orbis Cascade Alliance. The metadata for many of the objects comes from CONTENTdm installations. One of the most interesting collections included in Northwest Digital Archives are the items from the Oregon State University Herbarium (Figure 15.21).

Stanford University Libraries' implementation of Blacklight is primarily made up of materials from the library catalog, along with some digital objects. One of the most interesting features of

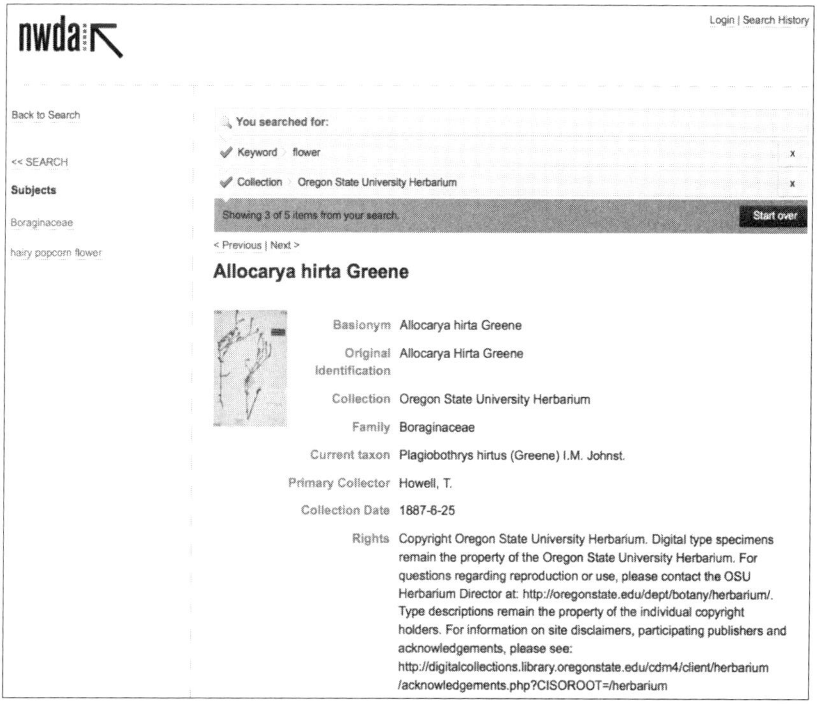

Figure 15.21 Item from Oregon State University Herbarium

Stanford's implementation is that it incorporates a tag cloud on the search homepage (Figure 15.22).

The tag cloud functionality is currently a Stanford-specific customization. However, a version of this functionality is scheduled to be incorporated into the 2.4 release of Blacklight. In addition, Stanford's Blacklight implementation also includes a variety of user interface enhancements, such as:

- Links to Google Book Preview
- Links to finding materials in another library via WorldCat.org
- Cite This link on records, which allows users to see citation in APA and MLA format
- Send This link on records, which allows users to send citation information as a text message or email or export it to RefWorks or EndNote

The University of Hull has also implemented Blacklight in order to better expose collections of digital objects in their Fedora repository. The collections currently being tested in the prototype include Electronic Theses and Dissertations, Digital Images, and a variety of other materials including presentations and journal articles (Figure 15.23).

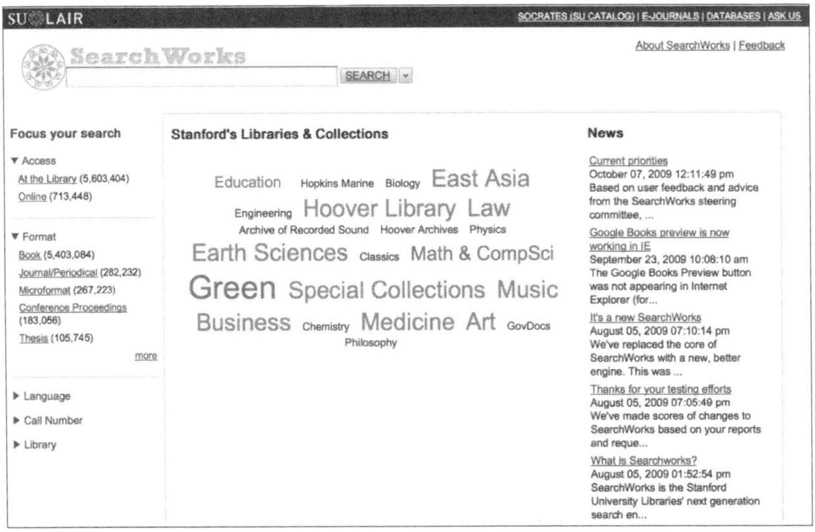

Figure 15.22 Stanford University Libraries' tag cloud from Blacklight

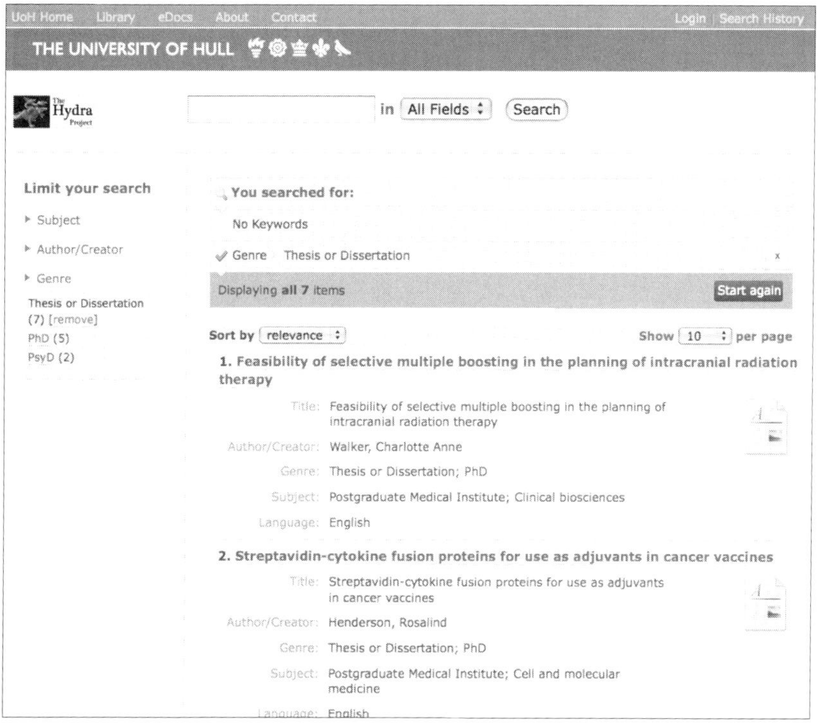

Figure 15.23 The University of Hull's Blacklight implementation

The project at the University of Hull is part of a larger effort called the Hydra Project. The goal of the Hydra project is to create a suite of tools for libraries to use to interact with Fedora repositories. Currently, the project collaborators include the University of Hull, University of Virginia, and Stanford University. Blacklight is being tested as a searchable user interface to Fedora objects.

University of Wisconsin (UW) has also implemented Blacklight, using it to search across the entire UW system, including all the UW library catalogs, several digital collections, and content from MINDS@UW, the institutional repository for the UW system. What is interesting, however, is that this implementation isn't merely a union catalog. Selecting a particular campus from the project homepage not only allows you to limit your search to that campus's resources but provides a uniquely branded interface for that campus (Figure 15.24).

This application demonstrates how easy it would be for state-wide university systems, such as the State University of New York or

Figure 15.24 Themed Blacklight interface used by University of Wisconsin

California State system, to implement Blacklight and provide both a union catalog as well as NextGen catalog functionality to all their campus libraries.

The diversity of Blacklight implementations demonstrates the software's flexibility and adaptability. It is likely that the Blacklight community will grow over time to include more libraries that use the software, to index a variety of materials, and to create interesting and unique user interfaces to meet their users' needs.

References

Blyberg, J. 2009. SOPAC 2.0: The thrashable, mashable catalog. In *Library Mashups: Exploring New Ways to Deliver Library Data,* ed. N. Engard. Medford, NJ: Information Today, Inc.

Hedges, S., L. Solomon, and K. Jendretzky. 2009. Federated database search mashup. In *Library Mashups: Exploring New Ways to Deliver Library Data,* ed. N. Engard. Medford, NJ: Information Today, Inc.

Houser, J. 2009. The VuFind implementation at Villanova University. *Library Hi Tech* 27 (1): 93–105. Library, Information Science & Technology Abstracts, EBSCOhost (accessed November 10, 2009).

Sadler, B., J. Gilbert, and M. Mitchell. 2009. Library catalog mashup: Using Blacklight to expose collections. In *Library Mashups: Exploring New Ways to Deliver Library Data,* ed. N. Engard. Medford, NJ: Information Today, Inc.

Sadler, E. 2009. Project Blacklight: A next generation library catalog at a first generation university. *Library Hi Tech* 27 (1): 57–67. Library, Information Science & Technology Abstracts, EBSCOhost (accessed November 10, 2009).

Glossary

Apache. An open source web server. For more information, see apache.org.

API. Application Programming Interface. An interface that creates a bridge between two programs to allow data transfer.

BitNami Stack. A software bundle that simplifies the installation of open source web applications. For more information, see bitnami.org.

Chmod. A Unix/Linux command that is used to set file or directory permissions or web access.

Cron Job. A Unix/Linux command that allows jobs to be scheduled for specific times.

Crontab. A text file that contains a series of cron functions.

FLOSS. Free/Libre Open Source Software. *See* open source software.

GNU General Public License (GPL). An open source license that gives users the right to use, copy, modify, and distribute a given piece of software.

GPL. See GNU General Public License.

.htaccess file. A configuration file used by the Apache web server software. An .htaccess file is used in a web directory to override the default server configurations.

httpd.conf file. A configuration file that is used by the Apache web server.

IIS. Internet Information Services. A web server designed by Microsoft and used on Windows servers.

JSON. JavaScript Object Notation. A text-based data exchange format based on JavaScript.

LAMP. A set of software services that includes the Linux operating system, the Apache web server, the MySQL database tool, and one or more of the following web programming tools: PHP, Perl, or Python.

Linux. A generic term that refers to an open source operating system based on UNIX. For more information, see www.linux.org.

MAMP. An Apache, MySQL, and PHP software package running on a Mac desktop. For more information, see www.mamp.info.

mod_rewrite. Apache module that rewrites URLs to be shorter and more user-friendly.

MySQL. A relational database management system. For more information, see www.mysql.com.

OAI-PMH. Open Archives Initiative Protocol for Metadata Harvesting. A protocol used to harvest metadata.

Open Source Software (OSS). Software that is free to download, modify, and redistribute.

PEAR. A programming language. For more information, see pear.php.net.

Perl. A programming language. For more information, see www.perl.org.

PHP. A web scripting language. For more information, see www.php.net.

Python. A programming language. For more information, see www.python.org.

REST. Representational State Transfer. An architectural style that defines and addresses sources of specific information, commonly known as resources. The World Wide Web is based on REST; web "resources" such as web pages are "transferred" to the client application (browser).

Root Access. Root access allows a user to log onto a server as "root," or with full administrative rights.

Ruby on Rails. A programming language. For more information, see rubyonrails.org.

SOAP. Simple Object Access Protocol. An XML-based protocol to let applications exchange information over HTTP.

Solr. An open source search server that is fast and features faceted search results.

SSH. Secure Shell. Used to connect remotely to a server.

VPS. Virtual Private Server. A virtual machine, or partition, on a server.

Wamp. An Apache, MySQL, and PHP software package running on a Windows desktop. For more information, see www.wampserver.com/en.

XAMPP. An Apache, MySQL, and PHP software package running on a desktop. For more information, see www.apachefriends.org/en/xampp.html.

XSLT. EXtensible Stylesheet Language. A style sheet language for XML documents. XSLT, or XSL Transformations, use XSL to convert XML documents into another form, such as an html or xhtml webpage.

About the Authors

Karen A. Coombs is a librarian and geek coder with an interest in mashups, web services, and library websites and interfaces. Currently she is the product manager for the OCLC Developer Network, a community of developers collaborating in a "sandbox" environment in order to propose, discuss, and test OCLC web services.

Prior to joining OCLC, Karen worked part time as a web application specialist for LISHost and as a library web technology consultant. She has an MLS and an MS in information management from Syracuse University. Karen has presented at many national and international conferences and written articles for a variety of journals. With Jason Griffey, she is the co-author of the book *Library Blogging*. In 2009, Karen was named a *Library Journal* Mover and Shaker. She blogs at www.librarywebchic.net.

Amanda J. Hollister is a librarian, photographer, and coder interested in web applications, open source software, and ebooks. She is currently the web application specialist for LISHost. Prior to joining LISHost, Amanda served as the web services librarian at State University of New York (SUNY) Cortland, where she was responsible for the development and maintenance of the library website and virtual presence. Amanda frequently teaches and presents at Internet Librarian and Computers in Libraries and recently co-taught a LITA preconference on open source content management systems at American Library Association's annual meeting. She has a PhD in biology from Binghamton University and a MSLIS from Syracuse University.

Index

A

AADL (Ann Arbor [MI] District Library), 233, 235
access control modules, 11
ACRLog, Association of College and Research Libraries, 53
ACRL wiki, 91
Activate Up Anchors function, LibData, 210
administration GUI, web hosting, 27
Agricultural Network Information Center, 246
Aiken library, University of South Carolina, 79, 80
Akeeba Backup extension, Joomla, 128, 130
ALA (American Library Association) wikis, 91
Allen County Public Library (IN), 235
All in One Video Pack, 47
AlphaContent extension, Joomla, 131–132
Amazon Elastic Compute Cloud (EC2) cloud computing web host service, 31–32, 33, 35
American Library Association (ALA) wikis, 91
Ann Arbor (MI) District Library (AADL), 233, 235
Apache open source web server, 10–12
Apache Software Foundation, 10
applications, selecting example, 7–8
archive.php file, WordPress, 100
Article Manager, Joomla, 118
Askimet spam-catching plugin, 40
assessment values, LimeSurvey, 175
Assignment Calculator, 163–166, 168
Association of College and Research Libraries ACRLog, 53
Atchison (KS) Public Library, 111–112
Atlantic City Free Public Library, 130, 131, 132, 133
audio, 46, 64, 86, 87–88. *See also* multimedia
AuthCAS add-on for PmWiki, 73
authentication modules, 11
Authoring Console, LibData, 201, 202, 203–204, 206, 207
AWStats tool for web use analysis, 25, 27

B

bandwidth, web host, 24–27
Best of Joomla, 120–121
Beyond Brown Paper, 231, 232
BibLibre, 235
Bibliography Module, Drupal, 145
Bibutils, 181, 182
Binghamton University Libraries, 70
Bisson, Casey, 229
Biz Wiki, Ohio University Libraries, 91, 92
Blacklight NextGen catalog, 243–250

blocks, Drupal, 146–147, 148
Blogroll Links plugin, 107
blogs, library, 39. *See also* WordPress
Blyberg, John, 233
Book Post module, Drupal, 144
Brigham Young University Library, 114
business models, open source, 6–7
BustAName domain name generator, 23

C

CakePHP open source framework, 15
calendar of events, 108, 110–114, 132–133, 144, 154
California State University—East Bay, 114
CAPTCHA spam blocking, 128
Cardinal Cushing Library, Emmanuel College, 195
Carter, Richard, 89–90
CAS (Central Authentication Server), 73
category.php file, WordPress, 100
Category Posts Widget, WordPress, 102
CCK (Content Construction Kit), Drupal, 141, 142, 157
Central Authentication Server (CAS), 73
Chudnov, Dan, 3
cloud web hosting, 28, 29–32
CMR Movable-Type-Styles, 65
CMS (content management system), 97. *See also individual products*
CodeIgniter open source framework, 15
coin information, Blacklight searching for, 245–246
Colby-Sawyer College, 231, 233
Collex, 243
Collingwood (NJ) Public Library, 231
Colorado State University Libraries, 239, 240
comments, moderating in WordPress, 40
comments.php file, WordPress, 99
comments-popup.php file, WordPress, 100
Comment Subscribe plugin, 68
community development of open source software, 3, 4
CommWiki, Ohio University Libraries, 91–92, 93
Comprehensive Perl Archive Network (CPAN), 16
conditional tags, WordPress, 101
config.php file, PmWiki, 71
config.php file, SubjectsPlus, 187
Connecticut Libraries, University of, 92
Contact Forms module, Drupal, 144
Contemplate module, Drupal, 142–144
Content Construction Kit (CCK), Drupal, 141, 142, 157
content management systems, 97. *See also individual products*
Cook Memorial Library (Tamworth, NH), 231, 232
copyleft, 6
Cortland (NY) Free Library website, 97
CourseLib function, LibData, 206, 209–211, 212, 213
CPAN (Comprehensive Perl Archive Network), 16
cPanel administration GUI, 27, 28–29
CPAN package manager program, 16
cron script, 140
cross-platform, Apache, MySQL, PHP, Perl (XAMPP), 17–18

Cumberland County (NJ) Library, 132
custom fields, WordPress, 105
Custom HTML module, Joomla, 127

D

Darby, Andrew, 185, 198–199
Darien (CT) Library, 151, 152, 153, 235
Dartmouth (MA) Public Libraries, 52–53, 111–112
databases, 16, 27. *See also* MySQL
db_inc.php file, refbase, 181
DBA Tools, LibData, 201
dbWiz federated search tool, 220–222, 227
dedicated server web hosting, 32, 34
DeKalb County (GA) Public Library, 133, 134
delete operation (SQL), 13
development web server, 21, 24, 35
DeWitt Wallace Library, Macalester College, 215
DHTML Menu module, Drupal, 150
domain names, 22–24
domain registrars, 23–24
Drupal
  blocks, 146–147, 148
  configuration, 139–140
  Content Construction Kit, 141, 142, 157
  content types, 140–141
  customizing, 145–149
  described, 97, 137
  events calendar, 144, 154
  example implementation, 151, 154, 156–159
  images, 144, 146, 150, 157
  installing, 137–139
  libraries using, 150–153
  maintenance, 140
  menus, 148–149, 150, 154–155
  modules, 141–146, 150–152, 154, 157, 159
  pages, 140
  stories, 140, 151
  tags, 149
  taxonomies, 149–150, 151
  themes, 145–146, 148, 157
  Web 2.0 functions, 158
  WYSIWYG editor, 144
Drupal4Lib LITA Interest Group, 151
Drupal4Lib mailing list, 150
Drupalib website, 150–151
Drupal Libraries Group, 151
Drupal Themes page, 145
dual license business model, 6
dynamic pages, 55

E

EC2 (Amazon Elastic Compute Cloud) cloud computing web host service, 31–32, 33, 35
editors, WYSIWYG. *See* WYSIWYG editors
Emmanuel College's Cardinal Cushing Library, 195
Equinox, 7
Event module, Drupal, 144, 154
events calendar, 108, 110–114, 132–133, 144, 154

F

Facet Search module, Drupal, 157, 159
Fantastico software install tool, 28
FAQ module, SubjectsPlus, 194–195
FCKeditor, 85
federated search tools, 219–220, 227. *See also individual tools*
Feed Display module, Joomla, 127
feeds, 106–109, 126–127
FlashMP3 MediaWiki extension, 88
Flexi Pages Widget, WordPress, 102
Flickr, adding images from, 46
FlickrAlbum add-on for PmWiki, 75

Flickr gallery, 46
Flickr MediaWiki extension, 88
FLOSS (free/libre open source software), 3
footer.php file, WordPress, 99
Forbes Library (MA), 79
Forum module, Drupal, 150
frameworks, open source, 15
free/libre open source software (FLOSS), 3
"From Zero to Wiki" (Haupt), 77
FTP support, web hosting, 27

G

gem packages, Ruby on Rails, 16–17
Georgetown University Library, 215
Georgia Tech Library, 239, 240, 241
Gimlet, 173–174
GMap add-on for PmWiki, 75
GNU General Public License (GPL), 6
GODOT OpenURL resolver, 220
GoogleMapExtension MediaWiki extension, 88
Google Maps for WordPress, 105, 106
Google Sites free web hosting, 22
GPL (GNU General Public License), 6
Grand Rapids (MI) Public Library, 92, 94
GRPLpedia wiki, 92–93, 94

H

Hansson, David Heinemeier, 16
Haupt, John, 77
header.php file, WordPress, 99
Health Sciences Library, Stony Brook University, 134
Heartland (FL) Library Cooperative, 70
Holland College, 186, 197
HostGator web hosting, 28, 29, 30, 34
Houston Libraries, University of, 53, 77, 225
.htaccess file, PmWiki, 72–73
Hull, University of, 247, 248–249
Hydra project, 249

I

images. *See also* multimedia
  in Drupal, 144, 146, 150, 157
  Flickr, 46
  in Joomla, 130–131
  in MediaWiki, 86–87, 88
  in Movable Type, 63–64
  organization example, 231, 232, 233
  in PmWiki, 75
  in WordPress, 45–46, 108, 110–111
IMT plugin, 68
Index Data, 222, 223, 227
index.php file, Joomla, 121, 126
index.php file, WordPress, 99, 100
Indian Prairie Public Library, 133
ini.inc.php file, refbase, 181
Inlinefeed plugin, 106–107
insert operation (SQL), 13
install tool for installing hosting software, 28
instructions.php file, Assignment Calculator, 164
instruction tools, 163. *See also* Assignment Calculator; Research Project Calculator
Insurge, 233, 234
Iowa State University Library, 77
is_front_page() conditional tag, WordPress, 101
is_page() conditional tag, WordPress, 101
Ithaca College, 189, 196

J

James E. Walker library, Middle Tennessee State University, 215
JCE (Joomla content editor) extension, 130
JEvents extension, Joomla, 132–133
Johns Hopkins University Libraries, 246
JoomGallery extension, Joomla, 130–131
Joomla
  advantages/disadvantages, 134–135
  components, 123, 131
  configuration, 115–117
  content, making available for searching, 119–120
  content, organizing, 117–118, 119
  customizing, 120–121, 124–126
  described, 97, 115
  events calendar, 132–133
  extensions, 121–123, 128–133
  feeds in, 126–127
  help features, 116
  images, 130–131
  installing, 115, 116
  libraries using, 133–134
  menus, 123–124, 125
  modules, 121, 122–123, 126–127
  photo galleries, 130–131
  plugins, 123, 130
  templates, 120–122
  WYSIWYG editor, 118, 130
Joomla content editor (JCE) extension, 130
JoomlaPack extension, 128, 130

K

Kaltura All in One Video Pack, 47
Kansas State Library, 112
Kete digital library tool, 7
Koha open source ILS, 7

L

label sets, LimeSurvey, 174–175
LAMP stack, 6, 9–13
Larson, Eric, 168
Latest Image block, Drupal, 146
LibData
  Activate Up Anchors function, 210
  advantages, 211, 215
  appearance, 211, 213, 214, 216
  Authoring Console, 201, 202, 203–204, 206, 207
  CourseLib function, 206, 209–211, 212, 213
  customizing, 203–204, 205, 206
  DBA Tools, 201
  described, 215
  development, 201
  guides, managing, 207–208
  installing, 201
  libraries using, 213, 215
  Manager Functions, 201, 206
  PageScribe function, 206–207, 209–211, 212
  Research QuickStart Assignments function, 207, 208, 209, 210
  resources, managing, 203–204, 206–207
  statistics, 211, 214
  users, managing, 202–203
  Vendor feature, 206
LibLime, 7
Library and Information Technology Association (LITA) Blog, 53
LibraryFind federated search tool, 221, 224–227
Library Success wiki, 91
Libstats, 168–174
licenses, open source software, 6
LimeSurvey, 174–180
Linux operating system, 9–10
LISHost, 34–35

LITA (Library and Information Technology Association) Blog, 53
LITA Wiki, 91
LitWiki, Ohio University Libraries, 91–92, 93
LocalSettings.php file, MediaWiki, 82–84, 86, 89, 90
Locum, 233–234
Loop tag in WordPress template, 103–105
Lucy Scribner Library, Skidmore College, 134
Lupton Library, University of Tennessee at Chattanooga, 134

M

Macalester College DeWitt Wallace Library, 215
Mace, Mark, 173
Maine, University of Southern, 190
MAMP installer, 18
MAMP model, 10
Manage Assets, SubjectsPlus, 193, 194
Manager Functions, LibData, 201, 206
MARC module, Drupal, 144–145
MARC records, Ruby libraries for, 17
Maryland Libraries, University of, 77, 78
MasterKey federated search tool, 7, 223–224
McCool, Robert, 10
McMaster University Library
  blogs, 53
  Drupal use, 151, 154, 156–159
  wikis, 77, 79, 80
MeanEditor MediaWiki extension, 85
MediaWiki
  audio in, 86, 87–88
  authentication, 84
  customizing, 88–90
  described, 81
  editing pages, 84–85
  extensions, 85, 88
  files, uploading, 85–86
  images in, 86–87
  installing, 81–84
  libraries using, 91–93
  permissions, 84
  users, 90
  videos in, 86, 87–88
  wiki farms, 90
  WYSIWYG editor, 85
MediaWiki Skins Design (Carter), 89–90
Melody, 69
Menu Manager, Joomla, 123–124, 125
Michigan Library, University of, 151–154, 155, 239
Middle Tennessee State University James E. Walker Library, 215
Millsaps College Library, 114
Minnesota Libraries, University of, 70, 77–78, 204, 205, 213
Minnesota State Colleges and Universities Libraries, 239, 240
mobile search interface, LibraryFind, 225, 226
mod_access module for Apache, 11
mod_auth_digest module for Apache, 11
mod_auth module for Apache, 11
mod_digest module for Apache, 11
mod_perl module for Apache, 11
mod_php module for Apache, 11
mod_rails module for Apache, 17
mod_rewrite module for Apache, 11
Model-View-Controller (MVC) paradigm, 15, 16
moderating comments in WordPress, 40

modules
  Apache, 11
  Drupal, 141–146, 150–152, 154, 157, 159
  Joomla, 121, 122–123, 126–127
  Movable Type, 66
  Perl:DBI, 16
  SubjectsPlus, 194–195
Mongrel web server, 17
Moniker domain registrar, 23
MorfeoShow extension, Joomla, 131
Mosets Tree extension, Joomla, 131, 132
Most Recent Poll block, Drupal, 146
Movable Type
  blogs, 60–61, 62, 64–69
  business model, 6–7
  described, 55–56
  images in, 63–64
  installing, 56–60, 61
  libraries using, 70
  license, 55
  media, adding, 63–64
  modules, 66
  notifications, 56, 68
  pages, creating, 63
  Perl-basis, 16
  plugins, 66, 68–69
  posts, creating, 61–62
  styles, 64–66
  tags, 55, 61, 64, 66
  templates, 65–66
  user community, 69, 70
  users, creating, 60
  widgets, 66, 67
  WordPress compared, 70
MultiBlock module, Drupal, 144
multimedia, 25. *See also* audio; images; videos
Murphy Library, University of Wisconsin—La Crosse, 215
music information, Blacklight searching for, 244–245
MVC (Model-View-Controller) paradigm, 15, 16
My Kansas Library on the Web (Kansas State Library), 112
MySQL, 6, 10, 12–13

N

Namecheap domain registrar, 23
Network Solutions domain registrar, 23
Newport Beach (CA) Public Library, 235
next generation (NextGen) catalogs, 229. *See also individual tools*
NextGEN Gallery plugin for WordPress, 46, 108
Nice Menus, Drupal, 154–155
NINES project, 243
NinjaXplorer extension, Joomla, 128, 129
Northwest Digital Archives, 247
Norwich Library, 91
notifications, 56, 68, 74, 235

O

OAI-PMH Module, Drupal, 145
OggHandler MediaWiki extension, 88
Ohio Public Library Information Network (OPLIN), 222–223
Ohio University Libraries, 91–92, 93
Ohio Web Library, 223
OpenBook Book Data plugin, 105, 106
OpenID WordPress plugin, 52
open source software (OSS), 3–7
OpenURL resolver, 224, 225
operating system, web hosting, 27
OPLIN (Ohio Public Library Information Network), 222–223
Oregon State University Libraries, 227, 247
Organic Groups module, Drupal, 151–152

Organize Resources, SubjectsPlus, 193
Orion Township (MI) Public Library Blog, 70
OSS (open source software), 3–7

P

page.php file, WordPress, 99, 100
pages, Drupal, 140
PageScribe function, LibData, 206–207, 209–211, 212
Palos Verdes Library District, 235, 236
Park County (CO) Library, 111–112
Park County (WY) Library System, 53
Patagonia (AZ) Public Library, 111–112
Pazpar2 federated search tool, 221, 222–224
PEAR (PHP Extension and Application Repository), 13–14
PECL (PHP Extension Community Library), 13–14
Perl:DBI module, 16
Perl open source programming language, 15–16
permissions, web hosting, 27
Phoca Gallery extension, Joomla, 131
photo galleries, 45–46, 108, 110–111, 130–131
PHP Extension and Application Repository (PEAR), 13–14
PHP Extension Community Library (PECL), 13–14
phpMyAdmin tool for MySQL, 12, 18
PHP/Perl platforms, 10
PHP server scripting language, 13–15
PHPSurveyor, 174–180
Picnik Photo Editing plugin, 68
Pirate Source, 185
PLA (Public Library Association) Blog, 53
Plesk administration GUI, 27
Plugin Googlemaps extension, Joomla, 130
plugins
  Joomla, 123, 130
  Movable Type, 66, 68–69
  WordPress, 40, 46, 49–50, 52
  WordPress as CMS, 103, 105–107, 108, 111
pluslets, SubjectsPlus, 192–193, 197, 216
Plymouth State University Library, 230, 231
PmWiki
  add-ons, 73, 75
  authentication, 73
  customizing, 75–76
  described, 71
  features, 74
  images in, 75
  installing, 71
  libraries using, 77–80
  notifications, 74
  URLs, cleaning, 72–73
  user community, 77, 79
  wiki farms, 76–77
pmwiki.php file, PmWiki, 71
podcasting, 46, 64
podPress plugin, 46
Poll module, Drupal, 146
programming languages, web hosting, 27
proof of concept server, 22, 24, 35
Public Library Association (PLA) Blog, 53

R

Rake (Ruby development environment), 17
Random Image block, Drupal, 146
reCAPTCHA MediaWiki extension, 88

Reese, Terry, 16–17
refbase, 180–183
reference tools, 163, 168–174, 180–183
Related Items module, Joomla, 127
reSearcher, 220
Research Project Calculator (RPC), 166, 168, 169
Research QuickStart Assignments function, LibData, 207, 208, 209, 210
robots.txt file, 25
RPC (Research Project Calculator), 166, 168, 169
RSS feeds, 106–109, 126–127
RSS Reader MediaWiki extension, 88
RubyGems package manager, 16
Ruby on Rails, 16–17

S

SaaS (software as a service) business model, 7
SAILS, 235
screen scraping, 219, 233
Scriblio NextGen catalog, 229–233
searching, 219, 227, 229, 234. *See also* federated search tools
Section Manager, Joomla, 117
SecureForm extension, Joomla, 128, 129
secure FTP support, web hosting, 27
secure shell (SSH) access, web hosting, 27
select operation (SQL), 13
server-side scripting, 11
shared web hosting, 28–29
Shibboleth WordPress plugin, 52
shortcode, 107, 108
sidebar.php file, WordPress, 99, 101–102
Signup module, Drupal, 144
Sigsiu online business index 2, 132
silos of library resources, 229
SimpleAntiSpam MediaWiki extension, 88
Simple LDAP Login WordPress plugin, 52
SimplePieDisplay add-on for PmWiki, 75
SimplePie MediaWiki extension, 88
single.php file, WordPress, 100
SiteGround tool for web use analysis, 26
SiteGround web hosting, 28, 29, 31, 32, 34
Six Apart, 7, 55
Skidmore College's Lucy Scribner Library, 134
SkinName.php file, MediaWiki, 89
skins, 75–76, 88–90
SkinsGallery, 75
Sniplets plugin, WordPress, 111
Sobi extension, Joomla, 131, 132
Social OPAC (SOPAC), 151, 153, 233–235
Sociotags plugin, 68
software as a service (SaaS) business model, 7
software vendors, changing, 5
Soir, 151, 236–237
Sooper Themes, 145
SOPAC (Social OPAC), 151, 153, 233–235
sopac-results-hitlist.tpl.php file, SOPAC, 234
South Carolina—Aiken library, University of, 79, 80
South Carolina Library Association, 79
South Carolina State Library, 134
Southern Queensland Library, University of, 239, 240, 242
spam, preventing web form, 128
SQL (Structured Query Language), 13
SSH (secure shell) access, web hosting, 27

Stanford University Libraries, 247–248
static pages, 55
St. Cloud State University Library, 213
Stevens Memorial Library, 111–112
St. Joseph County (IN) Public Library, 92, 94
Stony Brook University Health Sciences Library, 134
stories, Drupal, 140, 151
Structured Query Language (SQL), 13
style.css file, WordPress, 99
styles, Movable Type, 64–66
subject guide tools, 185, 215. *See also* LibData; SubjectsPlus
SubjectsPlus
  advantages, 216
  configuration, 187
  as content management system, 197, 198
  customizing, 195–198
  described, 186, 199, 216
  development, 185–186
  guides, managing, 192–195
  installing, 187
  modules, 194–195
  pluslets, 192–193, 197, 216
  resources, managing, 189–192
  support, 198–199
  tags, 197
  users, managing, 187–190
  versions, 186
support, software, 4–5. *See also* SaaS (software as a service) business model
SurveyMonkey, 176, 177
survey tools, 174–180
symbolic links, 90
Symfony open source framework, 15

T

tag cloud implementation, Stanford University, 247–248
tag.php file, WordPress, 100
tags
  Drupal taxonomy, 149
  Movable Type, 55, 61, 64, 66, 68
  PHP, 14–15
  Scriblio, 230, 231
  SOPAC, 234
  SubjectsPlus, 197
  WordPress, 45, 101, 102–105
Talkback module, SubjectsPlus, 194, 195
tar.gz files, 13, 81
taxonomies, Drupal, 149–150, 151
Taxonomy Menu module, Drupal, 150
templateDetails.xml file, Joomla, 121, 123
templates, 65–66, 99–101, 103–105, 120–122
Tennessee at Chattanooga's Lupton Library, University of, 134
Texas Libraries, University of, 77, 79
the_author tag, WordPress, 105
the_category tag, WordPress, 105
the_content tag, WordPress, 105
the_meta tag, WordPress, 105
the_permalink tag, WordPress, 105
the_tags tag, WordPress, 105
the_time tag, WordPress, 105
the_title tag, WordPress, 105
themes
  Drupal, 145–146, 148, 157
  Sooper, 145
  WordPress, 47–49, 98, 99–100, 103–104
Timeline module, Drupal, 157, 159
TinyMCE editor, 118
Token module, Drupal, 144
Torvalds, Linus, 9
Tyngsborough (MA) Public Library, 134

U

University of Connecticut Libraries, 92
University of Houston Libraries, 53, 77, 225
University of Hull, 247, 248–249
University of Maryland Libraries, 77, 78
University of Michigan Library, 151–154, 155, 239
University of Minnesota Libraries, 70, 77–78, 204, 205, 213
University of South Carolina—Aiken library, 79, 80
University of Southern Maine, 190
University of Southern Queensland Library, 239, 240, 242
University of Tennessee at Chattanooga's Lupton Library, 134
University of Texas Libraries, 77, 79
University of Virginia (UVA), 243, 244, 245
University of Wisconsin Library System, 215, 247, 249
Upcoming Events Widget, WordPress, 111, 113
update operation (SQL), 13
URLs, 11–12, 72–73
UThink project, University of Minnesota, 70

V

Vack, Nate, 168, 173
Vendor feature, LibData, 206
vendors, changing software, 5
videos, 46–47, 64, 86, 87–88
Views module, Drupal, 142, 157
Villanova University, 235–236, 237
Viper's Video Quicktags, 46
Virginia (UVA), University of, 243, 244, 245
virtual private server (VPS) web hosting, 32–34, 35
VuFind NextGen catalog, 235–242

W

Wake Forest University libraries, 239
WAMP model, 10
WampServer installer, 18
Web 2.0 features, 158, 229, 239. *See also* SOPAC
web addresses, 11–12, 72–73
Webalizer tool for web use analysis, 18, 25
Webform module, Drupal, 154
web form spam, preventing, 128
web hosting
  bandwidth, 24–27
  described, 21
  features, determining needs, 27–28
  free services, 22
  LISHost, 34–35
  recommendations, 35
  types, 28–34
  use of outside, 21–22
Web Links component, Joomla, 131
WEBrick, Ruby-integrated web server, 17
Web Robots, 25
web servers, 21, 22, 24, 32, 35
WestHost web hosting, 28, 29, 33, 34
Whatcom (WA) Public Library, 134
"What Librarians Still Don't Know About Open Source Software" (Chudnov), 3
Widget Logic plugin, WordPress, 103
widgets
  Movable Type, 66, 67
  WordPress, 49, 102, 103, 111, 113
wiki farms, 76–77, 90
Wikipedia, 81
wikis, library, 39, 76–77. *See also* MediaWiki; PmWiki

Wikiwyg MediaWiki extension, 85
Windows operating system, 10
Wisconsin Library System, University of, 215, 247, 249
"wisdom of the crowd," 4
WordPress
- administering, overview, 44
- advantages, 50
- appearance, 47–49
- blog features, 39–40, 51–52
- codex, 40, 105
- development, 39
- image gallery, 45–46
- installing, 40–44
- libraries using, 52–53
- moderating comments, 40
- Movable Type compared, 70
- pages, 40, 45
- plugins, 40, 46, 49–50, 52
- podcasting, 46
- popularity, 39
- posts, 45
- profile, 47
- Scriblio, use for, 229–230
- settings, 47
- tags, 45, 101, 102–105
- templates, 99–101, 103–105
- themes, 47–49, 98, 99–100, 103–104
- user community, 70
- user management, 40, 47
- videos, 46–47
- Web 2.0 features, 229
- web hosting, 22
- widgets, 49
- WYSIWYG editor, 39–40, 45

WordPress as CMS
- advantages/disadvantages, 114
- customizing, 98, 99–105
- described, 97–98
- events calendar, 108, 110–114
- feeds, 106–109
- homepage, 98–99
- images in, 108, 110–111
- libraries using, 111–112, 114
- page templates, 99–101
- planning, 98
- plugins, 103, 105–107, 108, 111
- widgets, 102, 103, 111, 113

WordPress Flickr Manager, 46
wordTube, 46
WorldCat Search API gem, 16–17
wp_list_authors tag, WordPress, 105
wp_list_bookmarks tag, WordPress, 105
wp_list_categories tag, WordPress, 105
wpCAS WordPress plugin, 52
wp-config.php file, WordPress, 51
wp-config-sample.php file, WordPress, 41–43
wpDirAuth WordPress plugin, 52
WPopac, 229–233
WYSIWYG editors
- Drupal, 144
- Joomla, 118, 130
- MediaWiki, 85
- WordPress, 39–40, 45

X

XAMPP (cross-platform, Apache, MySQL, PHP, Perl), 17–18
Xmap extension, Joomla, 130
XStandard Lite editor, 118, 130

Y

Yale University Library, 239, 242
YourLibrarySite, 235

Z

Z39.50 search protocol, 219, 227
Zend Framework open source framework, 15